WITHDRAWN

THE CONCEIT OF HUMANITARIAN
INTERVENTION

RAJAN MENON

THE CONCEIT
OF HUMANITARIAN
INTERVENTION

OXFORD
UNIVERSITY PRESS

OXFORD
UNIVERSITY PRESS

Oxford University Press is a department of the University of Oxford. It furthers
the University's objective of excellence in research, scholarship, and education
by publishing worldwide. Oxford is a registered trade mark of Oxford University
Press in the UK and certain other countries.

Published in the United States of America by Oxford University Press
198 Madison Avenue, New York, NY 10016, United States of America.

© Oxford University Press 2016

Cataloging-in-Publication Data is on file at the Library of Congress.
ISBN 978–0–19–938487–7

1 3 5 7 9 8 6 4 2
Printed by Sheridan, USA

For Lekha and Zoë

CONTENTS

ACKNOWLEDGMENTS

I am indebted to many friends and colleagues who have helped and supported me as I worked on this book. Not all of them necessarily agree with my conclusions, but they have, without exception, been generous and kind; and for that I am grateful beyond measure.

Michael Mandelbaum (School of Advanced International Studies, Johns Hopkins University) and Anne Mandelbaum have been ever-reliable sources of friendship, advice, and inspiration for many years. They lead busy lives but have never hesitated to set aside their work to support mine.

Jack Snyder (Columbia University), a scholar whose accomplishments are exceeded only by his modesty and readiness to help others, has long been a wellspring of ideas and an astute and constructive critic. More importantly, he is a valued friend to whom I owe more than can be recorded here. He arranged for me to join Columbia's Arnold A. Saltzman Institute of War and Peace Studies (SIWPS) as a Senior Research Scholar. SIWPS buzzes with intellectual creativity and energy, and I am grateful to its director, Richard Betts, and to other members of the Institute, in particular Alexander Cooley, Robert Jervis, Austin Long, and Kimberly Marten. Ingrid Gertsmann,

SIWPS's incomparable business manager, has been unfailingly welcoming, helpful, and kind.

I have been lucky to have exceptional colleagues in the Political Science Department at the City College of New York (CCNY), which I joined in 2010. Daniel DiSalvo and I have discussed and debated many of the questions covered in this book. His wide-ranging interests and knowledge and wicked sense of humor have enabled many delightful conversations. He is, beyond that, a close friend. Bruce Cronin has been a superb department chair; his unflappability, wit, and courage of conviction are admirable, his friendship invaluable. I am thankful as well to my colleagues Richard Bernstein and Nicholas Smith. I also wish to thank the dean of CCNY's Powell School, Vince Boudreau, and his superb staff, especially Dee Dee Mozeleski. Eric Weitz, dean of Humanities and Arts at City College and a Distinguished Professor of History, is a renowned historian of Germany and authority on human rights. He has been an invaluable source of intellectual fellowship and a wonderful friend with whom I have collaborated on various ventures, most notably the CCNY Faculty Seminar on Human Rights, which has been enriched by the participation of exceptional colleagues from CCNY, Columbia, Princeton, and New York University.

I am grateful to a number of individuals outside of my City College-Columbia circle: Andrew Bacevich (Boson University), Joshua Cohen (formerly at Stanford, now at Apple), Galia Golan (Interdisciplinary Center Herzliya), Thomas Graham (Kissinger Associates and Yale University), Vartan Gregorian (Carnegie Corporation of New York), Mel Leffler (University of Virginia), Alex Motyl (Rutgers), John Mearsheimer, (University of Chicago), Sam Moyn (Harvard Law School), Gene Rumer (Carnegie Endowment for International Peace), Mottie Tamarkin (Tel Aviv University), Daniel Terris (Brandeis University), and Chuck Ziegler (University of Louisville), with whom I have been friends since we first met in graduate school in 1975.

I am grateful to Josh Cohen, who invited me to present an early version of some of the ideas contained in Chapter 8 at Stanford in November 2009; to the editors of *Ethics in International Affairs* and the editors of the *American Interest*—in particular Adam Garfinkle and Daniel Kennelly—for permission to elaborate upon material that first appeared in their journals; and to Dan Terris, Director of the

International Center for Ethics, Justice, and Public Life, who invited me to present the main themes of this book at a conference on the Responsibility to Protect that he organized at the Center in March 2015. Jacob Heilbrunn, editor of the *National Interest*, his predecessor, Robert Merry, and Harry Kazianis, the magazine's executive editor, have provided numerous opportunities over the years for writing on an array of issues, some of which pertain to this book.

I owe a debt to Gareth Evans, whom I first met in 2000, shortly after he took the reins at the International Crisis Group, which he would transform, using his formidable intellect and energy, into a world-renowned organization of reporting and research on global crises and conflict. Some years later, after discussions with Gareth, I became interested in humanitarian intervention generally and the Responsibility to Protect—a concept that owes more to him than to any other individual—specifically. At the time, I was favorably disposed to both projects but had not had the opportunity to read and think about them systematically. The conversations I had with Gareth impelled me to do so and to start teaching a course on humanitarian intervention, which I continue to do. He and I now hold starkly different views on this topic but I wish to record here my admiration for what he has achieved in behalf of a cause about which he cares deeply. No one writing about humanitarian intervention will fail to be struck by how fundamentally he has shaped thinking and policy related to it.

I am grateful to the late Bernard Spitzer and to Anne Spitzer, whose generosity created the position I hold at CCNY and continues to support my work in many ways.

Simon Waxman's sharp editorial eye helped in numerous ways to improve the book's clarity and organizational structure. Lia Friedman prompted me to recast many sentences and thus proved, yet again, to be much more than a meticulous proofreader. I feel lucky to have been able to avail myself again of the skills of the peerless David Prout, who prepared the index for this book.

It has been a pleasure to work once more with David McBride, my editor at Oxford University Press. A historian as well as an editor, Dave raised valuable points on some matters of historical detail that helped improve the book. Katie Weaver, also of Oxford University Press, was efficient and attentive throughout. Maya Bringe, production manager at Newgen, expertly oversaw the production process down to the stage of publication. My thanks, as well, to Anne Sanow for her careful copyediting.

By their example, my teachers, Roger E. Kanet and Oles M. Smolansky, inspired me to choose an academic career and have been unswerving in their support for more than four decades, and close friends besides. Hugh Millard has been an inspiration through both his teaching and his art.

My good friends on Kezar Lake in North Sutton, New Hampshire, provided summertime companionship and merriment when the day's research and writing were done. I am thankful to Vic Del Vecchio and Lisa Lopez, John Herbert and Sarah Woolverton, Jon and Sherrie McKenna, Andrew and Heather Sideman, and to the inimitable Sandy Reilein. My dear friend Dick Reilein, always an engaging interlocutor, did not live to see the completion of this book.

My wife, Cathy Popkin, is the best writer and most perceptive reader I know; more importantly, she is the foundation on which I stand. Our daughters, Lekha and Zoë, have been incessant sources of love and laughter, and we have delighted in watching them become wonderful young women who have ventured forth into the world.

THE CONCEIT OF HUMANITARIAN
INTERVENTION

INTRODUCTION

"**M**ass atrocities" is an ungainly term. Still, as a catchall, it is useful because the large-scale violence that convulses societies comes in many forms. Ethnic conflict, as occurred in Rwanda and Darfur, is one kind. When it involves the expulsion of a culturally distinctive people from their homeland, as happened in Bosnia and Kosovo, we call it ethnic cleansing. Violent repressions during wars of secession, which occurred in Biafra in 1967–1970 and East Pakistan in 1971, are a second form of mass atrocity. The millions of lives consumed by state-directed revolutionary transformations—the 1932–1933 Ukrainian "terror-famine," now known as the Holodomor, or the death (from overwork, hunger, disease, and extermination) of 1.7 million in Cambodia under the Khmer Rouge from 1975–1979—are a third. Then there is genocide: the destruction in whole or part of a cultural community, exemplified by the Holocaust or the killing of the Ottoman Empire's Armenians in 1915. Mass atrocities can result from premeditated action by the state or from its inability to protect people living within the space it governs. It may be spurred by ideology, race hatred, tribal rivalry, and many other causes.

These forms of violence—the distinctions among them can be blurry—have claimed many more lives since 1945 than have wars among states.[1] They "shock the conscience," to use philosopher Michael Walzer's formulation. Most people therefore want something done to stop the bloodletting, an impulse that is understandable, even desirable. But when the complexities of stopping mass killing reveal themselves, the consensus born by outrage begins to fray. Well-meaning leaders and political thinkers have struggled to develop rules and norms of humanitarian intervention that would beckon world powers to end mass atrocities and inform their efforts to do so. Yet these attempts fail when one moves from general sentiments to operational particulars. Witness the most recent episode of large-scale slaughter: as I write, some 200,000 people have perished in Syria. Which great power is eager to enter those killing fields?

You could build a small mountain from the books and articles devoted to mass atrocity and humanitarian intervention. The subject has engaged journalists and political commentators (Roger Cohen, Noam Chomsky, Linda Melvern, Samantha Power, Bernard-Henri Lévy, William Kristol, David Rieff); historians (Ben Kiernan, Norman Naimark, Geoffrey Robinson, Davide Rodogno); political scientists (Gary Bass, Martha Finnemore, Aidan Hehir, Alan Kuperman, Benjamin Valentino, Nicholas Wheeler, Thomas Weiss); philosophers and political theorists (Charles Beitz, Gerald Doppelt, Terry Nardin, Henry Shue, Michael Walzer); international law experts (Ian Brownlie, Allen Buchanan, Simon Chesterman, David Luban, Anne-Marie Slaughter, Fernando Tesón, Geoffrey Robertson); and officials and military officers holding dramatically different views (Kofi Annan, Gareth Evans, Roméo Dallaire, Paul Wolfowitz, Richard Holbrooke). This list is not exhaustive, but I trust that it makes the point. Many of these individuals appear in the pages to follow, and readers will get to know their ideas.

In spite of the wide range of voices on humanitarian intervention, few who write on the topic question the overall project, which the overwhelming majority favors. Many of its supporters believe that now is a unique historical moment when the community of nations can develop a lasting solution to mass atrocities given that the normative and practical principles that support humanitarian intervention have gained worldwide purchase.

In fact, armed humanitarian interventions have, for reasons we shall see in later chapters, stirred considerable controversy among countries. As some of the project's proponents see it, however, the problem is that what intervention we have seen has not been frequent or muscular enough. They praise humanitarian intervention as a major advance in the defense of human rights; some even see it as a means to banish mass atrocities forever.

There are critics, to be sure—Anne Orford, David Chandler, Noam Chomsky, and David Rieff among them—but they constitute a minority. For their part, realist thinkers, such as John Mearsheimer, necessarily skeptical of humanitarian intervention, are prone to dismissing it as a woolly-headed idea that's not worth their time. That is a mistake. Big ideas can have big consequences. Humanitarian intervention certainly has.

This book presents a critique of the prevailing interventionist view. I am not morally disinterested when it comes to the slaughter of innocent people. Nor do I reject the conviction that it would be good, in principle, to have a universal consensus on when and how to respond to mass atrocities. I do not claim that nothing can or should *ever* be done in response to mass atrocities. Experience shows that it is sometimes possible to stop massacres. The difficulty arises in trying to find an all-purpose solution that rests on a global moral and legal consensus and that, in Evans's words, can stop mass killings "once and for all." Another challenge is to anticipate and to deal with the unintended consequences. The moral fervor of humanitarian interventionists is admirable, but it produces in them unwarranted confidence, even hubris. They seem to believe that if the objective is good, the outcome will be as well, and that their critics either lack ethical commitment or represent states that want the freedom to engage in repression without outside interference. One does not, alas, follow from the other: criticism of humanitarian intervention does not necessarily stem from cold-heartedness; not all of its opponents are brutal despots or apologists for them.

As we shall see, governments that cheer loudest for universal human rights and humanitarian intervention, and that themselves intervene, are capable of a great deal of hypocrisy and sanctimoniousness. Their reasons for entering some conflicts and not others do not simply reflect the facts or scale of the atrocity—consider Rwanda, the horrors of which would have compelled any principled intervener—but their own interests. They stay out because they don't want to act—because intervention is too dangerous, because the venue of slaughter is considered strategically unimportant, or because the offending government is an ally. Worse, liberal democracies have dealt with—and, indeed, actively supported—any number of brutal regimes guilty of killing their own people by the tens of thousands. Democracies may not go to war with other democracies, but their complicity in the massive violence perpetrated by nondemocratic states is undeniable. So is their willingness to exempt themselves from the universal values and legal principles they espouse and propagate. This less-than-honorable past is effaced by amnesia, explained away with rationalizations, and obscured by rhetoric directed at other states' crimes, making the double standard doubly distasteful.

The firm faith of interveners derives in part from the claim that since the Cold War, norms have fundamentally shifted in favor of universal human rights. This is questionable. Yes, treaties and declarations and resolutions record states' agreement that the evil of mass atrocity must be extinguished. But the signatories of these parchments have shown themselves unwilling to undertake concrete obligations with any degree of consistency. We are far from a universal norm that is reflected in practice. To recognize this we need but consider the millions who died, directly and indirectly, because of the violence the Democratic Republic of the Congo (or Zaire, as it was called from 1971 to 1997) has endured since 1994, the 800,000 slaughtered in Rwanda in 1994 in just one hundred days, and, again, the carnage in Syria.

The crass moral relativism that would present one person's mass atrocity as another's fight for freedom or security forms no part of my argument. I neither deny the seriousness of the problem nor celebrate its insolubility. Instead I aim to explain in detail why overarching solutions will prove elusive; to detail the harmful consequences that follow from believing otherwise; and, along the way, to expose some of the hypocrisy, smugness, and historical amnesia that pervade the paeans to humanitarian intervention.

The Consensus

The emphasis varies from one proponent of humanitarian intervention to another, but, in general, they base their arguments on a set of shared assumptions.

They assume that the end of the Cold War transformed international politics in ways that have made a universal approach to humanitarian intervention feasible. In the nineteenth century, the European powers intervened in support of Christian peoples persecuted by the rickety Ottoman Empire. Today any state may, in principle, intercede on behalf of any people. This transformation, we are told, owes to the spread of democratic ideals and human rights norms, the activity of transnational human rights organizations and "global civil society" more generally, and the emerging international consensus surrounding universal human rights. The result is an international context in which atrocities within countries can be deemed threats to peace and security and stopped by military means. This can be accomplished in two ways: under Chapter VII of the United Nations' Charter, which has traditionally been deemed applicable chiefly to wars among states; or, failing that, by a coalition of like-minded states, or even a single state, acting without the UN's blessing. Moreover, thanks to the creation of the International Criminal Court (ICC), perpetrators of atrocities can be brought to justice.

Interventionists argue that human rights norms are diffusing thanks to "norm entrepreneurs"—states and nonstate groups—and the information technology revolution. Among these norms is the belief that mass atrocities are intolerable and cannot be excused as the exercise of sovereign rights. States that flout this norm risk tangible and reputational losses. States of all types are increasingly inclined to embrace these norms, which are no longer rejected as Western or as the latest incarnation of cultural imperialism. Governments now covet legitimacy and value their standing in the global community. Their leaders are capable of acting as altruistic moral agents, not merely practitioners of cold-eyed realpolitik who think that all that counts is whether doing something benefits their country's interests.

Thanks to these transformations, long-standing "statist" conceptions of sovereignty are under assault as never before. Sovereignty can no longer serve only as a legal concept designed to protect the right of states to craft and implement policies within their boundaries without external interference. It now entails responsibilities; in particular, governments are expected to respect their citizens' basic human rights. Above all, they must not subject them to atrocities and must protect them from being killed arbitrarily. But the new understanding goes further than this. States can no longer claim to have negative rights— the right not to be interfered with—unless they also demonstrate that they can deliver on positive rights that extend beyond the minimal right to physical safety.

This concept of sovereignty provides the ethical and legal basis for humanitarian intervention in instances when states cannot or will not meet their basic obligations. Guaranteeing peoples' physical security is the duty of the governments that have legal jurisdiction over them, but when a government cannot or will not discharge this responsibility, it falls to the international community. To this end, foreign nations may use various means, including military force. This right of intervention from beyond results from universal agreement that there is a "Responsibility to Protect"—R2P, as it is called in human rights circles. If a particular state fails to uphold this responsibility, then the world must do so in its stead.

R2P advocates recognize that citizens may be wary of sending their soldiers abroad to end slaughter and produce peace in violent places. But they also believe that if leaders explain cogently and forcefully the need for armed humanitarian intervention in a given instance, citizens' reluctance can be overcome. Indeed, public opinion can be mobilized and turned into a legitimating, enabling asset. Leaders may demonstrate to their fellow citizens that—to borrow from the lexicon of just war theory—the standards of *jus ad bellum* (the conditions under which war may justifiably be waged) have been met: that there are morally defensible reasons to use force. Once the moral purpose becomes clear the public will support intervention, especially if leaders provide assurances that they will wage war in ways that minimize the death of innocents.

Concord among great powers is a precondition for universal norms, and the end of the Cold War, according to interventionists, has made that more feasible. That in turn makes it easier to gain the UN

Security Council's authorization before undertaking humanitarian interventions, as occurred in Bosnia and Libya. Obtaining that authorization became still easier in 2005, when the UN officially adopted the R2P doctrine at its World Summit. But in the eyes of some supporters of humanitarian intervention, if a permanent member of the Security Council should veto, or threaten to veto, an intervention, leaving the UN deadlocked, it is legitimate (from a moral standpoint), if not necessarily legal, for a country or coalition to act independently, as NATO did in Kosovo in 1999. Such interventions are morally valid and will, if repeated, eventually reshape customary law. That in turn will transform statutory international law so that humanitarian intervention cannot be held hostage to political discord within the Security Council.

Finally, interventionists repudiate theories of international relations rooted in "realism" or "neorealism," which they see as tone deaf to, or dismissive of, these normative and political changes. They contend that such theories rest on a worldview according to which states are the most potent participants in international relations; national interests alone, rather than altruism or ethical beliefs, define states' behavior; international law and organizations reflect the relative distribution of power among states and have little independent influence; norms and values are, in the main, rationalizations for the pursuit of states' interests; and cooperation among states is hampered by irreconcilable national interests and states' focus on relative gains, a proclivity that undermines cooperation even when every state could gain in absolute terms by joining hands. Realism, in this view, offers an outdated, impoverished, and inaccurate view of world politics. In particular it obscures, even denies, the new possibilities for humanitarian intervention and hence for a new model of international relations in which morality plays a pivotal role and is not an afterthought or rationalization.

Why the Consensus Is Wrong, in Brief

I reject each of the propositions underlying the consensus.

The end of the Cold War has been consequential, but the claim that it has fundamentally transformed the ways in which states think and act amounts, as E. H. Carr observed, to an instance of the wish fathering the thought. It is not that states are incapable of embracing altruistic and ethical precepts. It is that they rarely move from words to deeds when circumstances lead them to conclude that acting in the service of overarching moral principles, as opposed to concrete interests, will be costly in terms of blood, treasure, and strategic goals. Even democracies, whatever their avowed moral commitments, will not be inclined to intervene without popular support in instances when there are no compelling interests or when intervention could prove dangerous.

The interventions in Bosnia and Kosovo might be pointed to as counterexamples. But let us remember that three years of mass slaughter preceded intervention in Bosnia. During that time, Serbia and its Bosnian Serb paramilitary protégés acted with impunity and committed all manner of atrocities in defiance of a small contingent of hapless and poorly equipped UN peacekeepers. Armed intervention occurred only when officials in Washington and Brussels feared that allowing the carnage to continue would destroy NATO's credibility by demonstrating that its talk about adopting a new mission extending beyond Europe amounted to bluster, even when it came to the continent. These leaders were especially sensitive to that concern because the end of the Cold War put the alliance's value in doubt. Showing that it could offer solutions to conflicts beyond its treaty-defined realm was one way to counter claims that it risked becoming a relic.

NATO's Bosnia and Kosovo campaigns were also made possible by Russia's free fall. Russia opposed both interventions, but at the time the country was dependent on Western economic assistance. NATO probably would not have intervened militarily in the Balkans in the 1990s had Moscow's opposition been backed by commensurate power.

That Russia's weakness enabled a flourishing of seemingly humanitarian outreach in the 1990s becomes that much clearer in light of that country's recent opposition to the continuing calamity in Syria. Russian backing of President Bashar al-Assad has stymied intervention. Along with China, Russia has thwarted any UN resolution that would legitimize foreign military involvement. And in September 2015, President Vladimir Putin deployed military forces, including naval infantry, fighter jets, armored vehicles, and air defense missiles to Syria to shore up Assad's besieged, shaky government.[2] Russia and China learned their lessons in Libya. Neither country opposed Security Council Resolution 1973, which, in 2011, authorized military action, undertaken by a coalition of NATO and Arab states, to protect Libyan civilians; but they complained bitterly, well before the mission had ended, that "regime change" was afoot and had never been part of the mandate. They became determined not to allow a repeat performance in Syria and have acted accordingly. Iran, too, has aided Assad with weapons and advisers and encouraged fighters from Hezbollah to help as well. This makes Syria a more formidable adversary than Libya or Serbia, one reason why NATO has been unwilling to intervene and why there has been no serious talk of a "coalition of the willing" or a "league of democracies" acting in its place.

The claim that there is now a new level of great power consensus is hard to take seriously, especially when it comes to humanitarian intervention. It was not a commonality of values that enabled the Balkan interventions: both Russia and China opposed them as violations of sovereignty, and they were not the only countries to do so. What mattered was the West's massive advantage in power—the "unipolar moment," as columnist Charles Krauthammer famously put it. Likewise, Libya and Syria have, albeit in different ways, highlighted the disunity among the permanent members of the Security Council. So has the Darfur conflict, in which the Sudanese government of Omar al-Bashir has been shielded by China and Russia. Bashir has consequently been able to limit the size, capabilities, and mandate of the UN/NATO peacekeeping force deployed in Darfur, where the killing and displacement of people continues. None of the Western powers that have been at the forefront of touting the virtue and imperative of humanitarian intervention has been eager to intervene there, and indeed, no matter these countries' verbal support for universal rights, they continue to resist any treaty or declaration that could obligate them to act in defense of such principles. At the 2005 UN World Summit, these powers opposed any formulation of R2P that would have legally obligated them to stop atrocities.

This lack of consensus is evident more generally. For instance, there is little agreement on how to deliver aid to poor countries, in what measure, and when. Who knows exactly how far the obligations

of rich states extend? The central claim of intervention proponents—
the worldwide spread of universal norms and their acceptance by the
international community—therefore amounts to little more than a
conceit. Much of the world fears and suspects that the effort to legitimate humanitarian intervention by means of supposedly universal
norms is designed to camouflage the pursuit of power by the powerful. This sentiment is especially strong in non-European, ex-colonial
countries, which are understandably cynical about the true motives
underlying such ethical principles. They suspect that project interveners present as disinterested, universal, and beneficial to all of humanity may be driven by parochial self-interest. Whether this sentiment
is always warranted is beside the point. What matters is that it exists.

At first blush, the UN's endorsement of R2P appears to contradict
my skepticism regarding international accord. But the debates leading up to the adoption of R2P revealed deep international divisions.
Russia, China, India, a host of "nonaligned" states, and many from
the Group of 77 (G-77) were vocal in expressing their reservations,
particularly about the threat that the R2P doctrine posed to sovereignty. The eventual agreement produced a watered-down R2P that
imposed no obligations on states, refrained from mentioning *armed*
intervention, and insisted that R2P operations require Security
Council approval. In the aftermath of the Libya campaign, Brazil
introduced a coda: Responsibility While Protecting (RWP). While
often described solely as an effort to impose conditions that limit
civilian casualties during armed humanitarian interventions, RWP in
fact seeks to constrain interventions in the first place; I will discuss
this in later chapters.

This brings me to another axiom embraced by those favoring
humanitarian intervention: the emergence of an international community providing universal legitimacy to humanitarian intervention.

It is certainly possible to speak of a global community in which
states and an array of organizations are connected by the flows of trade,
investment, banking capital, migration, and information. It is also true
that international politics is not simply a Hobbesian struggle among
fearful, predatory, and ego-driven states in which, as Thucydides put
it in the Melian Dialogue, "the strong do as they will, the weak do
as they must." An account of world politics that dismisses the role

of international law and moral reasoning would verge on caricature. Yet the contention that the world is tending toward a convergence of norms and, in consequence, cohering as a community bound by common values is far-fetched. Despite the interconnections I have mentioned, the world—by virtue of power disparities among states, their varied historical experiences, and the strength and diversity of nationalism, culture, and religion—is pluralistic. The extent of the pluralism makes it hard to discern an international community united by a common morality or even universal mores and norms.

It is one thing to spot these norms in speeches and summit documents; it is another to establish that they actually enable collective action on problems such as mass atrocities. To take a case in point, the push for the redefinition of sovereignty as a source not only of rights but also of responsibilities is largely—though not solely—Western in its provenance and has met with skepticism in many parts of the world. The proposition that armed intervention is legitimate when a state fails to fulfill these sovereign responsibilities likewise lacks the wide support that proponents of humanitarian intervention pretend it enjoys.

Humanitarian intervention can never become an ethically driven pursuit disentangled from power and interests. Too many exceptions have been made for too many violators. Consider the West's two-faced approach in Iraq. The United States and its allies intervened militarily to protect the Kurds from Saddam Hussein's army after Iraq was defeated in the Gulf War of 1990–1991, an episode that receives prominent mention in interventionist literature. But those same powers stood by during the 1980s when Saddam razed the Kurds' villages, drove them from their homes, and slaughtered and, during the infamous 1988 Operation Anfal campaign, even gassed them. Indeed, during these years, the United States government under President Reagan provided Saddam with intelligence information and loans for food purchases as the latter fought Iran. The White House even discouraged Congress from issuing resolutions condemning his onslaught against Kurdish civilians or imposing sanctions.[3] What mattered at that time was that Saddam was fighting Iran. Once the alignment between Saddam and the United States turned to enmity—and once the declining Soviet Union was no longer able to serve as Saddam's patron—the Iraqi tyrant's abuse of his people became intolerable to American leaders. Fast forward to 2003. When Saddam was found not to have weapons of mass destruction following the American invasion, the justification for the war became Saddam's cruelty. Iraqis, so it was said, had been saved from tyranny by force of arms. But Saddam had been no less cruel in years past, particularly during Anfal, and, for all his faults, was not committing atrocities in 2003.

Rwanda illustrates the point in a different way. Some have argued that nothing could have been done to stop the 1994 genocide, a claim that has been challenged, not least by the UN commander on the ground, General Roméo Dallaire. In any case, studies of that orgiastic episode of violence make clear that no state contemplated intervention. The UN force (UNAMIR, United Nations Assistance Mission for Rwanda) deployed before the genocide began was small and poorly equipped from the outset, but none of the major powers favored beefing it up. The United States and Belgium, which pulled back its contingent after a few of its soldiers were tortured and killed, wanted the force withdrawn. Even lesser steps, such as the jamming of the Hutu government's hate-mongering radio station, which played a major role in orchestrating the killings, were not seriously considered, let alone attempted.

These examples suggest that humanitarian intervention has a weaker moral foundation than its supporters claim.

If context and national interests matter, so do power ratios. Powerful states such as Russia and China, to take but two of the most obvious examples, will be immune from armed intervention no matter what they do in their rebellious regions, whether the North Caucasus, Tibet, or Xinjiang. That's as it should be. It would be foolish—indeed, dangerous—to insist on a doctrine of humanitarian intervention that is absolutely consistent in its application. But in practice this prudence means that only weak states, and those lacking strong protectors, will be on humanitarian intervention's receiving end. One could say that that's still better than doing nothing, but one cannot then claim that universal norms nevertheless propel humanitarian intervention. These norms are selectively applied.

My point here is not to apportion blame but to reject the contention that ethics plays a decisive part in humanitarian intervention and that its practice has been enabled because states have revamped their motives and values. Realism may not be the perfect guide to understanding everything that happens in world politics, but there are occasions when it keeps us honest, restrains us from flights of fancy, and makes us face up to the tragic element in politics.

Ordinary citizens seem to understand this better than do influential proponents of intervention. When Western citizens sense that intervention does not defend or extend vital interests and could even end in bloody and costly quagmires, they reject it or offer tepid approval. Despite the much-vaunted "CNN effect," whereby viewers who are exposed to visceral televised images of atrocities demand that their leaders stop the butchery, no convincing evidence suggests that people are willing to undergo major hardships, spend a lot of money, or see many of their soldiers die in order to save strangers. In Somalia, the killing of a few soldiers led President Clinton to pull out American troops, with the American public supporting his decision. The West ignores Rwanda, Darfur, and Syria. Attention to Congo came late and remains insufficient. Leaders recognize the limits of their citizens' altruism, which is why they conduct humanitarian interventions from the safety of distance and high altitudes, using missiles and air strikes, not ground troops. That this mode of intervention can prolong wars and move perpetrators to ramp up the killing—as it did in Kosovo—has made no difference.

Then there is the problem of perverse incentives. The lesson that the Kosovo Liberation Army (KLA) took from NATO's intervention in Bosnia was that if it could intensify its attacks and induce the Serb state to escalate its military campaign and repression in Kosovo, NATO would come to the Kosovars' aid. Accordingly, the KLA set about conducting systematic attacks on Serb targets, including civilian ones, goading the Serbs to respond. Eventually NATO's cavalry did arrive. But the alliance was determined to limit its campaign to airpower so as to avoid casualties among its own troops. The result? The Serbs, seeing that they would not last long against air strikes, feverishly killed and expelled Kosovars, more of whom were killed or were expelled *after* the intervention than in the months preceding it. This dynamic—the attempt by one of the parties to a violent conflict to trigger an external intervention—is not peculiar to Kosovo. It revealed itself in Libya as well, where the anti-Gaddafi fighters turned to violence at an early stage, lobbied actively for external intervention following a crackdown by the regime, and publicized inflated figures on civilian deaths.

Alongside perverse incentives are unintended consequences. Interventions can lead to prolonged postwar occupations, costly and corrupting infusions of aid, and grandiose efforts to build state institutions and militaries from scratch. It is a protracted and frustrating business, and the citizens of countries footing the bill and deploying the forces tend to run out of patience, which makes *jus post bellum* (a just postwar order) hard to achieve. The hazards of state building and economic reconstruction have been revealed in Afghanistan, Iraq, and Bosnia.

Interventions can also have more immediate malign effects on the intended beneficiaries and their neighbors. Nowhere is this more evident than in Libya, where, since the toppling of Muammar Gaddafi, there is no functioning state to speak of. The resulting vacuum has been filled by militias that defy the central government and by armed Islamist groups that pursue a millenarian agenda and have no tolerance for those of different faiths or even for coreligionists following different interpretations of Islam. And the rest of the Maghreb has become a more dangerous place because of the fallout from Libya. Today the whole region is more hospitable to groups trafficking in religious extremism and violence than it had been while Gaddafi was in power.

The literature on humanitarian intervention is so suffused with moral certainty that it has not considered these problems in any depth. Such hubris makes intervention still more susceptible to the law of unintended consequences.

In Chapter 1, I explore humanitarian intervention's intellectual ancestry. The moral passion of the project, its ambition, and its confidence—indeed, its blindness—reflect the unfortunate side of a particular intellectual tradition, which has otherwise improved our lives. I discuss that tradition and how it has shaped the humanitarian intervention project. From this, readers will learn why this book bears the title it does.

Advocates of intervention may make the case that it can both serve states' interests and contribute to global stability. But what draws them to the idea is not pragmatism; it is principle. They contend that states can act in defense of people being persecuted even when the victims do not belong to communities, such as the religious group or nation, to which interveners attach special significance. Humanitarian intervention has placed a bet on the power of moralism—and that bet has a universal ambit. Chapter 2 is an inquiry into the soundness of this wager.

Chapter 3 takes up the debate on sovereignty and discusses the ways in which that concept is being rethought. Readers may be tempted to dismiss this debate as an academic tempest, but it has important practical consequence. Those who favor reframing sovereignty have a specific aim: to provide a moral defense for humanitarian intervention and to challenge the prerogatives of the state. To gain acceptance, policies require not just practical utility but also moral purchase and legitimacy. The revisionist account of sovereignty aims to provide humanitarian intervention with both. That's why the debate matters.

In Chapter 4, I turn to international law. International lawyers are prominent voices in the humanitarian intervention debate, and many seek greater leeway for action. One might say that if international law does not permit humanitarian intervention, then too bad for international law, which is bunk anyway. But for all its weaknesses—and there are many—international law actually does regulate state behavior in a number of ways. It provides rules of the road, and states collide less often and cooperate more frequently as a result. Besides, states seek to legitimize their foreign policies on the basis of international law; they don't want to be seen as outlaws. But whether, to what extent, and in what ways international law permits humanitarian intervention is hotly contested among lawyers. Understanding the dispute is not an arid exercise in legality; it provides a distinct vantage point from which to assess the limitations and controversies of humanitarian intervention and to assay the extent to which a global consensus supports it.

No proper discussion of humanitarian intervention can steer clear of R2P. No principle has shaped intervention discussions so powerfully, is so creative and ambitious, or has won as much international acclaim, which is precisely why it should be subject to close inspection. That is one goal of Chapter 5. After examining the use of humanitarian intervention in the nineteenth century, which proponents of the practice recall as a golden age, it turns to the emergence of R2P, tracing its origins and evolution, discussing the debates it has occasioned, and the degree of support it has won. The evidence suggests that R2P, and humanitarian intervention generally, is a far more contested concept than its proponents aver.

Chapter 6 segues into the real practice of humanitarian intervention, examines the gulf between states' proclaimed fealty to human rights principles and their actual policies. It considers the claim, common in the literature on human rights generally and humanitarian intervention specifically, that the end of the Cold War has produced a normative shift that has increased markedly the influence of universal conceptions of human rights on the conduct of states. In particular, it examines the extent to which this shift is reflected in the concrete policies of Western democracies, particularly the United States. To this end, the chapter discusses at length the 2011 intervention in Libya.

There's the intervention, and there's what happens afterward. One can knock down a brutal regime, but doing that and then decamping amounts to a demolition exercise. There are good reasons, practical and ethical, to think hard about what is needed to establish a stable, minimally efficient, and just postwar order. It's easy to come up with a checklist of dos and don'ts, but devilishly difficult to accomplish the former and avoid the latter. The humanitarian interventions of the last few decades make abundantly clear that there are no quick fixes: the task takes years, is expensive, and can be dangerous. When it's done badly, or not at all, the consequences for those whose lives have been saved, for their neighbors, and even for those farther afield can be dire. I take up the aftermath of intervention in Chapter 7, looking in particular at Bosnia and Libya. The 2003 war in Iraq, which offers valuable lessons, even though it is generally not seen as a humanitarian intervention despite the efforts of some influential defenders of the campaign to present it as such, receives attention as well. One of this chapter's themes is that humanitarian interventions, like war in general, produce many unforeseen and unintended consequences that their architects ignore or dismiss, whether from ignorance or arrogance. Another is that the aftermath of intervention poses massive challenges and that states underestimate their costs and severity and baleful consequences.

Chapter 8 considers two related issues. I turn first to the argument of those who believe that there exists an international community constituted not merely by the connective transactions of trade and finance, high-speed communications, and institutions of governance but also by common ethical values, particularly compassion, responsibility, and obligation. In a word, I am skeptical that an international community exists in the latter sense. It certainly can be—and ought to be—an aspiration, but it is not an actuality; nor is it likely to be anytime soon.

Second, I evaluate the effectiveness of global institutions to which humanitarian interventionists assign special significance for stopping violence within states and dispensing justice, specifically the UN's Department of Peacekeeping Operations and the International Criminal Court (ICC). I assess the latter's effectiveness in some detail given that those who write about human rights and humanitarian intervention believe that it will bring perpetrators of atrocities to justice and deter governments and groups from resorting to mass killing. As I see it, despite talk to the contrary, states don't want these institutions, particularly the Court, to have wide-reaching powers and thus routinely manipulate them and impair their effectiveness. States, while happy to see justice applied to others (providing they are not friends or allies), quickly balk and erect obstacles when they themselves come under scrutiny.

The concluding chapter begins by addressing two questions that critics of humanitarian intervention are often asked: If you don't like the solution on offer, what do you have in mind for a world in which governments and groups engage in atrocities repeatedly? You say that humanitarian intervention is applied inconsistently, but what's wrong with doing what one can where one can? After addressing these questions, I consider democracies' failure to live up to the human rights principles they support fervently and the effect that has on gaining a global consensus favoring humanitarian intervention.

I turn next to thinkers who believe that interveners should risk their soldiers' lives by requiring them to fight on the ground if necessary, and not solely from the air or sea, to save innocents. Those who make this case correctly point to the price that innocents pay when interventions conducted from afar inadvertently encourage perpetrators to ramp up the killing and prolong wars. But in my view their insistence that states should, when needed, send ground troops into places where mass killings are occurring is misguided and morally problematic.

I then consider the ideas of cosmopolitan theorists who favor humanitarian intervention. The adherents of this school share a bedrock principle, namely, that the fate of "others," no matter who and where they are, matters to all of us. Borders, states, and nationalism condition us to believe that our moral imagination and duties cannot extend beyond the frontiers of countries. Cosmopolitans insist that the unit of our moral concern ought to be the individual, regardless of nationality. Some go so far as to advocate "global citizenship." This worldview has important implications for humanitarian intervention, a subject to which some prominent cosmopolitans have turned their attention.

Our world brims with challenges and crises that affect the lives of billions, the prospects for peace, and the possibilities for justice. All of those engaged in the drama of world politics—states, groups, scholars, activists, leaders, soldiers, and citizens—want peace and fairness, but on terms that are not easily reconcilable and may even be incompatible. I hope to persuade you that the terms of peace and justice proffered by humanitarian interventionists withstand neither ethical nor practical scrutiny.

1

THE ANIMATING IDEAL

Armed humanitarian intervention manifests the belief that states are morally obligated to stop atrocities beyond their borders, by military means if necessary.

The resort to hostilities on behalf of foreigners in distress is a particular variety of humanitarianism,[1] the essence of which, as Michael Barnett has put it, is an "emancipatory ethics."[2] This takes many forms in practice: providing food, shelter, medicine, and other essentials to victims of war and natural disaster; combating cruelties such as slavery, sex trafficking, and genital mutilation; promoting economic development in poor regions; exposing human rights violators and mobilizing public protests; establishing democratic institutions and the rule of law in "postconflict societies," the leaden social science euphemism for countries that have been ravaged by war and have a shot at peace.

Uniting these diverse acts of rescue is the promise to render assistance wherever it is needed and without respect to who is in need. Again, following Barnett, "impartiality" is one of humanitarianism's "sacrosanct principles." From the standpoint of interventionists, the means may be diplomatic or coercive. Alone or in concert, with or without the approval of international bodies, states name and shame wrongdoers, and they offer rewards, assurances, safe passage, comfortable exile, and immunity from prosecution to dissuade perpetrators from killing. They may also impose economic sanctions and inflict violence.

This last recourse, armed intervention, is by its nature the most intrusive and controversial item in the humanitarian toolkit. It violates sovereignty as commonly understood since the modern state emerged from the 1648 Peace of Westphalia, ending Europe's Thirty Years War. After millions died as a result of kings battling to—among other aims—protect persecuted coreligionists abroad, Europe's rulers decided, in theory anyway, to leave one another alone, regardless of what was happening within their respective domains. By contrast, when states launch humanitarian interventions, the offending government is in effect told that what's happening within its territory is no longer its business alone.[3]

Boundaries of Sympathy and Duty

The disparate forms of humanitarianism emerge from a set of foundational ideas. One posits that humans are capable of moral reasoning and therefore of extending justice to people who do not belong to our communities, however we define them. Another principle asserts that we have a duty to help when others are suffering, even if we have not caused their distress. A third maintains that we are capable of exhibiting sympathy toward victims of violence and privation.

It may surprise readers to find that Adam Smith offers one of the strongest defenses of this universal sympathy. Though often marshaled in behalf of individualism and the single-minded pursuit of economic self-interest, Smith regarded sympathy toward others as an essential human attribute. Even in *The Wealth of Nations* Smith did not advocate selfishness, but his interest in compassion comes through most forcefully in the lesser-known *Theory of Moral Sentiments*. "Though our brother is on the rack," he writes, "as long as we ourselves are at our ease, our senses will never inform us of what he suffers. They never did and never can carry us beyond our own person, and it is by imagination only we can form any conception of what are his sensations ... His agonies, when they are thus brought home to ourselves, when we have thus adopted them and made them our own, begin at last to affect us, and we then tremble and shudder at the thought of what he feels."[4] In other words, we should not accord special moral significance to boundaries of belonging. This universalism is inseparable from humanitarianism.

Yet sympathy arises most easily in relation to those with whom we believe we have special ties. That word "we"—and relatives such as "us" and "our"—means different things to different people. It may refer to members of a nuclear or extended family; of a tribe, ethnicity, religious group, or civic organization; of a social club, professional association, or trade union. National political communities mobilize "we" solidarity through education, nationalism, citizenship, patriotism, and propaganda.

Communitarian philosophers look to national political communities as the outer limit—the largest collectivities toward which individuals can feel a genuine and distinctive attachment and obligation. As Alasdair MacIntyre puts it, "the case for making patriotism a virtue" is compelling. "Detached from my community," he writes, "I will be apt to lose my hold upon all genuine standards of judgment. Loyalty to that community ... is ... a prerequisite for morality."[5] Communitarians reject the charge that national patriotism encourages intolerance and jingoism and promotes callous disregard for outsiders' ideas, interests, and ways of life. Instead, they argue that a nation fosters an identity, which, precisely by virtue of its particularism, cultivates the moral and civic virtues and habits that enable citizenship.[6] The Greek philosopher Diogenes (fourth century B.C.E.) declared himself not an Athenian but "a citizen of the world"; communitarians consider such a claim unworkable because it demands that people identify with an airy abstraction. They would agree with Benjamin Barber, who holds that universalism, because of its "thinness," cannot satisfy people's innate desire for belonging.[7]

This debate bears on the program of humanitarian intervention because it takes on questions of who we are, what we owe and to whom, and what can realistically serve as the spatial boundaries of our obligations.[8] Humanitarians in general, and interventionists specifically, need not be world citizens like Diogenes.[9] But all are inspired by the ideal that compassion, duty, and assistance can and should be universal in practice.

The Enlightenment Ethos

In addition to its universalistic conception of compassion and obligation, humanitarianism rests on the conviction that human agency can transform the world. The roots of this optimistic perspective lie in the Enlightenment, the wellspring of individualism, rationalism, self-mastery, and the modern belief in progressive sociopolitical change, which originated in the latter half of the seventeenth century and extended through the eighteenth, leaving its mark on succeeding epochs.

In the Enlightenment tradition, humanitarianism assumes that people possess the moral, intellectual, and organizational capacities to end or alleviate ills such as violence, poverty, injustice, and unnecessary death, writ large. Cruelty toward innocents is not an inevitable, inescapable fact of life. Instead, from the standpoint of humanitarianism, such problems can be solved through the accumulation of knowledge and application of effort. Just as once-incurable diseases such as smallpox have been eradicated, so too can social ills be permanently relieved.

Humanitarianism is scarcely unique in embracing these postulates. Science, technology, and political ideologies as different as liberalism and socialism all owe a debt to the Enlightenment invention of social engineering. Humanitarian intervention represents a distinctive form of this engineering, relying on military force to stop mass killing. Where humanitarianism rejects the inevitability of poverty and exploitation generally, humanitarian intervention rejects the inevitability of a specific form of violence: mass atrocities. And in the aftermath of an intervention, it seeks to help create just governments and societies. The goal amounts to nothing less than the extirpation of tragedy—more precisely, an extreme variant of it—from international politics by means of human will and ingenuity.

Humanitarianism and Human Rights

Because humanitarianism entails a transnational conception of duty to those in trouble, it would be reasonable to infer a further humanitarian belief in a universal conception of rights. But a commitment to human rights—the idea that individuals everywhere are entitled to certain basic and inalienable rights simply by virtue of being human—was not among humanitarianism's foundational credos.

The intellectual historian Samuel Moyn argues convincingly that while the robust commitment to universal human rights is ubiquitous these days, it emerged only a few decades ago (in the 1970s, to be exact), notwithstanding references to this principle in the 1945 United Nations Charter and its subsequent adoption in the Universal Declaration of Human Rights (1948).[10] Moyn points out that when the idea of basic rights—such as freedom of expression, the right to own property, and the right to equal treatment under the law—was first articulated, it was understood that their precise content and ambit would be determined and worked out within individual political communities. Slaves, women, those lacking the property needed to qualify for full citizenship, and colonial subjects, among others, were long denied even these basic rights. Their struggle for inclusion proved long and hard, and only in the 1970s, with the help of transnational movements and organizations such as Amnesty International, itself founded in 1961, did the universal conception of human rights and the global movement to actualize them start to emerge.

Humanitarian intervention did not form part of the human rights movement's original agenda, which focused on governments' denials of basic rights and on the plight of prisoners of conscience. Nineteenth-century manifestations of humanitarian intervention were universal neither in concept nor in application. Only certain categories of people—notably the Christians of the Ottoman Empire—qualified for rescue, and the same great powers that dispatched their soldiers into the Ottoman Sultan's domains then forcibly colonized vast swaths of the globe, and with scant regard for their victims' humanness. They did not believe that the people they subjugated qualified for equal rights, or even compassion, by virtue of their personhood. Humanitarianism in this era had an acutely limited arc, making it a contradiction in terms.

During the 1970s, the same Western governments that today champion humanitarian intervention condemned the practice as illegal and destabilizing, even when it could have saved lives by putting an end to mass killings. Only after the Cold War—an era in which strategic calculations were the touchstone of foreign policy—has humanitarian intervention been regarded as desirable and permissible, powered by a commitment to universal human rights.

Against Realism

To believe in humanitarianism, then, is to reject the proposition, common in realist thinking, that certain immutable features of human nature and politics routinely and inevitably conspire to produce terrible outcomes.

Realists such as George Kennan, Reinhold Niebuhr, and Hans Morgenthau regard egoism, selfishness, and the impulse to dominate others, including through violence, as indelible human traits that, by extension, shape the conduct of states.[11] So elemental and powerful are these drives that they can at best be contained.[12] As realists see it, there is no basis for believing that human progress will eradicate these urges. Hence they view the humanitarian intervention enterprise with skepticism.

Despite appearances, realists are not enemies of idealism, or even of utopianism, and certainly do not dismiss the significance of normative values.[13] The realist E. H. Carr was careful to warn that taken to extremes, realism would "empty thought of purpose," "offer nothing but a naked struggle for power which makes any kind of international society impossible," and become "a disguise for the interests of the privileged."[14] Like Carr, Niebuhr valued idealism and hope, whether secular or religious, for the same reasons. Realism's distinctiveness lies in its insistence that power, self-interest, and hypocrisy (and for Niebuhr, the theologian, evil and sin) perpetually intrude, inevitably limiting the possibilities for changing international politics and ruling out categorical solutions to persistent problems, such as violence and war.[15] Schools of political thought energized by, and confident in, the promise of a universal community, do not deny that these limits exist but hold that they can be overcome and are contingent, not immutable.

Realists contend that a state's national interests, not overarching normative principles, ought to determine whether, when, and how its leaders use military power. The notion of universal moral principles, according to Morgenthau, "is either so vague as to have no concrete meaning that could provide rational guidance for political action, or it will be nothing but the reflection of the moral preconceptions of a particular nation and will by that same token be unable to gain the universal recognition it pretends to serve."[16] Indeed, to the realists, sweeping ideals offer not only an intellectually untenable basis for foreign policy, but also an unsafe one. They warn that utopian visions beget hubris and moralizing, endangering statecraft. Instead they emphasize diplomacy and prudence, making compromises when possible by taking account of other states' interests and ensuring that, as Kennan put it, one's own are "reasonably, not extravagantly, conceived."[17] Thus foreign policy ought to focus on the balance of power among states, not the nature of politics within them.

The classic, if extreme, exposition of realism appears in Thucydides' Melian Dialogue, a dramatic retelling of a diplomatic meeting during the Peloponnesian War, which dragged on, ravaging Hellas for over a quarter of a century.[18] Athenian emissaries arrive at the island of Melos and tell its leaders that they must renounce their fealty to Sparta and submit to Athens, or else be destroyed and enslaved. It is that simple—and, for the Melians, that complicated. The Athenian envoys proclaim an iron law of politics: the powerful do as they wish to the weak, and the weak have no choice but to comply. Virtue and morals and justice are all irrelevant, except as window dressing and verbiage. Submit or die, say the envoys.

By contrast, for proponents of humanitarian intervention virtue and justice are paramount. They understand that foreign policies can never be based on ideals alone, and they admit that altruism is rarely unadulterated. But they argue that justice matters deeply and need not be at odds with self-interest. Fernando Tesón, a scholar of international law and one of the most passionate and intellectually formidable advocates of humanitarian intervention, goes further. He deems purity of motive irrelevant; what matters is whether states are willing to act against a perpetrator of atrocities and whether the military action they take succeeds in stopping the carnage.[19]

Still, the humanitarian interventionist's call to arms is never, in the first instance, guided by calculations of self-interest or national security. The primary motivation must be the commitment to transnational moral responsibility, human rights, and justice. Order, while desirable, must not trump justice, which may necessitate war. As Thomas Weiss puts it, though humanitarian intervention may be undertaken for a number of reasons, the ethical objective must be "explicit and prominent," not incidental.[20] The supporters of humanitarian intervention are, in this respect, heirs to the natural rights tradition of Hugo Grotius, the seventeenth-century Dutch philosopher credited as the founder of modern international law. Grotius affirmed rulers' rights to intervene in the domains of others to stop grave injustices—though, oddly, he denied the oppressed the same right to overthrow or even fight the state. Humanitarian intervention bears similarity to the natural law tradition to the extent that both assert inviolable ethical principles—such as the impermissibility of committing atrocities—agreed upon through moral reasoning and applicable to all humankind, regardless of rules established by legislation and treaties.[21]

Humanitarian interventionists also regard norms of justice and human rights as independent forces in international relations, distinct in motive and efficacy from any legal or power factors at play. They fault realism for its supposedly narrow, materialist explanation of states' behavior and for its dismissal of altruism as a mere rationalization for foreign policy.[22] Norms, in the interventionist's view, constrain states by legitimizing certain acts and withholding legitimacy from others. This does not mean advocates of humanitarian intervention demand their preferred policy be undertaken whenever atrocities occur or that they are blind to risks, costs, and the odds of success; rather, they reject the power- and interest-driven view of politics that realists expound.

To those favoring humanitarian intervention, realism offers a soulless, deterministic, might-makes-right paradigm of politics that is as factually flawed as it is morally vacuous.[23] Virtuous violence can be turned usefully against injustice, and it ought to be, so that the weak are not condemned to a Melian world in which they are at the mercy of the strong.

An Elite Assault on Sovereignty

Given the centrality of justice to the humanitarian interventionists' project, they refuse to blind themselves to the internal politics of foreign countries. From the perspective of interventionists, sovereignty, to which realists attach great importance, has for too long protected predatory states from outside punishment. Tesón dismisses sovereignty as "the Hegelian Myth," a moribund principle designed to defend states, not citizens.[24] For him, the state that tramples on basic human rights loses legitimacy—and, potentially, immunity—from external intervention. As we shall see in Chapter 3, he is hardly alone in taking this stand.

In the classic Westphalian conception of international politics, states are immune from external interference unless they engage in aggression against other states.[25] This precept has frequently been violated in practice, but it has come under more fundamental and vigorous attack since the Cold War ended. So deeply has Westphalian sovereignty been undermined that Roberto Belloni argues it is no longer the default position. He notes that "up to the end of the Cold War [sic] states, international organizations, and nongovernmental organizations (NGOs) had to go to great lengths to justify their interference in the domestic affairs of other states." But "today the opposite is the case. States are under a great deal of pressure to explain why they do *not* want to intervene . . . to promote and protect human rights in the name of a nascent transnational morality by definition applying across borders. The assumption has turned in favor of such intervention, not against it."[26]

Belloni correctly points out that the traditional legal and philosophical barriers to intervention have come under fire in the last few decades. But he is wrong about the source of the change. Leaders in Western democracies, where the movement for universal human rights, norms, and humanitarian intervention has been most energetic, do not face overwhelming public pressure to defend human rights abroad by force of arms. Western citizens are in fact chary about the costs and consequences of rescue operations. Human rights groups, international lawyers, public intellectuals, journalists, and academics in Western democracies have been the true agents of change. By dint of expertise, political access, media clout, and money, they have promoted the idea that the balance between the rights of states and the rights of individuals must change, that states must be made accountable for massive violations of human rights, and that international organizations and states should intervene to hold them accountable and thus save lives.

Yet these elite voices rely on what they see as mass support. For instance, the legal philosopher Allen Buchanan maintains that the rights enjoyed by the citizens of liberal democracies flow from universal principles that perforce extend even to outsiders, entailing a positive duty to assist others when they are in harm's way.[27] Whether these duties are discharged depends on whether citizens of Western democracies wish to discharge them. Joshua Goldstein and Jon Western insist that this condition has been met and then some: there have been "deep changes in public norms about violence against civilians" and this has "altered global—not simply Western—attitudes about intervention."[28]

These views represent standard fare, if not gospel, within the humanitarian intervention community. Yet no evidence suggests that intervention has deep support among citizens of Western democracies, let alone those of other nations. This is particularly clear when the public fears that an intervention will be protracted, costly, and dangerous and that it is not justified by compelling demands of national interest. Consider the 2011 Libya intervention. A 2012 German Marshall Fund poll conducted in the United States and twelve European Union members found majority support for intervention in only five countries (Sweden, France, the Netherlands, Bulgaria, and Germany).[29] A March 2011 Pew opinion poll found 63 percent of Americans believed the United States had no responsibility to act in Libya.[30] Just 13 percent supported sending troops, 16 percent favored striking Libya's air defense systems, and 44 percent backed a no-fly zone. To provide perspective, the survey reported the level of support for intervention in previous conflicts: 30 percent in Bosnia, 47 percent in Kosovo, and 51 percent in Darfur. As I discuss in detail in Chapter 2, Americans and Europeans have consistently refused to become deeply involved in Syria, even as the conflict there has worsened. These numbers hardly point to a deep popular commitment to intervention.

Because the average Western citizen does not consider the advancement of human rights worldwide—let alone the use of military force to stop atrocities—a high priority, leaders have little to lose if they fail to intervene militarily in a given instance of atrocity. They know this. No Western democratic governments lost support at home for their failure to intervene in Rwanda, and none has thus far taken lumps for inaction on Darfur and Syria. Since President Obama's decision to not intervene in Syria—even following reports of the Assad government's repeated used of chemical weapons—aligned with the public mood, it did no noticeable damage to his political standing among Americans.[31] Thanks to humanitarian intervention's shallow political roots, leaders are not beset by public pressure to make the extent of suffering the criterion for intervention. And as we shall see, shaky popular support for humanitarian intervention affects not only *whether* it is pursued, but also *how*.

History as Progress

Flowing naturally from humanitarianism's insistence on the possibility and necessity of achieving a better politics is its vision of history as progress.[32] Humanitarianism rests on the belief that just as scientific advances have saved or improved countless lives, so too can ethical advances. There will be setbacks, to be sure, but history's progressive trajectory ultimately resumes.

Not for nothing did Gareth Evans title his book, arguably the most influential and thoughtful case for humanitarian intervention, *Responsibility to Protect: Ending Mass Atrocities Once and for All*.[33] Evans's word choice speaks to his confidence that humanity can *fix* the atrocity problem. It's only a matter of acquiring the knowledge, developing the techniques, and implementing them. In short, ending mass killings represents an engineering challenge.

This belief is now deeply embedded in our culture, even though citizens are ambivalent about putting it into action when opportunities to do so arise. But many prominent thinkers have challenged it in principle. Some, such as Niebuhr, reject the pursuit of perfection on the religious grounds that evil is ever-present in the world. Others take a secular perspective. Michael Oakeshott, for one, stresses that the limits of our knowledge about human and political affairs call for a more tempered view of transformational projects.[34] John Gray, another dissenter, concludes that ideologies grounded in progressive faith and given to comprehensive solutions—communism, capitalism, liberal democracy, and self-determination—have brought disaster and disappointment. As he sees it these results expose the myth of historical progress, the inability of humans to change abiding features of their nature, and the impossibility of banishing problems that spring from the essence of politics itself. If this is true—if historical progress is a myth—how do we account for people's persistent faith in grand political projects, humanitarian intervention among them? Here is Gray's answer:[35]

> If there is anything unique about the human animal it is that it has the ability to grow knowledge at an accelerating rate while being chronically incapable of learning from experience. Science and technology are cumulative, whereas ethics and politics deal with recurring dilemmas. Whatever they are called, torture and slavery are universal evils; but these evils cannot be consigned to the past like redundant theories in science. They return under different names: torture as enhanced interrogation techniques, slavery as human trafficking. Any reduction in universal evils is an advance in civilization. But, unlike scientific knowledge, the restraints of civilized life cannot be stored on a computer disc. They are habits of behavior, which once broken are hard to mend. Civilization is natural for humans, but so is barbarism.

Gray's somber assessment highlights the ineradicable tragic element in politics; the cyclical, rather than linear, nature of history; and the limits of human understanding and capacity. Yet in spite of these limits many of us maintain confidence in progress, which easily transmutes into hubris. This tragic theme appears across great works of literature, as readers of Dostoevsky or Conrad will recognize readily. And as Gray rightly argues, it is also evident in the thinking of Sigmund Freud, something the great psychiatrist's most perceptive interpreters reveal.[36]

For humanitarians, the tragic take on political life smacks of resignation and discounts the human capacity to overcome. It abdicates responsibility. It forfeits idealism and hope. Worse, by encouraging defeatist sentiments, it perpetuates injustice. It is moral cowardice masquerading as profundity.

The redoubtable men and women who campaigned to end the Atlantic slave trade would have been immobilized had they imbibed

Gray's view of history. Humanitarian interventionists, democracy promoters, and nation-builders would be unable to persist in their missions were they to accept his premises. Adherents of ideologies based on the belief in progress inevitably experience or observe failure, but the lesson they learn is not the one Gray would have them learn. Instead they learn that leaders chose the wrong policies or failed to implement them effectively. Their supervening belief in cumulative advances through social engineering remains intact. Their tendency to account for failure in this way—a species of cognitive dissonance—is evident in debates that have followed the wars in Vietnam, Afghanistan, and Iraq. Those who favored these campaigns never doubted that outsiders could remake societies wholesale; they attributed the failures to wrong choices about the means. The end was always achievable; what occurred resulted from technical blunders and managerial mishaps. Should Afghanistan devolve into chaos once American and allied forces withdraw, as Iraq has, this same pattern of reasoning will doubtless reemerge, just as it will in the case of postintervention Libya.

The tendency to rationalize rather than reassess basic assumptions persists across progressive ideologies, whether liberal internationalism, communism, or neoconservatism. When Marxist revolutions culminate in totalitarianism, the Marxist predictably blames contingent conditions or bad leaders, not the doctrine itself. The liberal will conclude from this same result that liberalism offers the only way to achieve efficiency, freedom, and justice. When interventions in conflict-ravaged societies, and the elections that inevitably follow, produce violence and extremism rather than stability based on compromise and reconciliation, the core convictions of interventionists remain intact. The same is true when nation-building produces massive waste, corruption, and cost overruns, as it did in Iraq and Afghanistan. Undaunted, interventionists and nation-builders move on to the next experiment, often blaming corrupt or incompetent locals for the failure of an ambitious project. It was both feasible and noble, and as such will be executed successfully elsewhere.

Consider the neoconservatives and liberal internationalists who agitated for Saddam Hussein's overthrow on the grounds that he was a brutal dictator. They have not abandoned the principles that led them to lobby for war and nation-building. Instead, they have cast blame on particular officials and policies, American and Iraqi, for preventing what could have been a happy ending—a stable, democratic, "pro-American" Iraq.[37] Similarly, post-Gaddafi Libya is awash in militias, free agents who are literally holding the government hostage. But humanitarian interventionists will doubtless insist that their motivating principles were, and remain, sound. The failures resulted from poor postwar leadership. This teleological belief in progress admits no doubts about the merits of humanitarian intervention and the triumph of universal human rights, no matter how many times the results confound expectations. As Weiss puts it, the problem consists not of too much intervention, but of too little.[38]

The Mindset Matters

Our debt to the Enlightenment mindset is too vast to describe comprehensively, yet it is recognizable everywhere. Life is better because of it. Yet its best attributes can also produce in humans arrogance and overconfidence in our capacity to master, predict, and transform. These goals run up against limits even in science, but in politics they encounter bigger, possibly immovable barriers.

This is not to suggest that improvement is never possible. Our error lies in believing that it *always* is. We fail to reckon with the limits of our understanding, the folly of certitude—what Niebuhr called "moral pride" or the "the pride of intellect," which, rather than the commission of particular bad acts, was what he meant by sin.[39] For their part, humanitarian interventionists are neither daunted nor humbled by the timelessness of mass killings. The resilience of this form of violence can be explained, in their view, by our lack of sufficient knowledge about the techniques required to eradicate it "once and for all." Interventionists cannot accept that mass killing may illustrate the indestructible dark side of human nature and the extremes to which people will go in order to protect interests they deem vital.

This Manichaean view of international politics leads interventionists to underestimate the capacity of the "good guys," whose cause they champion, for hatred, violence, and ineptitude once they attain power. They urge the refashioning of societies they often know little about, but belittle the time, effort, and resources required to achieve order—let alone democracy—in ravaged places where politics is propelled by score-settling and mistrust. More fundamentally, they tend to assume that the aftermath of an intervention will be stable rather than chaotic.

They are also naïve about the extent to which ethical considerations shape the foreign policies of democratic governments, which do not hesitate to cooperate with and to support regimes that have abysmal human rights records and have even committed atrocities. As we shall see, democratic states routinely exempt from punishment (even criticism) allies and friendly regimes that repress their people. In the name of post-9/11 national security, democracies have resorted to or enabled torture, "rendition," indefinite detention without trial, and "signature strikes" delivered by drones—acts that contradict the human rights values to which they claim allegiance and even the treaties they have signed. Democracies adeptly craft contorted legal defenses for these actions and appeal to extenuating circumstances to exculpate themselves. These practices erode both the legitimacy of humanitarian intervention and whatever prospects it may have for becoming a universal norm.[40] Undemocratic states perform worse in all these respects, but democracies cannot profess and propagate lofty principles and then reasonably expect not to be judged against them.

Those who are passionate about humanitarian intervention brim with certainty about their program's feasibility and its nobility. From there it is a short step to the conclusion that their values and solutions are universal values and solutions—or soon will be—and that resistance reflects the self-interest of repressive regimes, the cynicism of realists, or callousness toward the suffering of others.

Sometimes opponents of humanitarian intervention really are selfish, cynical, and callous. But opposition comes in good faith, too.[41] Weaker states may be justified in their fear that powerful democracies, above all the United States, employ their ideals capriciously and selectively. Ostensibly universal norms are bound to provoke resistance in a world of diverse polities and cultures, especially when the countries most fervently espousing those norms look the other way, in the name of their own security and interests, when these principles are trampled. In a pluralistic world, human rights agreements will, perforce, have to be stuffed with bromides and caveats if they are to gain acceptance, inevitably eroding their usefulness.

Interventionists, though, consistently refuse to recognize these practical challenges and counterarguments. Either that or, zealous and self-assured, they don't care.

ALTRUISM'S LIMITS

H umanitarians are not wrong to assume that people are capable of charity. We are social and moral beings, and people of means both great and small continually inspire us with their benefi- cence toward those facing hunger, poverty, disaster, and violence. But in considering the humanitarian mission the issue is not what good people are capable of, but the degree to which a universal ethic of care has or could become a powerful influence on the conduct of states. Humanitarians are more sanguine on this point than the facts war- rant. The argument that borders and boundaries must not make a dif- ference in whether and how governments help people is noble. It is also unrealistic.[1]

Poverty and Obligation

If benevolence really drove state policy, there would be much more poverty relief. That there isn't suggests that the humanitarian dream is far from realization.

In 2013 only five (Denmark, Luxembourg, Norway, Sweden, and the United Kingdom) of the twenty-eight leading donor nations devoted at least 0.7 percent of their GDP to foreign aid, the UN target. Nine, including the United States, devoted less than 0.2 percent, another eight less than 0.3 percent.[2] Though practices vary among donors, aid is often tied to purchases from the provider, and it is not directed toward the neediest but rather to allies and friendly regimes. Were helping the less fortunate an important value for the governments of rich countries, aid would go to the poorest, not those of the greatest strategic importance.

Americans' private giving exceeds their government's foreign development assistance by a large margin, but they focus overwhelmingly on the home front. The lion's share of US private philanthropy—95 percent in 2009—stays within the nation's borders, even though the world's poorest people need help much more than donors' fellow citizens.[3]

The relative unimportance of poverty alleviation abroad is clear in the electoral process. Few if any politicians in wealthy liberal democracies campaign on platforms that stress increases in foreign aid; nor do they suffer politically for failing to do so. They know it's not a smart way to win votes. Few voters would be moved by such promises, because citizens do not consider foreign aid a top priority, and political opponents would charge that those calling for beefed-up foreign assistance programs favor profligacy abroad even as needs at home go unmet.[4]

When poorer countries have sought systematic increases in aid from wealthy ones, they have generally been refused or accommodated to a minimal extent. For instance, as part of their campaign for a New International Economic Order (NIEO) in the 1970s, developing countries tried and failed, under the auspices of the UN, to require wealthy countries to commit 1 percent of GDP to aid. The NIEO campaign also pushed for wealthy countries to cut tariffs on raw materials and agricultural products exported by developing countries. This concession would have done even more than foreign aid, which can be wasted on showpiece projects or simply stolen by corrupt officials, to promote economic growth.[5] But barring the tariff reductions—qualified by various stipulations—under the Generalized Scheme of Preferences, developing countries did not make headway in securing unilateral tariff cuts. The idea has never gained popularity in developed countries that compete in the production of these goods. These producers are voters and political players, making it tough for politicians to give ground. Indeed, wealthy countries tend to impose high tariffs, quotas, and other restrictions on agriculture, food, clothing, textiles, and footwear. Increased exports in these products, enabled by more rapid progress in the elimination of tariff and nontariff barriers and subsidies, would have accelerated economic growth in poor countries and helped them gross a sum approximating the amount they receive annually in foreign aid—which, in 2013, totaled $134 billion.[6]

Since the Yugoslav civil war in the 1990s, the number of deaths related to poverty has far exceeded that of people killed by their governments. A 2013 report released by the World Bank, the World Health Organization, and the UN reveals that while the worldwide death rate of children under age five declined by almost 50 percent from 1990 to 2012, the tally was still 6.6 million, or 18,000 per day. Inadequate nutrition accounted for 45 percent of these deaths and poverty-related illnesses for most of the rest.[7] Cumulatively, these data describe a dismal state of affairs—but a day-to-day one, not the sort that competes with graphic images of large-scale killings, evictions, mass graves, and demolished cities purveyed by the 24-hour news cycle with its penchant for the sensational. So the quotidian deaths stemming from poverty do not generate the outraged calls for action from politicians and pundits or the media that the killings in Bosnia, Rwanda, Darfur, Libya, and Syria have.[8] Though poverty and hunger claim many more lives than do atrocities, they are not widely regarded as deprivations of basic rights, which tend to be seen, certainly in routine discussions and press coverage, in political rather than socioeconomic terms. They do not therefore generate fervent campaigns to "do something."[9] One can, of course, work to reduce atrocities as well as poverty-related deaths; doing one does not preclude doing the other. And the point is not that so much effort goes into humanitarian intervention—as we shall see, that's not the case— that no resources can be spared to combat poverty. It is that mass killings are headline-grabbing and arouse outrage in a way that day-to-day deaths caused by the lack of the most basic necessities do not, and that far more can be done to address the latter problem than is being done, and at minimal additional cost to wealthy societies.

The Reticent Public

The citizens of countries able to engage in humanitarian intervention don't consider saving lives abroad worth the expense in blood and
money: when asked to put military resources on the line, their altruism does not readily extend beyond their borders.[10]

Syria offers a clear case. According to a German Marshall Fund
(GMF) poll, American and European public support for intervention, or even for arming the opposition to Assad, declined even as
the death toll increased between 2012 and 2013. Opposition grew
in every country surveyed and ranged from 61 percent in Sweden
to 85 percent in Slovakia. The 2013 average for the entire EU was
72 percent—up from 59 percent in 2012—while the percentage of
Americans opposing intervention increased from 55 to 62 percent.[11]
When the mood shifted somewhat in mid-2014 to favor air strikes,
the source of the change was not the Assad government's continuing
killing of civilians. The catalyst was the rise of the radical Islamic
State of Iraq and Syria (ISIS), also known simply as the Islamic
State (IS). Its strongholds rather than the Syrian government's
forces were the target.[12] Self-defense, not altruism, led the United
States to launch air strikes against IS, and even then, there was slim
support among Americans and Europeans for sending their troops
to the battlefield, or, to use the now-ubiquitous expression, to put
"boots on the ground."

Surveying the wreckage Syria had become three years after the
uprising began, Jan Egelund, head of the Norwegian Relief Council
and a former deputy director at Human Rights Watch and UN official,
deplored this reticence in *The Guardian*:

> Politicians and diplomats declared that there would be "no
> more Srebrenicas and no more Rwandas." I started to believe
> in these declarations that "never again" would such atroci-
> ties be allowed to occur with impunity . . . The Syrian war is
> now threatening to erase this generation of progress . . . Who
> would have thought we, on our watch, would see people starv-
> ing in besieged cities with no accountability for the military
> and political leaders responsible? Perhaps the mindboggling

question is: where is the outrage we all saw in the 1990s? The public is not marching on the streets, nor collecting money.[13]

It is not hard to share Egelund's anger. Violence has claimed hundreds of thousands of lives in Syria and left 7.6 million displaced, according to a December 2014 UN report. But war fatigue from Afghanistan and Iraq weighs heavily, and Western citizens likely fear escalation, should their governments start small. If an initial step fails, calls for bolder action might follow. Fear of lost credibility, a kind of catchall excuse for hawks, would become a rationale for expansion. This concern was well expressed by a reader who, commenting on Egelund's anguish, remarked online: "'Outrage' is cheap. Effective action has a price. A price I, for one, do not want to pay—as I see no British interest that can be furthered by squandering British blood or treasure in this nasty sectarian civil war."

Egelund was not advocating military intervention, but the reader's reaction reflected broader currents. Western citizens do not worry about credibility, but about escalation and the possibility that a nonmilitary intervention might turn toward hostilities. Consider a September 2013 *New York Times*/CBS News poll conducted in the United States shortly after the news broke that Assad's government had used chemical weapons against civilians, prompting President Obama to consider air strikes as he faced pressure to make good on his warning, issued a year before the incident, that Assad would be crossing a "red line" were he to use chemical weapons. Despite the new circumstances, when asked whether the United States had an obligation "to do something about the fighting in Syria between government forces and anti-government groups," 65 percent of respondents said there was no responsibility to act. Only 28 percent said there was an obligation. Asked whether Assad's use of chemical munitions warranted an American military strike against his regime, only 30 percent favored the strike and 60 percent opposed it. Not surprisingly, 86 percent were against sending ground troops into Syria and only 12 percent favored it. Seventy-four percent of respondents said the United States ought not arm the anti-Assad forces; only 19 percent said yes. Other polls confirmed Americans' opposition to intervention in Syria and to arming Assad's opponents and demonstrated their view that the bloodletting in Syria did not affect significant American interests.[14]

President Obama's critics on the right, notably Senators John McCain and Lindsey Graham, criticized him for being weak in the face of civilian deaths, particularly in view of Assad's use of chemical weapons.[15] But, in their hesitation, Obama and his European counterparts were following public opinion, not defying it.

Documents, Declarations, and Delivery

States are willing to sign treaties that proclaim the importance of fundamental rights and collective measures aimed at ensuring them. They are also determined to see that these accords contain no language that obligates them to act in defense of these same hallowed rights.

Let us take two examples: the 1948 Convention on the Prevention and Punishment of the Crime of Genocide; and the Responsibility to Protect, which was adopted in 2005 by the UN General Assembly.

Advocates of humanitarian intervention assume, explicitly or otherwise, that American support is essential for the enforcement of international agreements to prohibit atrocities. But the United States, the self-styled leader of the free world, did not sign the Genocide Convention until 1988. It took the unflagging efforts of Senator William Proxmire—"nineteen years and 3,211 speeches," Samantha Power writes—to bring Washington around.[16] Successive American governments resisted for four decades because of politicians and groups who protested that the United States could be charged with genocide, as defined in the treaty, against Native American tribes. But even those countries that had long since signed the Convention knew they could have it both ways: subscribing to its noble ideals while avoiding any legal responsibility to uphold them.

The Convention defines genocide as an act aimed at destroying "a national, ethnical, racial, or religious group," categorizes doing so as a "punishable" crime, and stipulates that signatories agree to "enact national legislation" to provide for national courts or international tribunals in which genocide suspects can be tried. But the document is otherwise vague about signatories' obligations.[17] The lack of specificity and enforcement provisions does not reflect carelessness on the part the Convention's authors. Quite the contrary. States were determined to block mandatory language. The Convention sounds legally binding, but the text provides ample escape routes. Exploiting them does not require particularly clever lawyers. For instance, when states disagree about the terms of the Convention, they are enjoined to submit their disputes to the International Court of Justice. This body lacks compulsory jurisdiction and hears cases only when states have already agreed to seek and accept its judgment. It enforces nothing states haven't already agreed to.

In spite of the toothless Convention, American officials have been wary about characterizing mass killings as genocide, even when the facts left no doubt that doing so was appropriate. For example, though Rwanda's Tutsi minority was slaughtered in vast numbers and at horrific speed in 1994, the Clinton administration resorted to (sometimes absurd) verbal gymnastics to avoid using the word "genocide." According to David Scheffer, who served as senior advisor to then–UN Ambassador Madeleine Albright, the White House feared that calling the mass killings genocide would lead to more—and more impassioned—demands for intervention.[18] The Departments of State and Defense were likewise anxious that using the term in public statements would tie the country's hands. A secret State Department paper from May 1, 1994 noted, "Be Careful. Legal at State was worried about this yesterday—Genocide finding could actually commit [the United States government] to 'do something.'"[19]

In the end the administration took the position that the Convention did not, as a legal matter, require the United States to stop genocide beyond its borders.[20] But President Clinton could still have been convinced by the oft-repeated American commitment to global human rights. He wasn't. Having announced that American troops would be withdrawn from Somalia soon after eighteen Army Rangers and other soldiers were killed there in October 1993, Clinton was determined not to send Americans back into someone else's war. He knew that after Mogadishu the public would not stomach intervention in Rwanda.

The administration's public excuse was that the situation in Rwanda was too ambiguous. But documents obtained under the Freedom of Information Act by the National Security Archive show that as the killing progressed, administration officials, relying on

intelligence reports, were describing the bloodbath in Rwanda as genocide. But these officials were careful to confine their use of the term
to internal communications.[21] Thus the fear of being sucked into the
conflict, not a confusing situation in the country, accounted for the
administration's reticence about proclaiming genocide and responding
with military action.[22]

In her memoirs, Albright refers to the lack of clarity but concludes that by "the last ten days of April"—that is, about two weeks
after the start of the killings—she "realized along with most of the
world that what was occurring was not just terrible violence but
genocide."[23] Indeed, in a December 1997 speech in Addis Ababa,
Albright, who by then had been promoted to Secretary of State, con-
ceded that the United States should have used the genocide label.
So did President Clinton, speaking in Kigali the following March.
In his memoirs Clinton wrote that the legacy of Mogadishu—which
hovered over his administration like Banquo's ghost—led to "one of
the greatest regrets of [his] presidency": the failure, in conjunction
with allies, to send "a few thousand troops" to Rwanda, which "could
have saved lives." As the president acknowledged, "neither I nor any-
one else on my foreign policy team adequately focused on sending
troops to stop the slaughter." Congress, he noted, was opposed to
"military deployments in faraway places not related to our national
interests," Bosnia was a pressing concern, the memory of Mogadishu
still fresh.[24]

Like Clinton, Albright acknowledges the influence of Mogadishu's
legacy, noting, "Perhaps the only solution was a large and heavily
armed coalition led by a major power, but because of Somalia, the
U.S. military wasn't going to undertake that."[25] Nor, as it turned out,
was any other military. Albright observes that it would have taken a
"heavily armed, almost certainly U.S. led coalition" to stop the killing
and expresses remorse for not having pushed such a response. But she
adds, tellingly, "Many people would have thought I was crazy and we
would never have won support from Congress."[26] It's clear why hers
would have been a lonely voice. As Clinton concedes in his memoirs,
the bloodletting in Rwanda was not, to most Americans and their
elected representatives, an occasion for dispatching the American
cavalry. And given that the killers intermingled with the population,

which made them hard to distinguish from civilians and their own victims, air strikes alone would have not proved effective.

Rwanda is not an exception. The administration of George W. Bush showed the same hesitation for these same reasons to describe the killing spree against Darfur's African tribes as genocide, even though the House of Representatives passed a resolution with an overwhelming majority (422 affirmative votes and 12 abstentions) that labeled the violence in Darfur a genocide and urged the Bush administration to do the same and not to mince words.[27] In September 2004, nearly two months after the congressional verdict, Secretary of State Colin Powell used the word in his testimony before the Senate Foreign Relations Committee, placing the blame on the Sudanese government and the Janjaweed, a militia supported by Sudan's leaders and operating in coordination with the military. But Powell acted only after William Howard Taft IV, the State Department's legal adviser, informed him in a June 2004 memo that even if the killing in Darfur constituted genocide, the United States might not have to intervene. Taft pointed out that when the United States signed the Genocide Convention in 1988, it had insisted on adding a "reservation" designed to shield it from legal action stemming from failure to fulfill the responsibilities set forth in the treaty.[28] In other words, the State Department described what was occurring in Darfur as genocide only after making sure that it would not be required to do anything about it. Even then, other key departments, such as the Pentagon, did not embrace that position.[29]

The 2005 UN General Assembly resolution that adopted the Responsibility to Protect (R2P) offers another example of states' determination not to be pinned down by legal obligations to stop atrocities. Promoters of R2P trumpet the endorsement as a milestone in the effort to gain both universal condemnation of mass atrocities and universal agreement to prevent and punish them through collective action. But the resolution was a watered-down version of R2P, and even this was not enough to assuage states' fears of legal obligation. States with consistently poor human rights records were by no means alone in opposing any binding language. The United States did as well. The American ambassador to the UN, the redoubtable John Bolton, fought to exclude terms that might commit the United States to specific courses of action under R2P—indeed, to any obligations at all.[30]

In August 2005, not two months before the summit adopted its limp version of R2P, he wrote to other members of the UN:

> The [UN] Charter has never been interpreted as creating a legal obligation for Security Council members to support enforcement action in various cases involving serious breaches of international peace. Accordingly we believe ... that a determination as to what particular measures to adopt in specific cases cannot be predetermined in the abstract but should remain a decision within the purview of the Security Council ... We do not accept that either the United Nations as a whole, or the Security Council, or individual states, have an obligation to intervene under international law.[31]

That is to say, the United States would intervene only when it saw fit, and, through its Security Council veto, would control the implementation of R2P.

Bolton's efforts succeeded—and not just because of his tenacity. Other states shared his objective. Some joined the United States in opposing any formulation of R2P that might impose legal commitments. Others feared that a robust R2P might put them on the receiving end of intervention undertaken in its name. The diluted R2P formula articulated in the 2005 document was thus conducive to consensus. Everyone could go on accusing the Sudanese state of genocide without incurring obligations. No one wanted to forcibly intervene in Darfur—some, such as the United States, because they wanted to avoid the attendant risks; others, such as China, because they did lucrative business with Sudanese President Omar al-Bashir's regime. The reference to the brave new Responsibility to Protect doctrine in the 2005 declaration allowed those who signed the document both to assume responsibility and to avoid it—and to ignore those who needed protection.

No matter how committed they may be to human rights, democracies face a problem when it comes to intervening militarily to stop atrocities, the most egregious violations of these rights. They cannot easily initiate and sustain human rights–based military campaigns that do not have strong support at home. And so when humanitarian military operations do occur they are conducted from afar, with aircraft flying at high altitudes and warships stationed well offshore. The objective is a zero-casualty campaign. Such scrupulous care does not characterize wars fought to preserve the balance of power or protect national interests. But it typifies humanitarian intervention. When defending cherished moral values entails significant risks, democracies stay on the sidelines.

Continuing reticence despite years of well-documented mass killing suggests that humanitarian interventionists will fail to create a lasting global ethic of rescue. Intervention will remain in the toolkit of democratic governments, to be deployed only when risks are low. That won't satisfy intervention's most ardent proponents, who have grander ambitions. They want a binding legal and ethical commitment to stop atrocities, not a weak-kneed plan to be implemented when convenient. Their fate will be to oscillate, according to the whims of democratic citizens and their leaders, between the euphoria of Kosovo and the despair of Syria.

SOVEREIGNTY, LEGITIMACY, AND INTERVENTION

I n 1971, Pakistan sent its army into the restive province of East
Pakistan to prevent what officials saw as an impending secession.
The Bengali nationalist Awami League had won the December
1970 national elections—though it failed to prevail in any electoral
constituencies in the country's western wing—and Pakistan's leaders, particularly the army brass, were convinced that the party's true
objective was independence, not autonomy. Pakistan's president and
military strongman, General Yahya Khan, postponed convening the
national parliament, sparking continual demonstrations in the east,
where Bengalis, who comprised the overwhelming majority of the population, had long chafed under what they regarded as the domination
of the Pakistani state by the country's western flank, and the Punjabi-
dominated military in particular. The worst was yet to come: starting in March 1971, the army, following orders from Yahya, went on
a rampage, killing tens of thousands of Bengali civilians, possibly as
many as 300,000, displacing millions, and sending a total of ten million
refugees streaming into India.[1]

India invaded East Pakistan on December 3, after Pakistani
warplanes struck its western airbases, justifying its decision on the
grounds that it was being forced to absorb waves of refugees, a severe

and open-ended economic burden that it was shouldering, with only a small fraction of the costs being covered by assistance from abroad. Bengalis who had fled their homes could not, India asserted, be reasonably expected to return unless the killings stopped. The Indian military campaign culminated in the Pakistani army's surrender—after thirteen days of fighting—in the east and the eventual return of refugees. The newly independent Bangladesh emerged from the ruins of East Pakistan as a secure home for formerly oppressed Bengalis.

But it was no shining moment for humanitarian intervention. India's action was widely criticized—notably by Pakistan's allies, China, and the United States, but by the community of states more generally—as illegitimate and unlawful. It did not matter that a horrific slaughter had occurred in East Pakistan. In spite of the massacres, the prevailing international opinion was "to affirm Pakistan's right to sovereignty and the rule of non-intervention."[2]

During the bloodletting in East Pakistan, the singular preoccupation of President Richard Nixon and his secretary of state, Henry Kissinger, was preventing a shift in the balance of power in South Asia to the advantage of India, which was backed by the Soviet Union; the Bengalis were, to put it charitably, an afterthought. To that end, in December, Nixon dispatched the aircraft carrier USS *Enterprise* and escort ships into the Bay of Bengal to rattle India. He and Kissinger also secretly encouraged American-armed Iran and Jordan to meet Yahya's request for warplanes and broached with Beijing the idea of staging Chinese troop movements along the Indian border.[3]

Vietnam was castigated on these same grounds—violating a neighboring state's sovereignty—when its army swept into Cambodia in December 1978 and toppled the Khmer Rouge government. China and the United States once again led the criticism, joined by the Association of Southeast Asian Nations (ASEAN). Vietnam argued that the Khmer Rouge had launched numerous armed incursions into its territory. But the self-defense claim proved unconvincing internationally; nor was Vietnam applauded for uprooting a blood-drenched regime that had caused the deaths of nearly two million people.[4] Instead, its military intervention was decried as an act of aggression, just as India's had been. The leaders of China, Southeast Asia, and the West in particular viewed Vietnam's resort to war as a power play that resulted in the pro-Chinese Khmer Rouge government's replacement by a leadership beholden to Hanoi and Moscow. Vietnam received no commendations for removing a regime that had killed a quarter of Cambodia's population since taking power in 1975.

As it did in East Pakistan, realpolitik trumped humanitarian values. The United States, Britain, and China, joined by ASEAN, were the most vehement in insisting that the Khmer Rouge retain Cambodia's seat in the UN, which it did until 1992.[5] And, with American encouragement—which, ironically, began during the Carter administration, notwithstanding its trumpeting of the centrality of human rights in its foreign policy—Thailand provided the Khmer Rouge havens, and China arms and training, enabling it to regroup and wage guerrilla war against the Vietnamese-installed government, a decision that President Carter's national security advisor, Zbigniew Brzezinski, acknowledged to journalist Elizabeth Becker.[6] Beyond that, the United States pressed the World Food Program to use the Thai military as a conduit for providing aid to the refugee camps in Thailand that sprouted following the flight of the Khmer Rouge. Britain's Special Air Service (SAS) trained the anti-Vietnamese resistance forces, while the United States provided them intelligence information and supplies.[7] Because the Khmer Rouge constituted, by far, the most powerful part of the resistance forces, the distinction between supplying aid and training to their noncommunist allies and to them was murky at best.

The cold reaction to India's and Vietnam's interventions reflected the established view, embedded in international law and the UN Charter, that the use of force was justified only when a country's security and territorial integrity were in danger or when authorized by the Security Council under Chapter VII of the Charter. These stringent criteria were deemed essential because they safeguarded international stability, which in turn was seen as a precondition for the pursuit of trade, travel, foreign investment, and other transactions important to global peace and economic growth.

This is the legalist position: the legitimacy of an intervention is determined by its comportment with treaties and international law. In the previous chapter, we saw why the realist school of thought criticizes humanitarian intervention from a different standpoint.

Pragmatists who value order and prudence, realists do not valorize legal legitimacy; they value the preservation of state interests and the stability of the international system. Legalists, by contrast, believe that humanitarian intervention can be legitimized and that this legitimacy can serve as justification to act.

The Just War Paradigm

One of the sources of legalism is just war theory, which seeks a defensible balance between pragmatism and morality. While interests may guide foreign policy, leaders must not be allowed to throw ethics overboard.[8]

Michael Walzer—following John Stuart Mill, particularly in his essay "A Few Words on Non-Intervention"—is perhaps the most influential proponent of the theory.[9] In *Just and Unjust Wars* and other writings Walzer takes sovereignty seriously, but not for the security-based reasons adduced by realists, whom he chastises for being indifferent to morality. In his view, sovereignty deserves respect not solely because it is a pillar of stability in the international system, but also because it shields national communities from external interference. He considers such protection essential because it is within national communities that citizens deliberate on the decisions that, when added up, constitute their self-determination, which he deems a fundamental right. To expose states to intervention, except in exceptional circumstances, then, is to wrest self-determination from the national community and place it in the hands of outsiders.

By self-determination, Walzer does not mean the practice that prevails—or is expected to prevail—in liberal democracies. This is but one form of self-determination, which can be exercised in a variety of political settings and through various institutions. Likewise, the "fit" between the citizens and their states can be manifested in a number of ways that do not conform to the principles of liberal democracy, but are shaped by a country's particular history, customs, and culture. Outsiders, who are not always well informed about societies they would reshape, cannot determine what counts as a legitimate foreign state.[10]

This is not relativism, which holds that despotic governments, too, allow self-determination in their peculiar way. Rather, Walzer argues that people ruled by tyrannical regimes acquire authentic, organic self-determination "during an arduous struggle to become free by their own efforts."[11] As Walzer observes, "The recognition of sovereignty is the only way we have of establishing an arena within which freedom can be fought for and (sometimes) won. It is this arena, and the activities that go on within it, that we want to protect, and we protect them, much as we protect individual integrity, by marking out boundaries that cannot be crossed, rights that cannot be violated. As with individuals, so with sovereign states: there are things that we cannot do to them, even for their own ostensible good."[12]

Walzer's conception of the rights of a state within the international community derives from his conception of the rights of individuals within a national community of rights-bearing people. States must be immune from external military intervention unless they commit aggression against other states, just as individuals within a national community retain their rights unless they violate the basic liberties of other individuals in the community. Under the terms of liberal democracy, governments do not have the right to use force to determine how individuals live; similarly, states lack the right to determine how other states function. Walzer believes that people can rightfully revolt against their own cruel and repressive government, but he emphasizes that "that freedom does not easily transfer to foreign states or armies and become a right of invasion or intervention; above all it does not transfer at the initiative of foreigners."[13]

This might suggest that Walzer condemns meddling in the affairs of even a cruel foreign government, but he does not forbid external intervention aimed at rescuing individuals subjected to wanton violence. He deems intervention appropriate—even essential—when mass killing takes place. He has no sympathy for inaction in the face of atrocities, regardless of the ideology urging restraint: whether bloodless, interest-driven realism; isolationism; antiwar leftism; or pacifism. Thus he lauds India's intervention in East Pakistan, Vietnam's in Cambodia, NATO's in Bosnia and Kosovo, and Tanzania's 1978–1979 counteroffensive against Uganda, which culminated in the destruction of Ugandan president Idi Amin's tyranny.[14] Demonstrating the importance of the ethical charge to intervene, Walzer has argued that circumscribing campaigns to air and missile strikes is wrong because it prolongs the killing of innocents. In his view, interveners must be willing to court harm in defense of a fundamental principle.[15] Walzer therefore opposes on moral grounds what the conservative pundit Charles Krauthammer sneeringly called "immaculate intervention."[16]

Drawing on Mill, Walzer limits intervention to three specific circumstances: when there are within a country's borders "two or more political communities, one of which is already engaged in a large-scale military struggle for independence"; when "a foreign power" has already intervened militarily in a civil war, even if it has done so at the behest of "one of the parties in a civil war"; and when "the violation of human rights within a set of boundaries is so terrible that it makes talk of community or self-determination or 'arduous struggle' seem cynical and irrelevant, that is, in cases of enslavement or massacre."

Though Walzer constrains external military interventions to these three conditions, countries aren't obligated to invade whenever one of the conditions obtains. To insist that they must would be to violate just war theory's insistence on prudence. No state is required to protect others at peril to itself; leaders must ask and answer practical questions before intervening. Two such questions, which go back to just war theory's roots in the thought of St. Augustine and St. Thomas Aquinas,[17] are particularly important. The first is whether a war of rescue has a reasonable chance of success. The second is whether its objectives can be realized without doing more harm than good.

Despite the limitations Walzer imposes on humanitarian intervention, his paradigm permits a good deal more than he might have anticipated and consequences that he may not have foreseen. There are few ethnically uniform countries in the world, which increases the likelihood that one of Walzer's three conditions for intervention will be met. James Fearon finds that "about 70 percent of the countries in the world have an ethnic group that forms an absolute majority of the population, although the average population share of these groups is only 65 percent and only 21 percent of countries are 'homogeneous' in the weak sense of having a group that claims 9 out of 10 residents. The average size of the second largest group, or largest ethnic minority, is surprisingly large, at 17 percent."[18] To complicate matters, nationalities often straddle the boundaries of countries: Kurds, Russians, Baloch, and Pushtuns, for instance, are not confined to any one state. Under these circumstances "large-scale military struggle for independence" within nations is not inevitable, but it is fairly common, legitimizing intervention by Walzer's standards.

Thus Walzer's criteria in fact permit quite a lot and sit uneasily with his insistence on sovereignty as the incubator of self-determination. Indeed, the latitude to abet secession is remarkably wide, unencumbered by what would seem basic and obvious qualifications. How much popular support must the secessionist movement have among those it purports to represent? How does one ascertain the depth of popular support for a breakaway political movement? What circumstances justify a national community's quest for a state of its own? Must reasonable alternatives to secession, such as confederation and limited autonomy, have been tried and proved unworkable before outsiders intervene? Walzer does not explore—let alone answer—these questions in any depth.

As for counterintervention in civil wars, Walzer's criterion is again too broad. He has in mind cases when repressive governments call on outsiders to help them beat back uprisings. But a legitimate government might call for outside assistance in the face of an armed insurrection. Would other states therefore be justified in entering the fray? The mere fact that an external intervention has already occurred in a country caught up in civil war cannot itself justify a counterintervention. It also may not be prudent, especially if one assumes, as Walzer does, that limiting the conditions under which states can use force increases international stability. The same applies to his third condition: appalling human rights violations. This seems reasonable at first glance, but states have been divided on the question of whether even such a circumstance warrants intervention, and so Walzer's criterion can in practice be quite permissive. Some states will insist that the standard for intervention has been met while others will not; inevitably, states will invoke the standard when it suits them and ignore it when it doesn't.

Lowering the Bar

Walzer understands that he has provided a rationale for wars beyond those fought for self-defense or in defense of other states facing aggression. Yet he merely advises that we exercise intervention with "great care."[19]

Even so, critics have not taken him to task him for being too permissive. Instead they charge him with giving the sovereign state too much leeway—for exalting sovereignty and shortchanging human rights. This criticism stems in part from Walzer's claim that nondemocracies can be, in John Rawls's construction, "decent hierarchical regimes."[20] These governments don't enjoy the consent through the procedures—such as elections and the guarantee of an extensive set of rights—that democratic governments do. Still, they rest on an implied consent, and liberal states should respect them, providing that the regime is not involved in massive repression or aggression, offers forums for political consultation and participation, and respects citizens' basic freedoms. When these conditions are present, democratic states should work out rules for coexistence and even cooperation on matters of common concern. Regimes that systematically abuse their citizens and threaten and attack other states, on the other hand, fall into another category. Rawls calls them "outlaw states," and argues that they pose a threat to both liberal democracies and "decent" nondemocracies by virtue of being both internally repressive and externally aggressive.[21] He contends that the outlaw state "is to be condemned and in grave cases may be subject to forceful sanctions and even to intervention"—a stance compatible with Walzer's.[22]

The concept of a decent hierarchical regime has come under attack by, among others, Gerald Doppelt, David Luban, and Fernando Tesón. They make good, democratic governance the test of legitimacy and find no other form of consent meaningful. Tesón, for example, rejects "the traditional statist conception of sovereignty [that] leaves states free to adopt any form of social organization; states are thus legally and morally protected against moral interference aimed at criticizing or altering those internal social strictures."[23] As far as he—and others of like mind, such as Thomas Pogge—is concerned, governments that lack the consent of the people whom they govern are devoid of legitimacy and, when they commit egregious violations, have no legal or moral right to claim that other states do not have the right to intervene, militarily if need be.[24] Not surprisingly, those wedded to this position are less inhibited than Walzer and Rawls, to say nothing of realists, when it comes to relaxing criteria for intervention. For instance, while Luban concedes that potential interveners must account for "the empirical likelihood of escalation" before resorting to humanitarian war, he insists that "giving absolute primacy to the world community's interests in peace" subordinates the more important pursuit of individual rights and justice. His bottom line is that "a state must be legitimate in order for a moral duty of non-intervention in its affairs to exist."[25] Doppelt agrees that sovereignty and order must not override legitimacy and justice. "Whatever the moral or political character of this [national] 'community,'" he writes, "it is its 'independence' from external military intervention that Walzer values above all else in international relations. Hence, however oppressive a government and political community may be, Walzer would have its people, even if they are seeking to better their lot, maintain their strict independence from external intervention (or assistance) above *all else* even if the alternative is continuing oppression."[26] Tesón concurs. He has no patience with Walzer's view that sovereignty is valuable and must be defended because it enables a national community to practice its chosen form of self-determination. That, in Tesón's eyes, comes close to saying that "we must protect the enemies of freedom, that is, illegitimate, dictatorial governments, even when doing so means helping in the denial of freedom."[27]

This summary of Walzer's view by his critics is neither accurate nor fair; in particular, it conflates the importance he attaches to the political community created by citizens, whose interests he believes the state must serve, with an exaltation of the state per se.[28] But let's leave that aside. There is, given the focus of this book, a bigger problem: many states fail to meet the Luban-Doppelt-Tesón criteria for political legitimacy and hence for immunity from external attack. (Consider, for example, North Korea or Uzbekistan.) Doppelt believes intervention can be justified by "the more ordinary practices of tyrannical governments: imprisoning political opponents without trial, torture as a pervasive means of social control, systematic limitations upon freedom of movement, the prohibition of trade unions and the suppression of other civil liberties at the core of the liberal traditions."[29] Luban offers an expansive reading of human rights that would enable extensive intervention. Intervention requires no mass killings, systematic torture, or, indeed, physical coercion of any kind. States must provide not only security from violence, but also protect "subsistence rights, which include the right to healthy air and water and adequate food, clothing, and shelter." These "socially basic human rights," as the philosopher Henry Shue calls them, are, according to Luban, "worth fighting for not only by those to whom they are denied but, if we take seriously the obligation which is indicated when we speak of human rights, by the rest of us as well."[30] He assures us that intervention is justified "in defense of socially basic human rights" and would constitute a "just war."[31]

Surely not all states that fail to meet these stringent standards are fair game, but the antistatists never explain which circumstances, beyond those allowed by Walzer, would demand intervention. Whatever Doppelt's and Luban's and Tesón's alternatives to Walzer's paradigm—and the operational details are far from clear—this much is certain: they allow for a great deal more intervention than Walzer would deem justifiable and wise. They also gloss over the increased risk of disorder and conflict that would result from lowering the bar for intervention. After all, interventions justified by an uncompromising test of states' legitimacy and governance records will prove controversial, and are thus likely to encounter resistance.

Anne-Marie Slaughter reaches a similarly permissive conclusion via her "liberal theory of international law."[32] She contends that traditional international law is impoverished because of its "top-down" orientation; that is, it dwells on the equality and rights of sovereign states without regard for how they govern, and, in particular, ignores their records on human rights. Realists and legalists, she says, focus inordinately on the processes and rules that create order in international politics. They use international law to create institutions that enable better coordination among states, while ignoring the internal politics of those states. But, for Slaughter, international law primarily functions "to influence and improve the functioning of domestic institutions"— that is, to improve the degree to which governments respect the rights of their citizens and improve their lives.[33] This follows from her belief that "human rights law is the core of international law." Enforcement is not a source of controversy, in this reading: "humanitarian intervention is a natural concomitant of human rights law . . . necessitated by some radical breakdown in the functioning of domestic institutions— the failure of a state to provide essential services such as food and shelter to its citizens or the active mass oppression of its citizens."[34] Moreover, intervention can, as a legal matter, do more than ensure respect for these rights. It can "even rebuild basic state institutions to the extent such efforts have a reasonable chance of success."[35] This is an extravagant agenda, from a former high-ranking State Department official under Secretary of State Hillary Clinton and President Obama no less. The ideas of professors do matter sometimes.

Political theorist Charles Beitz's ideas reveal some additional problems that arise from vague and permissive attitudes toward intervention. Like Luban, Doppelt, Pogge, and Slaughter, Beitz rejects traditional sovereignty, seeing it as tyranny's shield.[36] He, like other intervention advocates, is careful to note that intervention is not morally required whenever there is injustice within states, but his criteria for intervention are nevertheless far more expansive than Walzer's. It is not enough that states avoid egregious abuse. For him, the privilege of sovereignty, and the immunity from intervention it guarantees, properly accrues only to "those states whose institutions conform to appropriate principles of justice and whose institutions are more likely to become just in the absence of outside interference than with outside assistance."[37]

But what does it mean to assert that state institutions must comport with "appropriate principles of justice"? Does it require an ongoing demonstration—satisfactory to outsiders—of popular consent and legitimacy? If so, need states be liberal and democratic, with free and fair elections and unfettered media and civic organizations? Must there be a just distribution of wealth, and if so, what constitutes a minimum level of economic justice? According to whom?

It should be obvious just how capacious Beitz's permission could be, though it is hard to say for sure what he would allow, since he has not answered the relevant questions. But if proof of ongoing democratic consent were required, a great many states would make the target list. The requirement that there be economic justice as well would make for an even longer list. His caveat that interveners should take costs into account seems a weak barrier to action since policy on his account must, above all, be just and moral.[38]

In fact, Beitz's framework courts injustice in its own way. A government able to make intervention costly may well be capable of a great deal of injustice, while a government that lacks the military means to raise the costs of intervention may be much less unjust, but perhaps enough to warrant intervention on the basis of Beitz's loose criteria. Beitz's prescription would appear to sanction action against the latter but not the former, given that it blends in just war theory to balance the normative principles he values with prudence based on contingent circumstances.

Assessing Expansive Interventionism

While some advocates of intervention, such as Walzer, have tight criteria, others set far more permissive limits and far more ambitious goals. They appear not to have considered carefully whether the public supports their agenda in Western democracies—the states most capable and most inclined to support humanitarian intervention—and what consequences their plans might have for world order, should they be pursued. Humanitarian intervention continues to elicit suspicion in the ex–colonial world; a more expansive version that poses even greater challenges to sovereignty can only increase that sentiment.

To some extent, that wariness reflects a covetous approach to sovereignty in much of Asia and Africa as well as the experience of having been colonized. Consider the Organization of African Unity's reaction to Tanzania's 1978–1979 military intervention in Uganda, which ended the brutal rule of the Ugandan dictator Idi Amin, who came to power in a 1971 coup.[39] Tanzania justified its invasion by invoking the basic right of self-defense against aggression—Amin's forces had seized 700 square miles of Tanzanian territory in the Kagera Salient in October 1978—not the humanitarian imperative of freeing Ugandans from a vicious government.[40] India and Vietnam had been widely castigated for their interventions but the Organization of African Unity (OAU, now the African Union) did not condemn Tanzania, though neither it nor the West applauded Tanzania for delivering Ugandans from tyranny. What troubled the OAU was that Tanzania had continued its campaign beyond the Kagera Salient and had pressed on into Uganda to achieve a goal that went beyond what appeared necessary for self-defense. That an infamous tyrant who had killed as many as 300,000 of his people had been removed as a result did not enter the considerations of the African grouping.[41] The OAU wanted to avoid creating a precedent by blessing, on human rights grounds, what we know today as "regime change." The organization wanted to uphold the principles of sovereignty and territorial integrity, which were mentioned early and prominently in its charter.[42] By contrast, the African Union, the OAU's successor, has incorporated into its Constitutive Act (adopted in 2000) the provision permitting it to intervene in member countries in the event of "war crimes, genocide and crimes against humanity."[43] Supporters of humanitarian intervention sometimes point to this shift as proof that support for the policy is not limited to the West. But in practice the AU chooses to uphold state sovereignty rather than protect human rights, especially when its most powerful members commit offenses.

Developing countries' suspicion of the doctrine of humanitarian intervention stems from more than unrepentant fealty to the Westphalian model. The power of interveners causes particular anxiety. Weaker states see that powerful ones control the levers of intervention, and thus fear that the policy will be used exclusively—and selectively—against them, in service of expediency rather than of human rights principles. They may not see mass killings as paroxysms of blind rage, as interveners do, and so will question rescuers' motives. Indeed, mass killings are arguably not irrational, nor do they necessarily stem from ethnic and religious animosity, both of which may persist for long stretches of time without leading to runaway violence. Instead, atrocities are an extreme measure that states and social groups choose to defend their power and status, broadly defined, against perceived threats to interests they deem vital.[44] In fact, the historical record shows that when the leaders of states and groups deem violence necessary to thwart such challenges, they are ready to risk external intervention. They see it as a prospective, uncertain threat as compared to the present, palpable ones.

There is little chance states will adopt, let alone implement, the human rights– and legitimacy-based model that Walzer's critics offer. But this doesn't render the ideas Beitz, Slaughter, Doppelt, Luban, and Tesón propose inconsequential. Their arguments have been extended, transformed, even distorted into a new, revolutionary amalgam of humanitarianism and power politics. According to its acolytes, traditional modes of diplomacy and peacekeeping are wrongly preoccupied with neutrality and brokering compromises and should concentrate instead on siding with victims and punishing oppressors. Even unilateral humanitarian intervention is a lawful, legitimate means for delivering justice and liberty; the veto-wielding members of the UN Security Council must no longer be allowed to hold victims hostage. This is an outlook that transcends the standard left-right ideological chasm.[45]

Yet as David Chandler points out, while the devaluation of sovereignty may appear impartial and altruistic, if the program underpinning it prevails, the rights of weak states will be eroded and those of powerful ones expanded.[46] States that decide when and by what means intervention will occur will never know the fear of being exposed to it themselves, or even have to worry about being targeted, no matter what they do to the people living within their borders. Thus a project that radiates the idealism of human rights and universality in reality perpetuates the very parochialism and realpolitik it claims to abhor and seeks to supplant.

THE LEGAL DEBATE

I f the normative aspects of humanitarian intervention remain contentious, its status in codified and customary international law also
continues to stir debate, with legal experts coming to starkly different conclusions after considering the same facts. A good part of this
disagreement centers on whether humanitarian intervention comports
with the letter and spirit of the UN Charter, which has attained the
status of a sort of global constitution. At first blush, the answer might
appear to be a straightforward no: states are prohibited from using military force except in self-defense or when authorized, under Chapter
VII of the Charter, by the Security Council.

In practice, however, the Council has not invoked Chapter VII
solely to deal with threats to the peace defined narrowly as aggression
by one state against the other, as it did in the Korean War and following
Iraq's invasion of Kuwait. It has also done so in instances of violence,
potential and actual, within countries, with increasing frequency following the end of the Cold War. Internal conflict inspired Chapter VII
missions in the Congo in the 1960s and, in recent decades, in such
places as Afghanistan, Haiti, Liberia, Somalia, Sudan, Sierra Leone,
Bosnia, Kosovo, and East Timor. Ninety percent of these operations
occurred after the Cold War.[1] This shift in the wider application of

Chapter VII owes in part to the changing strategic landscape: during the Cold War, the United States and Soviet Union made liberal use of their Security Council veto power to scotch UN-backed interventions that might advance the other's interests. The easing of that impediment does not, however, account wholly for the recent uptick in Security Council–authorized interventions in response to internal violence. States and civic groups, mainly in the West, have pushed hard for UN approval to stop atrocities, and their efforts fit within a larger program that seeks to make international law a more effective tool for promoting human rights.

States' Rights Versus Human Rights: The UN Charter

The UN Charter invites divergent readings and it is easy to see why legal experts on opposite sides of the humanitarian intervention debate have invoked the document in support of their claims.

According to the Charter, the UN's principal purpose is "to reaffirm faith in fundamental human rights, in the dignity and worth of the human person, . . . [and] in the equal rights of men and women."[2] This seems to permit the use of force to defend human rights, especially the basic right to be safe from wanton violence. Not so. The Charter contains no provisions for enforcement to guarantee human rights, and Article 2.7 of Chapter I prohibits the UN from intervening "in matters that are within the domestic jurisdiction of any state." This sounds like an unqualified defense of sovereign immunity, though, especially since 1991, the Security Council has affirmed on multiple occasions that upheaval within countries may threaten the larger peace and thereby justify intervention under Chapter VII of the Charter. The Council has not discarded the concept of sovereignty, but it has qualified it. It has not affirmed that military interventions to stop atrocities can, as a matter of law, now be authorized under the Charter. Instead, the Security Council presented the resolutions authorizing these missions as exceptional rather than precedent setting.[3] From the standpoint of customary law, humanitarian intervention, which does not have widespread support among states and has not become an established practice, cannot be deemed legitimate.

While the extension of Chapter VII to respond to violence within states has been accepted, claims that unilateral armed humanitarian intervention is legal as well have sparked controversy. Fernando Tesón, among others, has made this case with force and eloquence. Tesón believes the law must be the servant of morality, not a set of rules mechanically observed regardless of ethics and the consequences for human rights. He further argues that states comply with the law for normative reasons, not merely out of narrow self-interest.[4] Accordingly, Tesón, based on a distinctly Kantian approach to international law, insists that when liberal democratic states confront gross human rights violations abroad, they must be true to their values and defend the beleaguered—with or without UN authorization.

Tesón is not alone. International lawyers Philip Bobbitt and Geoffrey Robertson, President Obama's NATO ambassador Ivo Daalder, James Lindsay of the Council on Foreign Relations, Senator John McCain, neoconservative foreign policy expert Robert Kagan, and liberal scholars such as John Ikenberry and Anne-Marie Slaughter have argued that a coalition of democracies has the moral and legal ground to act unilaterally to stop mass killings when the UN cannot or will not act.[5]

Yet the Charter provides no basis for the claim that individual states or democratic coalitions can rightfully intervene militarily to stop mass killings when they choose to do so. The drafters of the Charter certainly did not intend to open the door for unilateral humanitarian military interventions. As Ian Brownlie observes, the drafters' deliberations were shaped by recent historical experience, most pertinently the tendency of leaders, such as Adolf Hitler, to invoke humanitarian values to legitimize wars of aggression.[6] According to Brownlie, during the Charter's creation, "the [drafters'] principal object was to avoid and rule out excuses for intervention."[7] Accordingly, at the 1945 San Francisco conference, where the Charter was drafted, committee members rejected a French proposal to allow unilateral intervention to stop egregious human rights violations.[8]

How then does one reconcile the evident tension in the Charter's language between states' sovereign rights and individuals' basic human rights? Tesón looks to Chapter I, Article 2.4, which prohibits "the threat or use of force against the territorial integrity or political independence of any state, or in any manner inconsistent with the Purposes of the United Nations." To Tesón, this language blesses unilateral interventions that comport with the purposes of the UN—namely, to defend and advance human rights. This interpretation amounts, at best, to a stretch. As Mary Ellen O'Connell points out, "[Tesón's] argument cannot withstand scrutiny. While the Charter's human rights provisions are aspirational and future-oriented, article 2.4 is emphatic and unconditional."[9]

If the drafters had wanted to authorize individual states or coalitions to stop atrocities at their discretion, without UN authorization, they would have said so. As a legal document, the Charter authorizes and constrains action with as little ambiguity as possible. Despite Tesón's claim, Article 2.4 of Chapter I more plausibly amplifies the ban on using force—except for individual or collective defense against aggression or when authorized by the Security Council under Chapter VII—rather than creating a loophole for permitting unilateral intervention in the name of human rights. Read beside other provisions prohibiting intervention without Security Council approval, Article 2.4 reinforces the point that the Council must follow UN purposes when deciding whether to approve intervention. This interpretation comports with the position that states adopted from the creation of the UN until the end of the Cold War. Hence in the 1970s, when India and Vietnam invaded East Pakistan and Cambodia, respectively, they invoked the right to self-defense rather than a right to intervene unilaterally in other countries to safeguard human rights.

The Unilateralists Persist

The most prominent effort to justify unilateral intervention occurred before, during, and after NATO's 1999 intervention in Kosovo. Though NATO acted without Security Council authorization, its leaders defended the campaign's legality on six grounds: 1) NATO is a collective security coalition, not a state; 2) it acted to stop atrocities, not to advance its self-interest or to violate a country's territorial integrity or to nullify its independence; 3) Serbia had failed to comply with Security Council resolutions 1160, 1199, and 1203, which aimed at protecting Kosovo; 4) twelve of the Council's fifteen members voted against the March 26, 1999, Russian resolution condemning the intervention; 5) the Serbs' attacks on the Kosovars constituted aggression; and 6) the Security Council effectively acquiesced to the intervention by accepting that it had happened.

International law specialist Louis Henkin rejects these justifications. Henkin argues that unilateral intervention violates the Charter's provisions whether it is carried out by one state or by a group. For the practice to become permissible in his view, Chapter VIII, specifically Articles 52.1 and 53.1, of the Charter would have to be revised. These articles permit the Security Council to authorize regional organizations, such as the African Union, to safeguard international security and peace through intervention; NATO is a military alliance, not a regional organization, hence the illegality of its actions.[10] What's more, legal scholar Simon Chesterman points out, aside from Belgium and the United Kingdom, no NATO country claimed that the Kosovo campaign constituted a humanitarian response justified under international law. Even Britain has presented an inconsistent position on unilateral humanitarian intervention. While the British government insisted that the Kosovo intervention was lawful, in 1986 the Foreign Office disputed the idea that unilateral humanitarian intervention was legally tenable, and following the Kosovo war, the House of Commons Foreign Affairs Select Committee did the same.[11] The other NATO members that supported the intervention either believed that the claim of legality would not withstand scrutiny—or, more likely, they did not want to advance an argument that could obligate them to intervene in future instances of mass violence.

These other NATO members typically focused on Serbia's refusal to comply with prior Security Council resolutions on Kosovo. But, as Chesterman notes, none of those resolutions contained provisions for enforcement. Michael Glennon, a scholar of international law who holds a more sympathetic view of humanitarian intervention than does Chesterman, also rejects the claims that the intervention was legal because of Serbia's noncompliance with Security Council resolutions and that the Charter permits unilateral intervention.[12] NATO also argued that Kosovo presented a special case and that the intervention did not set a precedent that would require it to deploy arms elsewhere to prevent other atrocities. This formulation revealed states' skittishness about being responsible for enforcing human rights abroad.

Some international lawyers insist that NATO's Kosovo intervention was lawful because it neither annexed a state's territory nor threatened its political independence. They insist that Chapter VII allows the unilateral use of force in such circumstances. Anthony D'Amato, for instance, argues that the United States had the legal right to topple the leftist government in Grenada in 1983 by force of arms and to invade Panama and arrest Manuel Noriega in 1989. D'Amato claims that both acts complied with international law because they were carried out on humanitarian grounds and neither led to the annexation of a state's territory nor compromised its independence.[13]

Let us leave aside the questionable assumption that an invaded country does not, in some measure, lose its political independence. No reasonable reading of the Charter could validate this tortured logic or the concomitant claim that the drafters of the Charter either intended to leave such a loophole or were just plain sloppy in their choice of words.[14] The Charter's text reflects the drafters' intent to limit the use of force to narrow circumstances, so as to protect states' independence and territorial unity, and to permit it in other circumstances only with the Security Council's authorization. They clearly did not intend to permit war outside the context of self-defense, providing it did not cross the critical threshold of depriving states of their independence or land; nor did they aim to enable unilateralism, providing it was not prompted by states' self-interests or aggressive intentions. Those who favor legalizing unilateralism—provided it does not grab a state's land or erode its independence—also seem to be forgetting the effect that such a principle might have on the international system. It is hard to imagine the world becoming more stable and less war-prone if governments can claim the legal right, based on normative values they profess to cherish, to intervene militarily in other countries to enforce human rights. Supporters of humanitarian intervention claim that repressive regimes invoke the principle of nonintervention to gain legal cover for engaging in brutality. While this claim has merit, it dismisses all too quickly the apprehension of weaker countries, particularly former colonies, about reverting to an age when powerful states used sweeping normative justifications, including the duty to civilize and enlighten,

to justify wars of expansion and conquest.[15] Nonintervention continues to have widespread support among states because it contributes to
justice and stability, not simply because self-interested, cynical tyrants
find it useful.

Human Rights, Reasons of State, and the Law

D'Amato avers that the American interventions in Grenada and
Panama represented "milestones along the path to a new, non-statist
conception of international law" that "may very well act as a catalyst in
the global revolution of popular sovereignty" and help create a world
in which law becomes the servant of freedom and justice rather than
of despots. These are appealing words; after all, who likes oppressors?
But the interventions he invokes to make his case were not motivated
by the noble, universal principles he admires. The claim of legality and
legitimacy requires that the intervener be motivated principally by the
desire to uphold human rights, and that other motives, to the extent
that they exist, remain secondary.

American aims in Grenada and Panama were not so pure. At one
moment the United States could not abide the Grenadian government's and Noriega's disregard for democratic rights, at others it suppressed this same revulsion when it came to dictators such as Saddam
Hussein, Anastasio Somoza, the Shah of Iran, Mobutu Sese Seko, and
Suharto, to name but a few. Washington cooperated for decades with
repressive rulers, and its material support and political backing helped
them maintain their grip on power.

The idea that the United States ousted Noriega because of outrage over his lousy human rights record cannot be taken seriously.
Washington had long known about the Panamanian strongman's unsavory qualities, but dealt with him anyway. He became an informer and
source of intelligence when President Eisenhower was in office and
continued in that role during the presidency of George H. W. Bush.
Noriega reportedly received payments from the CIA between 1971 and
1988, the year before his repressiveness and deepening involvement in
drug trafficking turned Washington against him.[16] His connections to
drug traffickers, including the notorious Medellín Cartel, could hardly

have eluded American intelligence, yet he stayed in good graces even during the Reagan years. Declassified US government documents establish that he played an important part in the Reagan administration's campaign to overthrow the left-wing Sandinista government in Nicaragua by allowing Washington to funnel arms and money to the anti-Sandinista Contras via Panama after Congress cut off aid to them.[17]

Noriega eventually proved uncontrollable and mercurial. Given Panama's strategic importance, the United States could not tolerate this. In December 1989 President Bush launched Operation Just Cause and dispatched troops to apprehend him, ending successive American governments' collaboration with a man who would later be vilified for the same transgressions that Washington had seen fit to ignore for years.

Grenada, for its part, was ruled by a leftist government with ties to Cuba and the Soviet Union, in a part of the world in which the United States had set the rules since the early nineteenth century. Yet there was no evidence that a fractious government rife with infighting was planning to embark on a killing spree, that it intended to harm American medical students based in Grenada or had rejected Washington's request to evacuate them, or that its human rights record was noticeably worse than that of the many repressive regimes Washington had backed over the years.[18] Grenada's leaders presented a problem not because they were committing atrocities or because they failed the test of liberalism, but because they broke the strategic ground rules that the United States had laid down.

Washington's dealings with Saddam, Noriega, and others of their ilk demonstrate that the defense of unilateralism as a lawful act rests on shaky ground: state leaders invoke and discard the humanitarian principle as needed. One can reasonably argue that national security interests necessitate moral compromises. But one cannot simultaneously maintain (at least plausibly) that tyranny is a morally intolerable crime that can legitimately and lawfully be punished by outsiders, except in the case of regimes that maintain friendly relations and have strategic value in the eyes of states asserting the legality of unilateral intervention.

Can Unilateralism Be Made Controllable and Accountable?

Some supporters of unilateral intervention recognize that it currently has no legal basis, but they argue that it ought to and that carrying out more such missions will change minds. The challenge, as they see it, lies in ensuring that unilateral intervention can be held accountable and that they advance humanitarian rather than purely strategic causes.

Michael Reisman, for example, understands that unilateral humanitarian interventions, clad in human rights robes, can be capricious, selective, and unrestrained by law.[19] Similarly, Glennon recognizes that far from becoming an effective solution, unilateralism could beget a backlash and fail to gain legitimacy, making it even harder for international law to evolve toward the effective, consensus-based solution to atrocities that is currently lacking.[20] Nevertheless, both believe that paralysis at the UN may necessitate unilateral interventions.

Yet neither offers solutions to the problems extra-UN remedies could create. Reisman rests his hopes on the new "international legal decision process," which involves not only states but also a network of NGOs, average citizens, and influential individuals committed to human rights. He believes that this process will prevent (or at least limit) arbitrary interventions that are not motivated by human rights principles.[21] As he sees it, it was the efforts of nonstate organizations that compelled states to intervene in Kosovo and East Timor on humanitarian grounds. But rather than proving that the international legal decision process will prevent states from using interventions to pursue goals unrelated to human rights while cynically exploiting lofty ideals to gain legal cover, this merely shows that civic groups and public pressure can help make interventions happen. Reisman's faith in the international legal decision process is belied by experience, including recent events such as the American intervention in Iraq in 2003 and the Russian intervention in Ukraine in 2014. Nor can the process he counts on—more commonly referred to as international civil society—impel intervention when leaders conclude that the risks and costs are too high (as in Syria) or the strategic interest minimal (as in Rwanda).

Glennon recognizes that unless unilateral interventions along the lines of NATO's Kosovo war gain international acceptance, "that solution will soon be resented" even when the interveners are motivated by altruism and horror over atrocities: "Justice, it turns out, requires legitimacy; without widespread acceptance of intervention as part of a formal justice system, the new interventionism will appear to be built on neither law nor justice, but on power alone. It will then be only a matter of time before the meddling of the illegitimate interventionist regime is rejected just as roundly as the one it replaced."[22] Precisely. But how might Glennon's model, variants of which other proponents of unilateralism favor, gain consensus-based legitimacy in a world of national communities that are rich and poor, strong and weak, and divided by ideas reflecting their cultures, political ideologies, and histories? The evidence suggests that these differences have produced considerable opposition to interventions that circumvent the United Nations and that nothing resembling a global consensus exists.

Glennon's response boils down to the claim that "if power is used justly, law will follow."[23] His axiom begs the principal question. Among the most vexing problems in politics, domestic and international, is that those who possess power are tempted to use it unjustly and selfishly. In national politics, particularly in democratic societies, institutions, laws, checks, balances, and elections ensure accountability, albeit imperfectly. In international politics, no comparable legal and institutional mechanisms exist. International institutions and rules—the United Nations, international law, and the International Court of Justice—may resemble those of nations, but their powers of enforcement are far weaker, especially when they must contend with opposition from powerful and willful states. Indeed, this weakness in part explains the calls for extra-UN interventions.

Chesterman argues that in a world divided on the proper balance between sovereignty and human rights, unilateralism, even when used intermittently, will not produce the anticipated evolution in customary law.[24] Instead, each instance of it will likely highlight the divergence of viewpoints and breed contention rather than consensus. This point seemed lost on the biggest boosters of NATO's air campaign in Kosovo, such as British Prime Minister Tony Blair, who presented it as an action undertaken in the name of the international community and in service of universal values. What international community? Chesterman correctly notes that "it was not the world but NATO that was acting. Despite the much-vaunted unanimity of the Alliance (reservations within the Czech Republic and Hungary, and massive unpopularity in Greece notwithstanding), states representing over half the world's population—and three of its seven declared nuclear powers—spoke out strongly against the action."[25] And Glennon himself concedes that when debate regarding humanitarian intervention emerged in the aftermath of the Kosovo campaign, "at least half of UN member states' delegations had nothing to say on the subject, one way or the other ... and of those delegates who did comment, roughly a third appeared to favor humanitarian intervention under some circumstances, roughly a third appeared to oppose it under any circumstances, and the remaining third appeared equivocal or noncommittal. Proponents, as one would expect, consisted primarily of Western democracies; opponents were primarily from Latin America, Africa, and the Arab world." His conclusion: "Simple mathematics reveals that the 'world community' as such has *no* view on the propriety of humanitarian intervention ... It is hard to see a 'developing norm' of humanitarian intervention; an equal number of states oppose such a norm as support it."[26]

New Rules?

Unilateral humanitarian intervention could become legal through new rules. International legal scholars tend to object to this possibility on the grounds that states could hijack any such rules in order to present interventions intended to serve their narrow interest as legitimate and as good for all. International law expert and intervention supporter Ryan Goodman concedes that the overwhelming majority of international legal scholars today subscribe to this view; moreover, 133 states and various UN General Assembly resolutions have opposed legalization. Yet he dismisses the concern that legal principles permitting unilateralism would serve as cover for capricious uses of force or trigger escalating wars.[27] Wars of humanitarian intervention, he argues, are much less liable to spread than those based on territorial, ideological, or ethnic disputes. Moreover, if leaders had to defend their interventions by means of robust humanitarian principles, they would be less likely to intervene for selfish reasons.

This line of argument presents at least two problems. First, we don't have any basis on which to predict that humanitarian wars won't escalate. We have abundant statistics—for instance, in the Correlates of War (COW) project database—on interstate wars,[28] so we can establish the frequency of escalation with some confidence. But unilateral humanitarian interventions have been rare, so we lack sufficient data to warrant Goodman's generalization. Second, his faith in the restraining powers of public opinion is misplaced. Governments have many means at hand to influence, and even manipulate, opinion—far more than the citizenry has to hold back leaders determined to go to war. And the impulse to rally around the flag remains powerful.

Tesón offers a variant of Goodman's argument. He insists that the question of whether states use humanitarian intervention as a cloak to advance self-seeking, nonhumanitarian interests is empirical and not a given and that interventions to stop atrocities must not, in any event, be ruled out based on a priori principles.[29] To keep states honest, he pins his hopes on "norms and institutions" that prevent governments from subverting the moral bases of humanitarian interventions.[30] But what if states fail to comply with agreed-upon rules and disregard the institutions entrusted with oversight, or bend both to their advantage? Tesón counters that "an intervention in which foreign troops abuse their power is not an instance of humanitarian intervention."[31] This tautology offers no solution to the problem of how to hold states accountable. Tesón in effect asks us to trust in the rules of the road, but, like Goodman, ignores the challenges involved in developing and enforcing them. Tesón does not worry about capricious war making because "intervention is very costly, so governments have a considerable disincentive to undertake *any* intervention."[32] If so, it is odd that he also believes that states ought to embrace humanitarian intervention out of normative conviction and that it should be used more frequently.

In his discussion of NATO's Kosovo campaign, the eminent German jurist and legal scholar Bruno Simma, who served on the International Court of Justice, offers another proposal for intervention without UN approval.[33] In his view, Kosovo-like interventions may be necessary as a last resort when a dire human rights crisis breaks out and veto-wielding members paralyze the Security Council. Simma believes that unilateralism is illegal but legitimate in exceptional circumstances. Jürgen Habermas took essentially the same position on the Kosovo War, as did the UN commission that investigated the campaign. It was, in the commission's words, "illegal but legitimate."[34]

Simma's careful, fair-minded account contains a major flaw (as does Habermas's position) that will prevent it from becoming a workable solution to mass atrocities. He assumes that Kosovo-like instances—massive violence within a country, gridlock in the Security Council—will rarely occur. But in the aftermath of the UN-sanctioned intervention in Libya, we may see a good deal of discord within the Security Council over humanitarian intervention. China and Russia concluded that the Libyan campaign went beyond its remit—protecting civilians—and helped overthrow a government. That assessment accounted for their unwillingness to allow any Security Council resolution that might open the door for intervention in Syria. Perhaps permitting unilateralism whenever the UN is deadlocked and certifying it as legitimate under appropriate conditions provides a solution. That, however, would amount to challenging one or more of the Security Council's permanent members on each occasion as well as those nonpermanent members of the Council and states in the General Assembly that oppose the intervention. But if one is concerned with legitimacy—and Simma is—blessing unilateralism even under these special circumstances won't provide a viable solution because it will not command a consensus among states.

Aligning Law and Morality

But surely, Allen Buchanan argues, law must not fail to respond to changing conditions and moral imperatives. Surely insisting on obeying the legal prohibitions against unilateral intervention at the cost of allowing mass murder is perverse. As Buchanan sees it, vulgar positivism—the tradition of seeing laws as rules detached from a moral purpose—amounts to ethical abdication.[35] He believes that violations of international law that strengthen the values of morality, justice, and equality among states deserve approval. Buchanan

points to Britain's use of naval power in the early nineteenth century to search foreign ships as part of its campaign to end the slave
trade and to the Nuremberg Trials, which punished crimes against
humanity, an offense that international law did not yet recognize.[36]
He dismisses concerns that condoning law-breaking in the name of
morality will undermine international order, permit powerful states
to "hijack" the international legal system for self-seeking ends, and
increase the vulnerability of weaker states. Such concerns, he insists,
rest on a false domino theory—essentially the claim that one violation
could start a chain reaction that eventually threatens the entire edifice
of international law—and overlook the multiple sources of order in
the international system.[37] Like Tesón, Buchanan rejects the formal-
ism (as he sees it) that treats international law as a corpus of treaties that requires compliance because it embodies the consent and
consensus of states. Law, in his view, should gain legitimacy by proving it can advance justice and be attentive to moral considerations.[38]
Buchanan believes that illegal acts can be defended rigorously and
persuasively—provided they are rooted in principles of morality and
justice and serve the greater good. What's more, they can set in train
practices, which, if sustained by states over a long duration, will create customary laws that strengthen human rights, eventually creating
treaty-based law as well.

Buchanan's case fails to convince. He claims that extra-legal
humanitarian interventions—which he defends in principle, though
not, curiously, in Kosovo—can gain global legitimacy and that the
differences in values and interests among states are overstated. After
all, he argues, in liberal democracies divergent views on many issues
abound, yet reach resolution. But here he skates over a critical point.
Liberal democracies have legislative institutions for reforming laws
and judicial ones for enforcing them; in international politics, no
institutions with comparable power and efficacy exist. Politics within
liberal democracies can be contentious, but its divisiveness pales in
comparison to that among states.

Buchanan's plan and vision contain another problem. He defends
law-breaking in international affairs (though in ways that meet his
strict standards of morality and justice) on the grounds that legal
reform takes time and encounters many obstacles. Yet he argues that

the norms he favors—state accountability for human rights and the permeability of the sovereign shield—are fast gaining ground, thanks to the transnational human rights movement, the spread of democracy and liberal norms, and the salutary effects of globalization. Yet this claim undercuts his plea for law-breaking to shape customary law so as to achieve justice. Time favors him, and the solution he advances therefore seems unnecessary.

Thomas Franck, another critic of the positivist perspective on law, offers a variation of Buchanan's thesis.[39] Franck argues that customary law can modify treaty-based law: the actual practice of states on a particular issue comes to be widely adopted, eventually producing new guidelines, standards, and expectations. This reproduces in the international arena the process by which domestic common law has developed. The essence of Franck's argument—which others make as well—is that while unilateral intervention may now be illegal under the UN Charter, the Kosovo campaign and other unilateral actions can, over time, create customary law, as long as the would-be interveners demonstrate the pressing need to save lives in each instance. But as Chesterman and Michael Byers point out, even when directed against abusers, unilateralism lacks supporters (the practitioners may turn out to be few as well)—but it does have numerous critics.[40]

During and after the Kosovo expedition, China, Russia, India, South Africa, and the G-77's 134 members roundly attacked unilateralism—and, more broadly, the right to engage in humanitarian intervention, which they declared lacked justification under the terms of the UN Charter.[41] The UN General Assembly passed resolutions in 1965, 1970, 1981, 1987, and 1991 opposing unilateral intervention for purposes other than self-defense.[42] Unilateralism's champions, in the main leaders and legal experts based in the United States, and to a lesser extent Europe, cannot claim to represent a global consensus, or even a significant number of states representing different parts of the world. They can claim—and some have—that action, not criticism, matters more, because it is what shapes the evolution of law. Those who believe that the powerful can and should shape law by exercising their might can comfortably make this argument and remain true to their view of politics. Not so those who see customary law as a means for creating new universal principles legitimized by the words and deeds of a wide range of states. In any case, the NATO states that waged the Kosovo war took pains to specify that they did not intend to set a precedent—which is to say, they did their best *not* to help create customary law.

What's more, international law experts disagree about the conditions under which customary law arises, the extent to which it shapes what states do, and why it influences their actions when it does.[43] Jack Goldsmith and Eric Posner argue that states may adopt certain practices, which then gain currency for various reasons: converging interests, a deliberate decision to cooperate in order to achieve a shared objective, or pressure from powerful states that stand to gain from the acceptance of a particular practice.[44] Even under these conditions, the greater the number of states involved, the more varied their political institutions and ideologies, and the more controversial the practice, the less likely it is that the practice will become widespread and routine. And as Goldsmith and Posner point out, evidence for the proposition that customary law exerts an independent and normative effect on states—shaping their conduct by virtue of its moral influence—is thin.[45]

Power Rules

If Western legal specialists are at odds on the legality of humanitarian intervention, how realistic is the prospect for a *global* consensus on humanitarian intervention? In the end, states will pick and choose, engaging in what Ian Hurd, in a perceptive analysis, labels the "strategic manipulation" of international law. Governments will, he says, select elements from the law that support what they propose to do for reasons of state and offer interpretations to justify their actions.[46] Power heavily shapes the laws among nations; the inverse is not true. States routinely invoke international law because they appreciate the advantage of presenting what they do as lawful and legitimate. And they adhere to many of its provisions because doing so provides the predictability needed for routine international transactions that benefit them. But this compliance does not stem from high-mindedness or a willingness to sacrifice national interests to the law.

When states choose not to intervene to stop atrocities, they will invoke contingent complexities and dangers (Syria) or infeasibility or the lack of reliable information (Rwanda). In cases where they want to block intervention against a friendly or allied state that is perpetrating atrocities, they will, as Russia and China have done in Syria, appeal to sacrosanct sovereign rights. In cases where human rights are not the prime motive for war, states will invoke them anyway so that principles camouflage power plays (Panama). This sort of rationalization has occurred regularly, despite the end of the Cold War and the supposed spread and strength of human rights norms worldwide. For instance, Russia invoked R2P, a concept for which it has scant enthusiasm, to defend its war against Georgia in 2008.[47]

The world's political and cultural plurality rules out universally accepted principles, let alone laws that legitimize and legalize humanitarian intervention. Against any such laws, dissenting states, whether democratic or not, will invoke existing international law, especially the centrality of sovereignty. Whatever international human rights treaties states may sign will, as they have in the past, emerge after much debate and dueling. As a result, the texts will contain enough loopholes and caveats to allow multiple interpretations, enabling states to evade concrete obligations. Universality—in the form of declarations and treaties—will amount to a lowest common denominator. Governments will engage in humanitarian intervention when it serves their interests or when the price that they expect to pay is tolerable. Power and interest, not law, will prove decisive.

5

HUMAN RIGHTS AND INTERVENTION

Trying to get experts on humanitarian intervention to agree on which historical figure deserves to be recognized as the project's progenitor, and just how far back in history one needs to reach to accurately trace its intellectual lineage, will produce nothing but end-less hair-splitting. There will be lots of heat, but little light. Thankfully, we needn't subject ourselves to any such painful and pointless ordeal here, for there is a period that most of them would readily accept as one that featured analogues to present-day humanitarian intervention and fervent debates about the rights of strangers and the duties of powerful states to rescue them from butchery.

Scholars who stress the salience of human rights and liberal norms in world politics—Gary Bass and Martha Finnemore are prominent examples—point to the nineteenth century as an exemplar, portray-ing it as an epoch in which compassionate, altruistic European pow-ers launched humanitarian interventions to stop atrocities abroad. The politics among nations, they add, isn't about power and strategic purpose alone. Ideals, human rights, and transnational norms exert a powerful influence on states' foreign policies, and discounting their importance amounts to accepting the cynical, materialistic, myopic—indeed wrongheaded—worldview of realists.

Is this interpretation of the nineteenth century tenable or tendentious? Does it improve our understanding of international politics? And what light, if any, can that era shed on the current debates about humanitarian intervention, particularly as regards the much-touted Responsibility to Protect (R2P), which we will turn to later in this chapter?

Nineteenth-Century Saviors: Altruism or Humbug?

In three instances, Britain, France, and Russia dispatched troops abroad to stop mass killings in the Ottoman Empire.[1] Between 1821 and 1827 Greeks fought for independence from the Ottomans, and Ottoman soldiers committed mass atrocities while suppressing the rebellion. In response, Russia, France, and Britain sent a maritime force that defeated the Ottoman navy at Navarino in 1827. In 1860–1861, over ten thousand Maronite Christians who had earlier risen in revolt against their Druze overlords were massacred, with the participation of Sunni Muslims and the complicity of Ottoman troops. France intervened, honoring an agreement that had been signed by the major European powers and the Ottomans to help the Sultans stop bloodshed and restore order within their non-Muslim domains. Then, in 1877–1878, Russia, the self-styled defender of the Empire's Orthodox Christians, intervened after Ottoman troops killed thousands of Bulgarian subjects.

The details of these various crises and wars are too complex to cover here. Suffice it to say that the European powers' concern for the Empire's Balkan Christians mingled with their rivalry over the fate of a decaying Ottoman colossus. Austria-Hungary and Russia, previously committed to upholding the Empire's unity, changed their stances and instead hoped to annex chunks of the Balkans. Britain wanted to keep the Empire whole, or at least out of Russian and Austrian hands. Through it all, the interventionist powers displayed remarkable sanctimony and hypocrisy in presenting a morality play, the theme of which was the sympathy among Britons and Russians for the Greeks, French compassion for Maronite Christians, and Russian outrage over the killing of Bulgarians, and the resulting triumph of humanitarianism.

Sympathy comprised only part of the story.

For one thing, the interveners did not apply within their own empires the humanitarian ethics that they invoked to defend their interventions abroad. Then, as now, calculations of self-interest and the circumstances created by the balance of power were paramount. The European powers and Russia were able to wage war against the Ottoman Empire because, by the mid-nineteenth century, it provided an easy mark. An empire whose armies had once conquered vast swaths of Europe, unto the gates of Vienna in 1683, had become the "sick man of Europe." Powerful European states insinuated themselves steadily into its internal affairs by many means, including arrogating the right to define the terms under which the Ottoman state would rule the Balkans.[2] Serial rebellions and secessionist uprisings by Balkan Christian subjects exacerbated the Empire's predicament, as did tensions between the Empire's Muslims and Christians. These revolts gained strength once European powers made clear that they supported the Christians, were prepared to intervene in their behalf, and that the Ottomans would prove unable to parry the Europeans' demands, to say nothing of their military power.[3]

By contrast, Russia faced no such foreign pressure when it crushed the 1830–1831 and 1863–1864 revolts in its Polish domains, even though Russian troops killed civilians en masse, deported them, and destroyed entire villages. The Ottoman Empire offered little resistance; military intervention against Russia presented substantial risk. Hence there was war against the former but not the latter in this supposed time of norm-based humanitarianism.

Second, even as the European powers trumpeted their humanitarianism, they understood themselves to be in competition for strategic gains in the Ottoman Empire, especially in the Balkans and the Turkish Straits. The British in particular were suspicious of their rivals' invocation of humanitarian principles, seeing them as a cover for activities aimed at shifting the European balance of power. It is impossible to disentangle the European powers' noble motives from their interest in preventing competitors from gaining strategic advantages. Consider the 1875–1878 Eastern Crisis and its aftermath.[4] It was precipitated by the Turks' suppression of rebellions that erupted in Herzegovina in 1875 and the following year in Bosnia and Bulgaria. The Empire's killing of Bulgarian Christians and the Sultan's spurning of European demands that he end repression and institute reforms led Russia to declare war on Turkey in 1877. As part of the postwar settlement, the Congress of Berlin, the European powers divvied up Ottoman real estate. Russia gained Batum, Kars, Ardahan, and southern Bessarabia, Britain took Cyprus, and Austria-Hungary gained Bosnia and Herzegovina.[5] Altruism, as it happened, paid well.

Third, tens of thousands of Muslims were driven from their homes, tortured, and killed by Christians during the nineteenth century in the course of ethno-religious violence and movements for national independence in the Ottomans' Balkan domains, yet the European powers' humanitarian sentiments focused exclusively on Christians.[6] Indeed, while Russia was championing the rights of Balkan Christians, it was pitilessly colonizing the Muslim North Caucasus. General Alexei Yermolov, who commanded the Tsar's North Caucasus forces from 1817 to 1827, boasted of his deliberate wanton violence, designed to strike terror in the hearts of the North Caucasians. (It succeeded: mothers were said to warn disobedient children that Yermolov would seek them out.) The Russians killed several hundred thousands of Circassians and others during the subjugation of the western outposts of the North Caucasus region abutting the Black Sea, and deported 460,000 others to the Arab and Turkish domains of the Ottoman Empire, where their descendants live to this day.[7] Of those expelled, many thousands died from disease or drowned during perilous voyages undertaken in makeshift boats. Circassians comprised a majority of the deportees, and an estimated 75 percent of them perished in the war or en route to exile.

Finally, the nineteenth century witnessed a wave of European (and American) empire building that involved war, subjugation, and massacre, all of which went unchecked by fellow powers.[8] For example, European powers knew of the horrific cruelties, including murders, amputations, and rapes occurring routinely in King Leopold's Belgian

Congo. These acts were integral to a system of economic exploitation (including forced labor) described as "one of the most destructive and all-encompassing *corvée* institutions the world has known."[9] Between eight and ten million Africans may have perished, halving the Congo's population by 1910.[10] Yet the European powers did not speak of humanitarian intervention, much less act. As colonial overlords, they themselves lived in glass houses. Moreover, they practiced a deeply parochial, if supremely practical, version of humanitarianism: some peoples deserved humane treatment, but not others, who were seen as lower than European Christians in the hierarchy of human societies. As the historian Davide Rodogno observes:

> It is worthwhile for readers to bear in mind that when Europeans dealt with massacres taking place in the Ottoman Empire, they ignored the appalling violations of the right to life in their respective colonies. They forgot, whether deliberately or not, the fact that equality before the law and religious freedom in their own states, let alone colonies, did not exist ... In a former Ottoman territory like Algeria, French authorities ruled in a far more intolerant, discriminating, and despotic way than the Ottomans ever had done. Europeans intervened militarily when the "barbarous" Ottomans used the same "savage" methods to repress insurrection they systematically used in their own colonies ... After Indians massacred Britons in Delhi and Kanpur in the summer of 1857, the British sadistically slaughtered Indians by the hundreds, burning old women and children alive, and smearing Muslims with pig fat before killing them. The Earl of Carnarvon, Disraeli's colonial secretary, spoke inside the cabinet for the Bulgarians in 1876, just a few years before he launched widespread brutal reprisals against the Zulus in 1879. In 1876–79, at the height of British public rage over the Bulgarian horrors, an epic drought took the lives of untold millions of Indians.[11]

Indeed, the European powers agreed that they would not intervene against one another no matter the extent of the brutality they resorted to in conquering and keeping their colonies. Sovereignty, sacrosanct in the relations among European states, did not apply outside of Europe and the United States, where its breach was justified in the name of humanitarian or civilizing missions.[12]

The rendition of the nineteenth century as a golden age of humanitarian intervention and a wellspring of the norms that motivate military missions of rescue today rests on romanticization and a few decidedly ambiguous cases. This is true as well of present-day humanitarian intervention, which, for reasons that will become apparent, cannot be understood properly without taking stock of the R2P doctrine.

How Much Universalism?

R2P represents the most creative and comprehensive formulation of humanitarian intervention yet developed and posits an admirable goal. It embodies the work of smart, well-meaning people who are serious about saving lives and should be commended for their commitment. Unsurprisingly, boosters of humanitarian intervention point to R2P's cachet as proof of the worldwide diffusion of human rights norms, which in turn has laid the foundation for a global consensus that has already made strong headway.[13] They insist that this augurs well for agreement on universal principles and procedures for intervention to stop atrocities.[14]

The facts belie their optimism.

To get a fix on just how much international consensus exists on humanitarian intervention, let's start by considering human rights, of which R2P is an ancillary. The supposed transnational concord on human rights enjoys its strongest support among governments, intellectuals, and NGOs in the West, and in Latin American democracies; elsewhere attitudes vary considerably. This should hardly be surprising: too many nationally specific circumstances are at play in a culturally and politically pluralistic world to make robust worldwide agreement feasible on so sensitive an issue. In reality, contending views on the substance and scope of human rights, the appropriate procedures and institutions for implementing and adjudicating them, and the proper role of other states and international institutions in setting standards and evaluating and enforcing compliance all render accord implausible. In consequence, at best a patchy universalism prevails.[15]

For example, the mainstream—especially Western—international human rights agenda turns on political rights, transnational cooperation among advocacy groups, and the role of international organizations, such as the International Criminal Court (ICC). But activists in non-Western countries often focus on the social and economic facets of rights and on local laws and courts as vehicles for enforcing them and often resist external, supposedly universal norms.[16] Citizens' attitudes toward local human rights organizations vary.[17] That, too, makes claims about the deepening appeal of human rights norms suspect. So does the gap between declarations and deeds. What states proclaim that they will do does not necessarily betoken their behavior—whether in living up to human rights ideals and accords themselves or taking steps to ensure that others do so.[18] Signatories, democracies included, routinely violate human rights treaties, even those pertaining to such basic principles as the ban on torture.[19] As Oona Hathaway concludes, "If one compares states that share otherwise similar economic and political characteristics, it turns out that—if anything—those that ratify the Convention Against Torture are reported to engage in *more* torture than those that have not ratified."[20] The Covenant on Civil and Political Rights and the International Convention of Economic and Social and Cultural Rights, both adopted in 1966, have little effect: they employ ambiguous language, contain numerous loopholes, lack enforcement mechanisms, and are overseen by committees containing states that themselves violate the same principles the texts espouse.[21] And as we shall see in later parts of this book, agreement on how to enforce human rights rules has proved elusive. For now, suffice it to note that the two largest countries, China and India, and the United States, home to the organizations and intellectuals most active in promoting the idea of universal rights, have not ratified the 1998 Rome Statute, which created the International Criminal Court. Nor has Russia. Together these four countries contain three billion people, 44 percent of the world's population.

The lack of consensus and the contrast between ideals and reality is no less evident in the theory and practice of humanitarian intervention. Yes, R2P was incorporated into the "Outcome Document" that emerged from the UN General Assembly's 2005 World Summit.[22] But as we shall see, the formula had to be watered down to gain the necessary support for inclusion, and the discussions on R2P that preceded the Outcome Document's passage exposed bitter divisions among states. R2P rests on a fragile foundation, and, for reasons we shall see in this chapter, states' misgivings about it have only increased since the 2011 intervention in Libya, which R2P's fans nevertheless hail as a "textbook example" of the plan's successful implementation.[23]

The chances that states will ever agree on a more substantive scheme to stop atrocities—one that contains specific obligations backed by determination and power—remain slim for three reasons. First, it is difficult to get a large proportion of the UN's 193 members to assent to a concrete plan of action on anything that involves duties and sacrifice but does not provide tangible benefits except in the abstract long run. Second, states continue to disagree about the normative and operational principles that ought to underlie humanitarian interventions. Third, military intervention (and prolonged postwar trusteeships that maintain order and promote economic reconstruction) lacks strong public support in powerful Western democracies, the very states most capable of practicing it with the regularity that would be required to end atrocities. Fourth, it does not help that humanitarian interventions have been selective in their application, poorly executed, strategically naïve, morally incoherent, and sometimes pernicious in their consequences. This chapter and the following one discuss the bases for these conclusions.

The Road to R2P

The 1990s saw several horrific civil wars, which led directly to the R2P debate and the 2005 World Summit.

The Bosnian war raged for more than three years by the time NATO got around to intervening in the late summer of 1995. By then 100,000 people, the vast majority of them Bosnian Muslims, had perished.[24] Additionally, thousands had been raped, forced from their homes, and corralled in concentration camps. Marauding Bosnian Serb troops had assaulted or captured Bihać, Goražde, Sarajevo, Srebrenica, Tuzla, and Žepa, the "safe areas" that the UN Protection Force (UNPROFOR) had vowed to defend. Despite the carnage, NATO did not intervene; it finally acted because the credibility of a Cold War alliance—whose purpose was already unclear—was on the line and because of fears that streams of refugees would unsettle neighboring countries and perhaps reach other parts of Europe.[25]

In the years preceding the intervention, the UN and NATO displayed fecklessness in the face of serial provocations and atrocities by Bosnian Serb forces. But the West had made a prior diplomatic mistake as well: precipitously recognizing Croatia and Bosnia, both of which contained significant Serb minorities. Germany jumped the gun, recognizing Croatia as early as December 1991. The rest of the European Community (EC) soon followed, recognizing Croatia in January and Bosnia in April, the same month in which the United States overcame its hesitation and recognized both Croatia and Bosnia. The Western powers acted before either country had made even minimal political arrangements to allay the fears of their Serb communities. By then, the signs of the coming disaster were amply evident. The disaffection of the Serb minorities in Croatia and Bosnia, which included demands for autonomy and even secession, was being fanned by the nationalist leadership in Serbia and was on display as early as the spring of 1990. And by the beginning of 1991, the Serbian leader Slobodan Milošević proclaimed that were Croatia and Bosnia to secede, he would annex their Serb-majority territories.[26] Western efforts to use recognition as leverage to push for, and help mediate, political arrangements in Bosnia and Croatia aimed at addressing Bosnian and Croatian Serbs' apprehensions may well have proved fruitless.[27] We shall never know; amid the West's rush to recognition, which buoyed Bosnian leaders, no such efforts were made. When a country whose independence the West encouraged came under attack, it was left to its own devices.

At about the same time, killing on a much more massive scale erupted in Rwanda. In just a hundred days between April and July 1994, rabid Hutu nationalist militias, principally the Interahamwe, and the army slaughtered 800,000 people, the overwhelming majority from the Tutsi minority. Western countries with the power to intervene stood watching, entering the conflict zone only to airlift their diplomatic staff to safety. Once Belgium withdrew its troops serving in the United Nations Assistance Mission for Rwanda (UNAMIR)—they were the best-trained and best-equipped serving in that UN force, which had been deployed to Rwanda starting in August 1993—after ten were killed, other countries followed, and none volunteered forces to fill the void. Belgium's government was pleased; it would have been shamed had troops from other countries moved in. Like Belgium, the United States opposed UNAMIR's expansion, even though the force did not contain any American soldiers.[28] An already feeble UN force was slashed from 2,500 in August 1993 to 250 in April 1994, precisely when the butchery started surging. Following the genocide, many claimed that nothing could have been done to prevent it because the pace of the slaughter made it impossible to deploy a sufficient number of troops in time. But no evidence suggests that any Western power seriously considered, let alone actively planned or prepared for, an intervention; the United States certainly did not. Declassified US government documents depicting official deliberations leave no doubt that large-scale violence was anticipated in Rwanda after President Juvénal Habyarimana's plane was shot down—that event triggered the genocide—on April 6, 1994, and that, once the massacres began, American officials were well aware of what was going on yet reluctant to label it a "genocide" for fear that the United States might then be obliged to intervene.[29] When the French, who would intervene with UN authorization in June and later open a humanitarian safe zone, asked for American transport planes to help ferry their troops, the US government turned them down. Thus, a solution to which no serious thought had been given—for want of political will to act, through the UN or without it—has, ex post facto, been declared infeasible.[30]

By late June, when France's UN-approved Operation Turquoise was underway in the southwest and northwest, the worst of the killing in Rwanda had peaked. Though France's ostensible aim was to save lives, local Hutus, including the Interahamwe, welcomed the French troops. So did the beleaguered members of the Hutu nationalist government—it had by then decamped to Gisenyi in Rwanda's northwest—which France had supported for years, even after the killing began.[31] These leaders and their followers feared capture by the Tutsi Rwandan Patriotic Front (RPF), led by Paul Kagame, which was already ensconced in northern Rwanda, having swept into the country from its Ugandan redoubts in 1990.

Once the genocide began in the first week of April 1994, the RPF fanned out in an attempt to stop it, but the French intervention permitted many of the perpetrators, civilian and military, to escape amid the refugee exodus to neighboring Zaire, through the humanitarian safe zone France created in July.[32] Worse, in the French occupation zone local Hutus leaders who had been part of the genocide retained their positions and armed Hutu bands continued their killing spree, notably in Bisesero.[33]

France's military intervention undoubtedly saved thousands of lives, and for that it deserves credit, especially since no other major power would intervene, but it was driven by the fear that the Hutu government's forces were being routed by the RPF, which would consolidate control over Rwanda.[34] What motivated the French, certainly at the early stages of Operation Turquoise, as the meticulous account of the late Alison Des Forges makes clear, was preventing the impending rout of the Hutu-dominated government. The armaments that French soldiers brought with them—mortars, armored vehicles, and ground-attack aircraft— suggested that they were even prepared to fight the advancing RPF, while the paucity of trucks suggested that evacuating Tutsi who were under attack or in danger of being slaughtered mattered less.[35] In particular, the French hoped to prevent the RPF from overrunning Gisenyi, where the government had relocated, and deployed there in addition to the southwest. French soldiers were told by their commanders, several of whom had in past years trained the Rwandan army in its fight against the RPF, that the RPF was committing atrocities and expelling Hutu, thus keeping in the background the magnitude of the massacres that had been perpetrated against Tutsi by the Rwandan army and Hutu militias. French troops made no effort to detain the Rwandan government or disarm its troops or the militias. French commanders declared that doing so would amount to interfering in Rwanda's politics and choosing sides.

Initially, local Hutu officials whom the French knew had been involved in the genocide were kept in place, ostensibly because France lacked sufficient troops on the ground to replace them. But once the French decided to burn their bridges with the Hutu government, they administered the zones they occupied using their own personnel and Hutus that they selected. Initially, French commanders claimed that putting the hate-mongering Radio Rwanda out of business was not part of their mandate; later, once its broadcasts began vilifying France, they did precisely that. Once the French decided to create a safe zone, in July, Rwandan troops, their arms intact, were allowed, and in some instances helped, to use it to escape to Zaire. In at least one instance French troops were seen refueling trucks carrying the Rwandan government soldiers, even though the vehicles were laden with pillaged property.[36] Whether and to what extent France enabled Hutu officials, central and local, who were implicated in the genocide to flee through the safe zone remains unclear, though Des Forges notes that "a high ranking French officer" told a Western reporter that French troops arranged for Colonel Théoneste Bagosora, who played a major part in the killings and would be convicted by the International Criminal Tribunal for Rwanda in 2008, to be airlifted to safety.[37] The French also helped evacuate several senior members of the Rwandan government, but the extent of these officials' culpability for the massacres remains unclear.

Des Forges appropriately credits the French intervention with having saved several thousands of Tutsi in the southwest, whom the RPF, despite its rapid advance, could not have reached in time. But she adds: "Like members of the UN, the French could and did save lives when it suited their interests. And, when it did not, they too hid behind excuses of insufficient troops and concerns for their safety or they used a supposed commitment to adhering to the mandate or to preserving neutrality as pretexts for inaction."[38]

A few years later, in 1997, Serb forces were battling the secessionist Kosovo Liberation Army (KLA), which had sidelined Ibrahim Rugova, the "Balkan Gandhi" who advocated nonviolent resistance to achieve Kosovo's independence. The aim of the KLA's armed struggle—which was not limited to military and police targets—was not to defeat the Serbs on the battlefield, something it lacked the firepower to achieve, but rather to elicit external intervention, based on the calculation that neither Rugova's peaceful campaign nor the KLA insurgency could free Kosovars, given Serbia's superior military might. The strategy proved sound. In 1999, amid increasing fighting between Serb soldiers and the KLA, NATO, acting without the Security Council's authorization, launched air strikes, forcing Serbia's capitulation, albeit after a 78-day campaign.

With the Balkan and Rwandan atrocities—and the global community's failure to respond speedily and effectively—in mind, the UN sought to construct a new policy to get serious about humanitarian intervention. Secretary General Kofi Annan called on his organization's members to draw up a plan that would allow a better choice than inaction (Rwanda) or freelancing (Kosovo). Inaction, he believed, would make a mockery of the UN's paeans to human rights; freelancing would corrode the UN's authority and perhaps even call into question its relevance for tackling serious international problems.

The Canadian government rose to Annan's challenge by sponsoring the International Commission on Intervention and State Sovereignty (ICISS), a cluster of global notables convened under the chairmanship of former Australian Foreign Minister Gareth Evans and veteran Algerian diplomat Mohamed Sahnoun. In December 2001 the ICISS issued the report that introduced the world to the Responsibility to Protect doctrine.[39]

The distinctiveness and creativity of R2P lies in its attempt to reconcile two perspectives on sovereignty that we have already encountered. One hews to the more traditional conception: sovereignty protects states, particularly weaker ones, from external interference and military intervention; proposals to redefine it open the door to conflict, domination, and disorder. The other position seeks to prevent brutal regimes from using sovereignty as a defense against external interference; it demands that sovereignty be reformulated so that it safeguards states from external intervention, yet requires that the rest of the world assume an ethical commitment to protect citizens from murderous states. R2P's moral logic combines two of Michael Walzer's basic premises: first, respecting states' sovereignty and immunity from intervention enables international order and the exercise of self-determination; second, in exceptional circumstances, particularly a government's egregious violation of basic human rights, overriding sovereignty can be the morally correct choice.[40] R2P owes even more to Francis Deng and his coauthors, who, in their 1996 book *Sovereignty as Responsibility*, proposed that states that inflict wanton violence on their people ought not to be allowed to avert external intervention by claiming sovereign immunity.[41]

The growing attention to managing violence within states—as reflected in the 1992 *An Agenda for Peace*, produced for the UN, and the 1995 report of the Commission on Global Governance, *Our Global Neighborhood*—through early warning mechanisms, crisis diplomacy aimed at averting violence, peacekeeping to enforce agreements reached by warring parties, and post-war rebuilding provided a propitious context for the ICISS's labors. So did the intellectual trend in academe favoring the rethinking security to emphasize the needs of individuals ("human security") rather than of states alone.[42]

Still, the ICISS recognized that the traditional conception of sovereignty retained abundant support among states and would not go away quietly. The commission also understood that humanitarian intervention still elicited suspicion, not only in powerful China and Russia and in mammoth India, but also among many smaller African and Asian states. So the ICISS report bowed to the shrine of sovereignty, affirming that the obligation to protect people rests, first of all, with the governments that have jurisdiction over them, not with other states or with international organizations.

But the ICISS also asserted that states' sovereign rights entail duties, above all protecting their people from, and not subjecting them to, unjustifiable physical harm. When a state fails to uphold these duties, because it perpetrates atrocities itself or because it cannot stop them, responsibility shifts to the international community. The ICISS wanted this duty discharged through the UN Security Council but proposed that when the Council's approval could not be secured because of a deadlock or its failure to act for other reasons, regional organizations could intervene to stop mass killings, provided they sought the Council's endorsement later so as to legitimize their action. Alternatively, the General Assembly could convene a special emergency session (under the 1950 "Uniting for Peace" provision) to deliberate and recommend further steps, including the use of armed force.[43]

R2P's proponents stress that their plan isn't a cloak for justifying, let alone encouraging, freewheeling military intervention. Force, Gareth Evans has reiterated tirelessly, should only be used during human rights emergencies, when—barring extraordinary circumstances—diplomacy, mediation, naming and shaming, and sanctions have not worked. Even then, he emphasizes, interveners must not automatically launch military campaigns, but must first weigh the feasibility and risks and, should they decide to use force, do so in a proportionate manner. R2P's expositors also recommend various non-violent measures, some of which are designed to prevent atrocities from occurring in the first place. These include early-warning mechanisms that enable advance planning for diplomatic responses; mediation before or following the initial outbreak of violence; peacekeeping to safeguard cease-fire agreements signed by the warring parties; economic assistance as an inducement to prevent or stop bloodshed; and assistance for post-conflict reconstruction, in part to prevent new cycles of violence.[44] These ideas predate R2P, of course, and add nothing new to the doctor's bag of diplomacy. The controversy sparked by R2P stems from the doctrine's distinctiveness—namely, the reformulation of sovereignty and the legitimization of armed intervention in defense of human rights.

Reassurances from R2P's proponents that force would be a rare, last-ditch response have not calmed critics, who respond that R2P cannot make good on its commitment to universality. Weak states will remain at the mercy of powerful ones, while the latter will have no cause to fear, despite the magnitude of their misdeeds. Witness the international community's unwillingness to take even nonmilitary steps in response to Russia's two wars in the North Caucasus, the first between 1994 and 1996, the second ongoing since 1999. The first, confined to Chechnya, included the reckless bombardment of Grozny, the capital city with a population of 500,000. Thousands of civilians died, there and elsewhere. The second war has featured civilian deaths, torture, executions, and abductions across the North Caucasus, with the state security forces playing a fulsome role. Precise numbers are impossible to obtain, but estimates of civilian deaths in Chechnya alone range between 50,000 and 75,000.[45] These cases provide further evidence that idealism and power are inextricably intertwined, with the latter frequently manipulating, even trumping, the former. As a result, R2P may provide powerful states a script for playing the Good Samaritan when intervention promotes their interests or stirs their compassion but also appears safe enough. Moreover, these states know that the underlying normative principles won't ever apply to them. By contrast, weak states and those lacking powerful friends have good reasons to fear. Despite its egalitarian allure and homage to justice, in practice R2P will simply reinforce existing hierarchies.

R2P stalwarts regard such complaints as products of misunderstanding or as the artifice of dictators who declaim about sovereignty and legality but in truth seek to escape accountability for their brutality.[46] In the end, though, it doesn't matter which side is right: moralistic interventionists or cynical and cruel rulers who lean on sovereignty as a defense against intervention. In a world of multiple polities and cultures, the objections to and anxieties about humanitarian intervention carry enough weight to prevent R2P from acquiring universal approval and legitimacy. Thus, any version of R2P that stands a chance of gaining general acceptance will have to be diluted by reassuring qualifiers, caveats, and loopholes. Precisely this scenario has played out.

R2P and the 2005 World Summit

The General Assembly debates on R2P at the UN's 2005 World Summit revealed the extent of global divisions. Many states—China, Russia, and members of the Non-Aligned Movement and the G-77—were leery of any formulation that might lay the groundwork for interference in states' internal affairs or impose obligations to intervene to stop atrocities.[47] Objections to R2P did not, however, come solely from non-Western and authoritarian states. The United States, through its pugnacious UN ambassador, John Bolton, also opposed any formulation that might be interpreted as obligating states to stop mass killings. Ex-colonial countries, in particular, objected.[48] Their dissatisfaction targeted R2P's numerous ambiguities: Who would decide whether a state had failed to meet its responsibility toward its citizens? What standard would be used in making judgments? How would decisions on interventions reflect the international community's sentiment rather than the preferences of a few great powers? What would prevent the definition of "responsibility" from expanding and progressively eroding sovereignty and legitimizing the toppling of governments? How would the rescued people hold accountable a UN that, under R2P, could acquire considerable power over their lives?[49]

Because these concerns had to be addressed, the version of R2P approved in the summit's "Outcome Document" amounted to a dilution of the original ICISS formula. Security Council approval was made a prerequisite for the implementation of any R2P measures. The international community was required only to "encourage and advise" states to discharge their responsibility to protect, and no obligations were placed upon UN member states. No wiggle room was provided for unilateral intervention. No explicit reference was made to the use of military means for enforcement.

R2P has certainly gained influence. It has been invoked in eleven Security Council resolutions during conflicts in such places as Darfur, South Sudan, Côte d'Ivoire, Liberia, Libya, Syria, and Mali.[50] It was praised, though not uniformly, during the debate devoted to it at the 2009 UN General Assembly session and was also the evident inspiration for a resolution at the conclave on regional cooperation on conflict prevention in Africa.[51]

But the 2005 Outcome Document's anodyne language and states' variegated interpretation of it have been critical to creating consensus on R2P. As Alex Bellamy, a thoughtful proponent of R2P, has put it:

> Although the principle enjoyed strong support in Europe and the West, parts of Africa and parts of Latin America, a significant portion of the UN's membership remained cautious and unconvinced. Perhaps a majority among those in the global south that did not advocate the principle merely "mimicked" support for the norm in 2005—choosing to accept the new norm rhetorically but without actually changing their behavior to take account of the norm. Others simply calculated that the principle had been watered down so much as to make it practically meaningless. Finally, some, such as Cuba, Sudan, Pakistan, and Nicaragua argued that they had not, in fact, endorsed the RtoP and that the World Summit agreement only committed states to further consideration of the norm.[52]

Geoffrey Robertson, a prominent supporter of universal human rights and humanitarian intervention, rejected the claim that the 2005 conclave produced a big victory for R2P:

> Was this, as some immediately dubbed it, "R2P lite" or was it R2P at all? The ICISS definition had been cut off at the knees … Everything had been left to the Security Council to decide, without guidelines or preconditions, on a "case-by-case

basis." There was no presumption, as in the ICISS formulation, that the Security Council would act at all, no leeway for NATO to bomb first and ask questions afterwards, and certainly no suggestion that any state might heed the cry for action in "conscience-shocking situations." The danger, of course, in this new, watered-down but UN-approved version is that it places all responsibility on the shoulders of an unreformed Security Council, without any obligation on "big five" members to withhold a veto if intervention has majority support, and virtually implies that humanitarian intervention without Security Council Chapter VII authorization is unlawful.[53]

Of course, had the tougher provisions Robertson favors been included in the document, it would never have won approval—not just because Russia, China, and various authoritarian regimes in Asia, Africa, and Latin America would have opposed it, but also because the United States would not have backed it either. The international sentiment favoring sovereignty remains more powerful, the anxiety that R2P will legitimize humanitarian interventions that erode sovereignty deeper, and states' interpretations of R2P more variegated than the bulk of the human rights literature would have us believe. This was apparent both in the lead-up to R2P's incorporation into the 2005 Outcome Document and the 2009 General Assembly debate on the doctrine. If anything, the 2011 intervention in Libya will increase the international divisions over human-rights-based interventions.

Flies in the Ointment

One need not have read Johann Gottfried Herder (who celebrated the varieties of national identities and values) or Isaiah Berlin (who underscored the incommensurability of values) to see why the diversity of the world makes R2P so hard to implement in a meaningful way—even amid globalization, whose multifarious connections are said to have shrunk time and space and created a "global village." China, Brazil, India, the member states of ASEAN (the Association of Southeast Asian Nations), South Africa, and Russia engage in all manner of international transactions, but nevertheless reject the proposition that sovereignty must be redefined so that states become legitimate targets when they contravene what certain other states have certified as transcendent norms. When these countries, which account for a big chunk of the world's population, support intervention and other forms of coercion used in the service of human rights, they do so under specific, narrow conditions. And they are not alone in having reservations about R2P.

Brazil's 2011 proposal, "The Responsibility While Protecting" (RWP), demonstrates some of the concerns surrounding R2P-style humanitarian intervention. R2P proponents claim that RWP seeks to limit the damage done to noncombatants during armed interventions—in short, to refine and polish their doctrine—and that it does not raise fundamental concerns about armed intervention in general or R2P in particular. But a close reading of RWP reveals the shakiness of this claim.[54]

Offered in the wake of Brazil's criticism of NATO's expansive interpretation of UN Security Council Resolution 1973, which enabled the March 2011 intervention to protect civilians in Libya, RWP seeks to ensure that the Security Council exercises stricter start-to-finish control over the civilian-defense missions it authorizes. The proposal expresses an underlying concern, expressed by a number of countries during and after the Libyan intervention, that R2P will become an excuse to achieve other goals. "There is a growing perception," the Brazilian document notes, "that the concept of the responsibility to protect might be misused for purposes other than protecting civilians, such as regime change." RWP also seeks to limit the circumstances under which force can be used to begin with. Mass killings must in fact threaten international peace, and the Security Council must authorize intervention under Chapter VII of the Charter: "The international community must be rigorous in its efforts to exhaust all peaceful means available in the protection of civilians under threat of violence." The document also warns that interventions risk ratcheting up violence and encouraging terrorism. If Brazil's post-Libya coda to R2P endorses the doctrine, it does so strangely indeed.

Brazil did not vote against a May 2013 General Assembly resolution condemning the bloodshed in Syria, something proponents of humanitarian intervention have noted with satisfaction. But that does not necessarily mean that its misgivings about the potential misuse of R2P had vanished.[55] In explaining Brazil's abstention, its UN representative stressed that Syrians themselves must resolve the conflict and questioned whether the resolution would help foster a political dialogue and an eventual settlement between the warring parties. India also abstained; its delegate insisted that Syrians should be the ones to devise any political solution, not the General Assembly, which should steer clear of regime change.[56] Both countries, along with Lebanon and South Africa, also abstained from an October 4, 2011, EU-drafted Security Council resolution, vetoed by China and Russia, condemning the Syrian government and threatening sanctions if the Assad government did not cease attacking protestors. India and Brazil no doubt feared that the European initiative would serve as a thin wedge to open the door to intervention. Had the resolution mentioned or even alluded to armed intervention, both states would most likely have opposed it.

Brazil and India also abstained from a March 2011 Security Council resolution authorizing the creation of a no-fly zone over Libya, as did China, Russia, and Germany. That outcome prompted *The Guardian* to report that there had been "a global split" on a military response.[57] The abstentions and the debates that preceded the vote reflected a wider suspicion, by no means confined to these countries, that no matter R2P's homage to universal values, the doctrine will be applied inconsistently and directed solely at weak states. The five countries that abstained rather than oppose the resolution did so because Persian Gulf states and the three African states then on the Security Council (Gabon, Nigeria, and South Africa) supported it. The Arab League also backed the creation of a no-flight zone over Libya. These circumstances increased the resolution's legitimacy by demonstrating that it had local purchase, something that proved crucial in persuading China and Russia to not veto the resolution. Still, their abstentions served as a reminder that a doctrine that presents itself as principled and impartial elicits skepticism, even hostility, in many quarters.

These divisions within the Security Council—and more so with in the General Assembly, a better gauge of international opinion—

underscore the ultimate problem facing humanitarian intervention. Countries are too numerous and too different to agree on a common standard for intervention; the resulting compromises will perforce produce R2P-related accords that are nonbinding, full of wiggle room, and susceptible to self-interested interpretations.

THE PRIMACY OF PRAGMATISM

A nother Arab Spring sweeps through the Middle East. This time the protests rock Saudi Arabia, particularly the oil-rich Eastern Province, where the majority of the Kingdom's Shi'a (who account for 10 to 12 percent of the population) live, a place where revolts and violence have occurred since at least the late 1970s, and more recently following the Arab Spring.[1] The crowds swell and refuse to be cowed by the regime's shows of force. Demonstrators occupy government buildings. The House of Saud goes into full battle mode. Blood starts flowing in the streets. Would the Saudis ever face a Security Council–approved R2P resolution? Would the United States, Britain, or France vote for an R2P resolution condemning Israel's use of force, and the resulting deaths of noncombatants, in the West Bank or Gaza? Would Russia allow the doctrine to be applied in authoritarian Belarus or Uzbekistan? Surely not, just as China would not have when the Sri Lankan army launched an offensive in 2008–2009 that eventually destroyed the violent Tamil Tiger separatist movement but also killed numerous civilians—according to a UN panel's report, "tens of thousands"—and uprooted thousands of others from their homes.[2] During and after the Sri Lankan war, China insisted, within the UN and in other venues, that the conflict was an internal matter and that external interference, even an inquiry, was unwarranted.[3]

When friendly states commit atrocities, the great powers are wont to look away, offer political cover, or even provide material assistance. Those inclined to disagree might meditate on a few examples that show how closely the post–Cold War era, supposedly characterized by the growing influence of universal human rights norms, in fact resembles the period that preceded it.

The Long Ride With Suharto

The West began supporting the Indonesian dictator Suharto after he took power following a 1965 coup and didn't stop backing him for more than three decades. The United States had been determined to see Suharto's predecessor, Sukarno, ousted long before the army pushed him out. His nonaligned foreign policy, anti-imperialist speeches, and leftist economic policies antagonized Washington. American officials were also agitated about the strength of the Indonesian Communist Party (PKI), which put its grassroots operations and millions of followers behind Sukarno. To hasten the fall of Sukarno and the PKI, successive US presidents and foreign policy officials banked on the Indonesian army, providing it with arms and economic support and arranging for anti-Communist army officers to be trained at US bases.[4]

Tensions peaked in 1965. A group of left-wing officers and a few PKI members feared, not without justification, that the army would overthrow Sukarno. To avert a coup, they foolishly arrested and killed some senior officers, unleashing a nationwide military crackdown on the PKI. The army, together with the civilian militias it organized, killed as many as 500,000 people. Washington did not plan the coup, nor even know of its precise timing, but welcomed it, even though the generals clearly did not intend to cede power via free and fair elections. Indeed, the United States, which monitored the progress of the coup using the radio frequencies of the telecom equipment it had sold to the anti-Communist officers, abetted the massacres by providing the army with lists of PKI members and lending the military material support.[5]

The United States and key allies, notably Britain and Australia, continued to back Suharto until the political upheaval that the 1997 East Asian economic crisis brought to Indonesia rendered their once-stalwart partner a liability. They did not jettison Suharto the following year because of an epiphany that his human rights record didn't pass muster; rather, Washington, Canberra, and London calculated that nothing would be gained—and much would be lost—in Indonesia and the surrounding region by clinging to a leader who was fast becoming a political corpse and was forced to resign in May 1998.

But back in the day, Suharto had the fulsome support of these same democracies. When the Portuguese relinquished control of East Timor in 1975, Suharto ordered his army to conquer the territory and the Western democracies stayed conspicuously silent.

To break the back of the armed resistance, the Indonesian military "bombed and strafed" the population relentlessly and also created a massive food crisis by attacking farms and depopulating arable areas, driving people into areas controlled by the anti-Indonesian insurgency that was soon overwhelmed.[6] By 1991, East Timor's population, excluding the 140,000 Indonesians who emigrated there following the 1975 annexation, was 12 percent smaller than it should have been based on the average pre-invasion rate of growth.[7] Between 1975 and 1999, when Australia led a UN-sanctioned military intervention in response to a new round of killing that started after voters in East Timor overwhelmingly approved a referendum on independence, Indonesian forces killed 18,600 Timorese civilians. Another 102,800 died from war-related hunger and disease. The vast majority perished prior to the 1999 intervention.[8]

Australia rightly received praise for leading the multilateral force (to ensure that it would not run into resistance, the intervention proceeded only once the Indonesian government consented) that helped bring stability, and eventually independence, to East Timor. But its policy toward Indonesia prior to Suharto's fall was different, to say the least. Australia's government documents reveal that its leaders, including its ambassador in Indonesia, knew Indonesia was preparing to conquer East Timor in 1975, may have provided tacit approval, and were willing to arm Suharto's regime in the years preceding the conquest. Seven months before Indonesia's invasion, Australian Prime

Minister Gough Whitlam indicated during a meeting with Suharto that he favored East Timor's absorption into Indonesia.[9]

Geoffrey Robinson puts it bluntly: "For most of the twenty-five year occupation [of East Timor], a succession of Australian governments sought to deny or downplay reports of gross human rights violations in the territory ... Australia also provided substantial military training to Indonesian forces, including the notorious Kopassandha and Kopassus."[10] Moreover, Australia was the only major Western democracy to officially recognize Indonesia's conquest of East Timor. In 1989 Gareth Evans, then Australia's foreign minister, signed an agreement with his Indonesian counterpart, Ali Alatas, which gave Australian energy companies drilling rights in the seabed off East Timor.[11] Portugal, acting on behalf of its former colony, challenged the legal validity of the treaty before the International Court of Justice in 1995. Australia's defense was that it was not legally obligated to refrain from signing agreements relating to a forcibly annexed territory.[12] Canberra apparently cared little that Indonesia had appropriated East Timor following a ruthless war.

The United States took a similar attitude toward Suharto and its material support proved more consequential, not least because American-supplied weapons enabled the Indonesian military's offensive against the pro-independence insurgents in East Timor and its bombing of Timorese civilians.[13] Declassified documents make clear that the Ford administration knew about and acquiesced to Indonesia's conquest of the Timorese.[14] The Carter administration made much of its commitment to foreign policy shaped by human rights, but once-classified documents show that it handled Suharto in the same way its predecessors did.[15] Likewise, American arms sales to Indonesia persisted throughout Bill Clinton's first presidential term, despite cutbacks in training and in the sale of certain armaments in response to Congressional concerns over Suharto's human rights record. The total value of American arms sold to Indonesia amounted to $1.1 billion, an average of $53 million per year for twenty-one years following the annexation of East Timor.[16] For its part, Britain established itself as an important arms supplier and lent Suharto money to finance purchases of British tanks and aircraft. Post-Suharto governments inherited unpaid bills totaling £304 million.[17]

On top of all this, notes Robinson, the Western democracies "also abetted the genocide by aiding the Indonesian army's cynical manipulation of information, humanitarian assistance, and access to the territory. Pursuing a policy of deliberate silence and obfuscation, the United States, Britain, Australia, and other states sought to suppress or dismiss information regarding the widespread dislocation and famine [of 1977–1979] in East Timor."[18] Having observed the famine up close, the American ambassador, Robinson adds, failed to acknowledge it for nearly a year and even then shielded the Suharto regime, blaming the calamity on "'backward' East Timorese agricultural practices, erosion and drought, and Portuguese colonialism."[19]

Humanitarian interventionists would say that all of this occurred when strategic exigencies created by the Cold War necessitated realpolitik and the concomitant moral compromises. To substantiate their claim (rather, their rationalization) that a new dawn has emerged they point to the Australian-led, UN-sanctioned intervention in East Timor in 1999. That campaign did help stop the slaughter in East Timor. But as Aidan Hehir notes in contrasting the interventions in Kosovo and East Timor, "NATO's intervention was greeted with jubilation by proponents of global civil society who clearly believed that it heralded a new era. Within two months of Operation Allied Force [the code name of NATO's operation], however, the international community demonstrated a profound unwillingness to intervene in East Timor in the wake of the violence sparked by the results of the [August 1999] independence referendum. Not until Indonesia had given its consent did an international force deploy, by which time thousands of people had been killed."[20] By then, the TNI and militias that it employed had killed as many as 2,000 people, and 500,000 more were forced to flee their homes. There could be no doubt that the TNI was adamantly opposed to East Timor's independence, but none of the major Western powers pressed the Indonesian authorities to permit an international peacekeeping force to be deployed before the vote. As for the intervention having occurred only once the Indonesian leadership acquiesced, later in this chapter we shall see that NATO would show no such hesitation in Libya—not because the killing was worse than in East Timor but because Libya's army, far weaker than Indonesia's, was a safer target for NATO to strike.

Moreover, in the former Yugoslavia and in Rwanda, the Western democracies pushed for international tribunals to bring perpetrators to book but no such court was created for Indonesia, whose leaders rejected the idea. Though the country moved toward democracy after 1999, given the political power that the TNI wields, it was hardly surprising that the Ad Hoc Human Rights Tribunal for Timor Leste created by Indonesia did not convict any of the senior leaders of the military or intelligence services who were responsible for the killing of civilians following the August 1999 referendum, let alone during and after the 1975 invasion. In 2004, the convictions of three officers and one policeman were overturned and an East Timorese militia leader's jail term was reduced from ten years to five.[21] Thus, only five people faced justice, and all of them got off lightly.

Turkey, Algeria, Bahrain

Turkey's war against the Kurdistan Workers' Party (PKK) insurgency in the 1980s and 1990s emptied or destroyed thousands of villages. Thousands of civilians were killed.[22] The Turkish government itself estimates that the war displaced 378,335 people, while other tallies put the number closer to a million.[23] Yet the plight of Kurdish civilians never prompted the Americans to cut aid to Turkey, nor did it produce a political crisis between Washington and its ally. As Stephen Zunes observes:

> The Clinton administration justified its eleven-week bombing campaign of Yugoslavia in 1999 on the grounds that atrocities such as the Serbian repression of Kosovars must not take place "on NATO's doorstep." Ironically, similar ethnic-based repression on an even larger scale had been already taking place within a NATO country without U.S. objections.
>
> During the 1980s and 1990s, the United States supplied Turkey's army with $15 billion worth of armaments as the Turkish military carried out widespread attacks against civilian populations in the largest use of American weapons by non-U.S. forces since Israel's 1982 invasion of Lebanon.[24]

Pragmatism again pushed principle to the periphery in Algeria. In 1990 the Islamic Salvation Front (FIS) won Algeria's local elections. At the end of the following year it swept the first round of national parliamentary elections and strengthened its position in the second round. The political change was electrifying. An elected Islamist government seemed poised to run a country that since its independence had been governed by secular socialists, the National Liberation Front (FLN), whose roots reached back to the struggle for independence from France. But the FLN-dominated Algerian military didn't wait for the next electoral round: it voided the outcome of the vote by forcing the president to dissolve the National People's Assembly, detained FIS members, and ignited a decade-long civil war. Tens of thousands of people were killed in battles between government security forces and radical Islamists belonging to the Armed Islamic Group (formed by members of FIS committed to violent resistance against the coup) and the Salafist Group for Preaching and Combat. Civilians were killed and antigovernment demonstrators "disappeared." By the end of 1998, the Algerian government, which blamed the Islamists, put the death toll at 26,536; the US State Department estimated 70,000.[25] Throughout all this, what mattered to the major Western democracies was that the Algerian military's usurpation had saved the day by blocking the FIS from taking power.[26]

Strategic considerations prevailed yet again in 2011 amid the upheaval in a small Persian Gulf sheikhdom. During the Arab Spring, Bahrain's Sunni-run monarchy, which has long lorded over a Shi'a majority underclass, faced a popular uprising. Though the United States and its European allies quickly denounced Gaddafi's violence against the Libyan opposition as R2P-worthy, they blinked at the Bahraini regime's repression of peaceful, unarmed protestors seeking basic political rights. Washington's stance is unlikely to change if Bahrain's rulers suppress protestors in the future—with or without Saudi assistance and with greater brutality than in 2011. The United States has important strategic interests in Bahrain that any Washington administration will be determined to protect: the US Fifth Fleet is headquartered there, and American leaders believe that a Shi'a revolution in Bahrain would extend Iran's influence decisively into the vital Persian Gulf region.

Three days before NATO launched its Libya intervention in liberty's name, Saudi Arabia—which played a crucial role in mobilizing Arab backing for Security Council Resolution 1973, authorizing the intervention against Gaddafi—sent its troops, which were joined by soldiers from several other states belonging to the Gulf Cooperation Council (GCC), into Bahrain to quash the popular uprising that the government, despite its efforts, had failed to suppress. UN diplomats and Saudi officials confirmed that Washington and Riyadh had cut a deal: the Saudis would muster Arab backing for the attack on Gaddafi, and the United States would not object when the Saudis moved into Bahrain.[27] Qatar, which also marshaled support in the Arab League for the fight against Gaddafi and even provided combat aircraft to bolster NATO's intervention, was among the Persian Gulf states that dispatched troops to supplement the Saudi march into Bahrain.[28] The Gulf sheikhs intended to block the rise in Bahrain of a Shi'a government that might align itself with Iran. Self-determination and liberty, scarce commodities in the Persian Gulf polities in any event, could wait—and the West didn't mind.

Western democracies reacted no less pragmatically when Egyptian security forces killed 840 unarmed civilian demonstrators and injured another 6,000 during the anti-Mubarak revolution of 2011.[29] None of them invoked R2P, even as a shot across the Egyptian regime's bow.

Since Mubarak's fall, strategic calculations have continued to overshadow human rights idealism. Consider the American and European response to the July 2013 military coup: The army, which was led by General Abdel Fattah el-Sisi, ousted the elected Muslim Brotherhood government of President Mohammed Morsi, suspended the constitution, and cracked down on the opposition. In July and August, troops fired into crowds of pro-Morsi demonstrators, "killing at least 1,150, most of them in five separate instances of mass protestor killings," according to Human Rights Watch. Mass arrests became standard practice: as many as 41,000 people had been incarcerated by April 2014, following Sisi's takeover.[30] Protestors and political dissidents were stuffed into overcrowded detention rooms and tortured routinely by jailers in the employ of the Interior Ministry and armed forces, not the regular state prison system.[31] Egyptian rule soon reverted to another Mubarak-like strongman. Sisi stepped down as army chief to run in the June 2014 presidential election, winning an improbable 96 percent of the vote. Despite the façade of civilian rule, the army still calls the shots, and arbitrary arrests and torture continue, rendering meaningless the due-process provisions provided on paper. Human Rights Watch concluded that the army's repression "likely amounted to crimes against humanity, given both their widespread and systematic nature and the evidence suggesting that the killings were part of a policy to attack unarmed persons on political grounds."[32] Capitalizing on the West's fears of violent Islamic radicalism and its yearning for a stable Egyptian bulwark, Sisi was quick to tie the Muslim Brotherhood as well as the democratic opposition movements to the upsurge in terrorist attacks mounted by jihadist groups such as Ansar Beit al-Maqdis (Champions of Jerusalem) and Ajnad Masr (Soldiers of Egypt) despite the lack of evidence.[33] He calculated that the liberal democracies would not rush to hold him accountable for his draconian methods by exerting economic or political pressure.

His logic proved impeccable. Although the EU and the United States did stop arms sales to Egypt in August 2013, by November, Britain had resumed export licenses for twenty-four out of forty-nine categories of weapons whose sale to Egypt had been banned.[34] Washington restarted partial arms sales in June 2014, authorizing the delivery of Apache helicopters and the release of $575 million in military aid, nearly half the total earmarked for Egypt that year. When Secretary of State John Kerry met with Sisi in Cairo that month, he expressed confidence that Congressional restrictions on military assistance would end and that Egypt would "ultimately [be] able to get the full amount of aid." He spoke of Sisi's "strong commitment" to improving human rights.[35] Sure enough, in March 2015, President Obama ended the freeze on arms sales to Egypt, clearing the way for Sisi's regime to get tanks, fighter jets, and missiles as part of the $1.3 billion military support package Egypt has long received.[36] In February 2015 France, which had been among the most ardent proponents of intervention in Libya on human rights grounds, reached an agreement with Sisi's government on a €5.2 billion arms deal, which included twenty-four Rafale fighter jets.[37]

Brussels and Washington phrased their criticism of Sisi's seizure of power, killings, and detentions delicately. Certainly, no Western or Arab government slammed him for flouting R2P's principles. No permanent member of the Security Council proposed a resolution condemning the Egyptian generals' conduct or invoking R2P. Western leaders had criticized the Muslim Brotherhood government's authoritarianism and swiftly condemned Gaddafi's violence during the Libyan uprising, but when Sisi and his troops spilled blood they responded differently. Their rapprochement with him will continue, for Egypt has emerged as a prime opponent of the Islamic State and a critical player in creating order in post-Gaddafi Libya, which has descended into chaos and violence. The West's attitude toward Sisi's coup and the aftermath bears a striking resemblance to its reaction to the Algerian army's anti-Islamist coup in 1992.

A Dinner, a Death, a Dictator

At a state dinner in Tehran on December 31, 1977, Jimmy Carter, who styled himself as the human rights president, gushed about the deep cooperation between the United States and Iran—never mind that the Iranian secret police, the notorious SAVAK, used torture routinely. Carter praised the Shah's Iran as an "island of stability." "This," he continued, "is a great tribute to your leadership, Your Majesty, and to the respect and admiration and love which your people give to you."[38] Just over a year later, the Iranian monarch would flee his country to escape a popular revolution. That the cruel reign of the Ayatollahs followed must not obscure the relevant point here: the stark gap between Washington's liberal principles and its policy.

Yes, Carter's encomium to the Shah occurred during the Cold War, and we supposedly live in more ethically enlightened times now. But do we? The examples of Bahrain and Sisi's Egypt, which are not aberrations, show that much less has changed than those who behold a universal normative consensus on human rights would have us believe.

When Saudi King Abdullah died in February 2015, President Obama truncated his visit to India and flew to Riyadh, an unusual move for a president who had only once before visited a country to pay his respects immediately following the death of its leader: South Africa after Nelson Mandela passed away. The president sought to underscore the importance of America's long-running alliance with Saudi Arabia.

It has not mattered to American leaders that the Kingdom forbids women from driving, let alone voting, and punishes citizens with public floggings, amputations, and beheadings.

Nor has the Saudi leadership shown much regard for human rights abroad. In March 2015, it began air strikes in an effort to prevent the Houthis, a tribe adhering to the Zaydi sect of Shi'a Islam, from winning Yemen's civil war and establishing control over the country, which adjoins Saudi Arabia. As in Bahrain in 2011, so too in Yemen four years later, the Saudis were determined to prevent political forces supported by Shiite Iran, its archenemy, from taking power.

Yemeni civilians paid dearly. By October 2,355 had died, the bulk because of air attacks carried out by the Saudis and their GCC allies, who supplemented the Saudi-dominated campaign. There is scant evidence that the bombings were conducted so as to minimize the killing of noncombatants; certainly some of the buildings and areas that were struck—such as a water-bottling plant, suburban residential zones, and the Old City in the capital, Sana'a—suggested that they were not. The use of cluster munitions, previously provided to Saudi Arabia by the United States, its principal arms supplier, further increased the chances that civilians would be maimed or killed.[39] Yet the destruction and death caused by the GCC's air campaign in an already dirt-poor country provoked no expressions of outrage, let alone calls for sanctions, from the United States or other Western powers. Indeed, as the Saudi-led air war got underway, American officials stated that they would provide "intelligence and logistical support." The United States was also then engaged in discussions with the Kingdom about the sale of two US frigates worth $1 billion or more, having already closed deals or nearly reached agreement on supplying attack helicopters and air defense missiles.[40] President Obama received King Salman in September, and the monarch also met major American business leaders. The discussions between president and king appeared to have centered on calming Saudi fears about the agreement that the United States, the EU, China, and Russia reached with Iran in July on its nuclear program. The Saudi-led air campaign's killing and displacement of Yemeni civilians seemed a sideline.[41]

Human rights didn't count in these instances, but they did in another.

On December 18, 2014—not long before his visit to Saudi Arabia—President Obama signed legislation that would clear the way for sanctions on several of Venezuela's civilian and military leaders.[42] The purpose was to punish them for repressing the protests that erupted in early 2014, in large part because of an economic crisis, and continued into 2015.[43] President Nicolás Maduro's government arrested more than 3,000 people, though most were soon released. The state security forces used tear gas, water cannons, and rubber bullets to disperse demonstrators, who were also attacked by armed pro-government groups (*collectivos*). By March 2015 more than 40 demonstrators had died, though not all of them at the hands of the security forces (for example, one was electrocuted while building a street barricade; another died when a makeshift bomb that he was building blew up).[44] Most of the demonstrations were peaceful, but some protestors did throw Molotov cocktails, makeshift bombs, and rocks at the security forces.[45] The protestors also erected street blockades (*guarimbas*) built from debris to block traffic. There is no denying the Venezuelan state's crackdown against the protests. Yet the arrests, repression, and violence it used and the resulting death toll cannot compare even remotely to the mass arrests, violence, and killings perpetrated by Egypt's army and police during and after the revolution that deposed Mubarak in Egypt. Maduro, for all his faults, is no Sisi. Washington nevertheless reacted differently toward Venezuela. It had deemed Maduro's predecessor, Hugo Chávez, a menace, but Chávez's death did not change its attitude; indeed, in March 2015 Obama declared Venezuela a threat to American national security. His administration lost no opportunity to condemn human rights violations there. Sisi, by contrast, has been embraced as an ally—and armed to boot.[46] Human rights principles, it appears, shape policy toward some states but not others. So much for the much-vaunted post–Cold War normative shift.

Then there is Washington's cooperation with Uzbek president Islam Karimov, whose dictatorship systematically uses torture. Despite Karimov's abysmal human rights record, after the 9/11 attacks he became a partner in the American war against terrorism. Washington provided aid to Uzbekistan, and even "rendered" terrorist suspects to it.[47] Karimov even made an official visit to the United States in 2002. Concerns over human rights did prompt the White House to cut aid in 2004, and the relationship worsened after Karimov quashed a 2005 revolt in Andijon, in Uzbekistan's Ferghana Valley, killing numerous people—estimates range from several hundreds to 1,000—in the process.[48] (The Uzbek strongman reacted by expelling the United States from the Karshi-Khanabad airbase, which the US began using for operations in Afghanistan in 2001.) In 2008, once Washington started developing the Northern Distribution Network (NDS) through Russia and Central Asia to supply American troops in Afghanistan and to reduce its reliance on the route through Pakistan, the Obama administration moved to mend fences with Uzbekistan, through which the overwhelming majority of the supplies flowing to Afghanistan via the NDS would pass.[49] Following her (scarcely credible) claims that human rights in Uzbekistan were improving, Secretary of State Hillary Clinton visited Tashkent in 2011, and US diplomats dutifully pointed to her discussions with Karimov about the importance of continued progress and his solemn assurances to her on that score.[50] By 2012 the US had lifted the ban on American arms supplies to Uzbekistan, and Karimov started receiving military equipment once again.[51] For its part, in 2009 the EU scrapped the sanctions it had imposed on Uzbekistan following the Andijon killings. Karimov visited Brussels in 2011 and met with José Manuel Barroso, the European Commission's president.[52]

The upshot of these examples is that the realpolitik of the Cold War remains alive and well. Contrary to R2P boosters' claims about new norms, states' strategic calculations still prevail over their ethical proclamations.

Friendless Gaddafi

Being powerful matters as much as it ever did; the same goes for having powerful patrons. Many people fall victim to wanton violence, but only those ruled by regimes not strong enough to make intervention risky and not backed by a major power can expect to be saved by foreign cavalry. Libya offers a case in point.

Having alienated his fellow Arab autocrats for decades with taunts, threats, and megalomaniacal antics, Muammar Gaddafi had no friends left by the time the Arab Spring came to Libya in February

2011. The leaders of the Libyan opposition, however, had close connections to Saudi Arabia, Qatar, and the United Arab Emirates
(UAE). These sheikhdoms in turn were aligned with the major
Western powers, above all the United States. Gadaffi's stock was
not much higher in Africa. Though he lavished aid on some countries, he also backed various African coups, supported insurgencies
in Sudan and Ethiopia, invaded and occupied northern Chad (a war
that proved to be a debacle), and alienated his fellow African leaders
during the African Union's meetings with his bombast, buffoonery,
and effrontery.

Still, at first Gaddafi beat back the rebellions that had erupted
along Libya's central and eastern coast. Had he stopped there, he
might well have escaped Western intervention. But he soon ordered
his forces to storm the eastern city of Benghazi—a longtime anti-
Gaddafi bastion, the second-largest municipality in the country, and
the first to raise the banner of rebellion. Eastern Libya also housed the
political base of the Senussid monarchy that Gaddafi had overthrown
in 1969 and of those elites who regarded the onetime colonel as a par-
venu and usurper from society's lower ranks. Though the rebels in the
town of Misrata were still fighting, by mid-March Benghazi remained
the last antiregime stronghold.[53] And because its example had inspired
the other rebellious towns, the city had attracted Gaddafi's ire.

American and European officials feared a looming slaughter.
Human rights groups, political commentators, and various intellectuals sounded the alarm, the ubiquitous Bernard-Henri Lévy prominent
among them.[54] Anxiety peaked following Gaddafi's March 17 speech
beamed at Benghazi. By that point the Western press was reporting,
and the Libyan opposition was charging, that his forces had deliberately shelled and bombed civilians during the counteroffensive en
route to the city. One senior Obama administration official, Dennis
Ross, warned—without a shred of evidence—that 100,000 people
would be killed in Benghazi, a city with a population of about 700,000,
were Gaddafi to conquer it.[55]

In fact, in the initial counterattack, the government's forces had
not targeted civilians purposely or systematically. They directed their
firepower at armed insurgents, though civilian casualties certainly
resulted. Nor had the regime killed unarmed Libyans en masse.[56] Of

course, there is no telling what might have happened had Gaddafi's troops stormed Benghazi. Still, his much-cited warning to the city was directed at its armed fighters—not, as is routinely portrayed, the civilian population. He pledged that fighters who laid down their arms would not be punished for their previous violence and ordered his troops not to harm those who fled.[57]

By then, however, Benghazi's rebels knew that intervention was already under discussion in Western capitals and that the United States would make the final decision. Accordingly, the rebels, in that city and elsewhere, did their best to tip the balance in favor of the strongest advocates of intervention within the Obama administration—among them UN ambassador Susan Rice and National Security Council staffers Samantha Power and Michael McFaul—and against the skeptics, most prominently Defense Secretary Robert Gates. Thus, the rebels falsely claimed that 30,000 people had already been killed.[58] This outlandish figure equaled that which the opposition National Transitional Council (NTC) offered at one point *after* the war as its upper estimate for all deaths (civilian and combatant) during NATO's entire eight-month war against Gaddafi.[59] Apparently no American official thought it worth asking how Gaddafi's small and lackluster army, fighting an armed rebellion on multiple, widely separated fronts, could have managed such a feat in only two weeks. Still more dramatic was opposition leader Mustafa Abdul Jalil's assertion on March 12, that the regime would kill 500,000 people unless a no-fly zone was promptly established.[60]

Between February 15, when the uprising began in Benghazi, and March 17, when Security Council Resolution 1973 authorizing a no-fly zone over Libya was approved, Western and Arab leaders made no serious and sustained efforts to explore nonmilitary steps aimed at ending the fighting and securing a political settlement. Yet R2P requires precisely such diplomatic initiatives before intervening with force—the last resort—and indeed, Resolution 1973 called for an end to the fighting and for a political solution.

Neither that resolution nor the February 26 Resolution 1970, which sanctioned Libya's government for violence against protestors, authorized regime change as an objective or military aid to insurgents determined to achieve that outcome. But by the end of February,

Secretary of State Hillary Clinton had already told the UN that Gaddafi had to quit. Less than two weeks later, EU and American leaders discussed plans for removing him.[61] Never one to be upstaged, President Nicolas Sarkozy, at the urging of Bernard-Henri Lévy, met in Paris on March 10 with Mahmoud Jibril and Ali Al-Essawi, leaders of the NTC, which five days earlier had already declared itself Libya's legitimate government. The group by no means controlled the country or had established viable institutions of governance, but Sarkozy recognized its claim anyway.[62] British, American, and French demands for Gaddafi's abdication grew more frequent and fervent in March and April. The rebels, whose goal was regime change, were in effect assured that the Western powers were fully behind them, and that assurance reduced whatever chances there may have been for a political solution.[63]

Early signs that Western and Arab governments would arm and train them steeled the rebels' resolve to fight on until Gaddafi was vanquished. Egypt began equipping them, with American knowledge, in early March or even late February, and also dispatched its Special Forces to instruct them—before the passage of Security Council Resolution 1973, and despite the arms embargo mandated by Resolution 1970 (paragraph 9).[64] In mid-March President Obama signed a presidential "finding" permitting covert assistance to the rebels.[65] On March 6 news broke of the seizure in eastern Libya of two British MI-6 agents and six British Special Air Service soldiers. According to their Libyan captors the interlopers carried weapons, ammunition, explosives, and fake passports from multiple countries. An embarrassed UK government, having secured their release, explained sheepishly that the intelligence agents and troops had been helping British diplomats connect with Gaddafi's opponents in the Benghazi area—the very people who apprehended them.[66] At the end of March the *New York Times* and Reuters reported that American intelligence personnel and "dozens" of Britain's Special Air Service and Special Boat Service soldiers had been operating in eastern Libya.[67] Thereafter, Western and Arab countries ramped up arms shipments to Gaddafi's opponents, with tiny Qatar playing an outsized role, especially in the east. By April trainers and Special Forces from Britain, France, Italy, Qatar, the UAE, and Egypt were assisting the rebels.[68] In his thorough account of the war, the Rand Corporation's Christopher Chivvis notes:

> Egyptian forces were reported in the country from the start, arming and training rebels in the east. In early April there were reports that French forces were active in securing weapons sites in southern Libya. On April 19 Britain announced that it would send a small advisory team to Libya to "advise the NTC on how to organize their military organization structures, communications and logistics." France and Italy followed suit with small numbers of military advisors.
>
> In June, in a significant increase in its commitment, France airdropped weapons and ammunition along with humanitarian supplies to Misrata and the Nafusah Mountains. French aid included assault rifles, machine guns, rocket launchers, rocket-propelled grenades (RPGs), and Milan antitank missiles. Previous arms shipments to the *thuwwar* [revolutionaries] from Qatar and the UAE had gone primarily to Benghazi. At the end of the month Britain also sent nonlethal supplies ... Small teams of French and British Special Forces were then deployed into the Nafusah Mountains to train the rebels in the use of these weapons and other equipment.[69]

These foreign personnel may have numbered only in the hundreds, but their activities extended from Libya's east to its west. Some even fought alongside the insurgents on occasion, including, in the case of the Qataris, during their final march on Tripoli.[70] Even supporters of the intervention acknowledge that external assistance played a crucial role in unifying and strengthening a disparate, scattered resistance. Training, arms, and equipment from outside Libya boosted the anti-Gaddafi groups' capacity to coordinate their operations, gather intelligence, and locate and target loyalist troops.[71] Though the rebels' external backers had started down the road to regime change even before the UN authorized the mission to protect civilians, the momentum increased after March 17 and the goal was soon firmly in place and became unshakeable. The interveners would interpret paragraph 4 of Resolution 1973, which authorized states "acting in cooperation with the Secretary General, to take all necessary means, notwithstanding paragraph 9 of resolution 1970 (2011) to protect civilians and civilian populated areas under threat of attack," creatively and expansively in order to achieve their objective.[72] In the heat of battle the stipulations related to the Secretary General's oversight and the Security Council's role in authorizing measures that exceeded the terms of the two resolutions amounted to verbiage. Effectively, the interpretation of what constituted "all necessary measures" was left to NATO and the Arab states conducting the intervention. By then, what they had in mind was something more ambitious than protecting civilians.

The UN Secretary General had appointed a special envoy to mediate a political solution in Libya. But at no point did military operations halt in order to ascertain whether Gaddafi had been persuaded by the aerial bombardment and missile strikes to accept a ceasefire and negotiations toward a political solution, both of which were mentioned in Resolution 1973 (paragraphs 1 and 2). Indeed the rebels and the Western and Arab governments supporting them dismissed Gaddafi's proposals—offered in March, April, and May—for ending the fighting and starting talks on a transitional government. The rebels insisted that the Libyan leader had first to withdraw all of his troops from the recaptured cities; even then, their goal was to remove him and his entourage and to establish the opposition's authority over all of Libya. They rejected out of hand not only any peace plan that included the participation of Gaddafi or his family members in an interim government, but also proposals from the regime that called for talks aimed at reconciliation but, conspicuously, did not mention a role for Gaddafi.[73] Peace proposals proffered by third parties, such as the African Union (AU) or Venezuela, fared no better.[74]

When the rebellion broke out, the AU, like the Arab League and the Organization of Islamic Cooperation (OIC), condemned Gaddafi's repression, and the three African states on the Security Council in 2011, Gabon, Nigeria, and South Africa, supported Security Council Resolutions 1970 and 1973. But as the war between the regime and the opposition in Libya intensified, especially following NATO's intervention and the flow of Arab and Western arms and other assistance (money and training) to the rebels, the AU sought to broker talks between Gaddafi and his opponents, fearing that continued war would bring chaos to Libya and eventually threaten its neighbors' security. The AU formed an Ad Hoc High Level Committee in March to bring the warring parties in Libya to the bargaining table. By the end of that month the Committee had developed a "roadmap."[75] But by then NATO had started its air strikes and the flow of training and arms to the rebels from abroad was well underway. Buoyed by this support, the opposition's umbrella group, the National Transitional Council (NTC), rejected repeatedly the Committee's various proposals for negotiations with the regime, insisting that Gaddafi had to first relinquish power and leave the country. Despite the Committee's repeated efforts, the chances for an interim government including members of the regime and figures from the NTC began to evaporate, especially because, NATO and the opposition's Arab backers having made their lack of enthusiasm for the AU's diplomatic efforts plain, the NTC refused to budge from its position. The AU's diplomatic efforts may well have failed: its members were divided in their attitude toward Gaddafi, the Libyan leader was cagey about what he was prepared to do and when, and no AU state was keen to provide peacekeepers in the event that a deal proved possible. But the American and European leaders were dismissive of the AU's efforts from the get-go—and that loaded the dice against the Committee given the leverage that they and the Arab states had over the Libyan opposition.

In May, the various efforts of its Ad Hoc Committee having failed, and with NATO and the Arab states determined to oust Gaddafi, the AU criticized what it regarded as the transformation of an intervention authorized by the UN to protect Libyan civilians into one aimed at toppling Libya's government and, effectively, shaping the country's future political order. The mission's metamorphosis, in the AU's eyes, violated Resolution 1973 and also set a dangerous precedent. The AU was not alone. By the end of March, Argentina, Brazil, China, India, and Russia were among the countries that had already begun to criticize the intervention on these same grounds.[76]

The AU and other like-minded states had a point about the morphing of the mission. Hugh Roberts argues in an important analysis that the interveners' claim that their supply of weapons to the resistance (and deployment of Special Forces) complied with the UN-mandated arms embargo rested on tortured logic and confirmed their true goal: overthrowing Gaddafi.[77] In their minds, deposing Gaddafi and defending civilians, the goal of Resolutions 1970 and 1973, quickly became one and the same—a case they would make publicly. Accordingly, the United States and the European and Arab states conducting the intervention backed, and reiterated, the NTC's dismissals of Gaddafi's ceasefire offers and Secretary of State Hilary Clinton closed the door on negotiations with Gaddafi despite overtures and proposals from his regime.[78] The interveners and Gaddafi's armed opponents, Roberts points out, were essentially demanding that he deliver a ceasefire singlehandedly. Beyond that, they insisted that Gaddafi withdraw his troops from Benghazi and Misrata, as well as from Ajdabiya and Zawiya and other cities, which his forces had retaken from opposition fighters. The upshot, Roberts concludes, was that "he had to accept strategic defeat in advance. These conditions, which were impossible for Gaddafi to accept, were absent from Article 1 [of Resolution 1973]." A split within the international community soon followed. China, Brazil, India, South Africa, Russia, and Uganda criticized the mission for transmuting from one designed to save civilians into another whose objective was to uproot a regime and bring its opponents to power through a revolution midwifed from abroad. That metamorphosis amounted to deciding Libya's future—but, as we shall see in the next chapter, without any commitment to assuming responsibility for its postwar fate.

The dominant narrative presented in much of the Western press and by human rights organizations and the anti-Gaddafi opposition was that from the start of the rebellion, Gaddafi had attacked civilians using airpower and artillery deliberately and without restraint. The resulting atrocities and the supposed threat of a bloodbath in Benghazi, it was said, necessitated military intervention. But this rendition—that Gaddafi was perpetrating mass atrocities by ordering his forces to kill civilians—at best oversimplifies the situation and indeed contradicts the assessments of officials within the Defense Department and of the intelligence community.[79] The claim of the American ambassador to the UN, Susan Rice, made in April at a closed session of the Security Council, that Gaddafi had provided Viagra to his soldiers so as to pursue a systematic policy of rape was another story that gained wide currency but was then, and still remains, unsubstantiated by evidence.[80]

Undoubtedly, there were instances in which government troops shot unarmed protestors, some as they sought to escape war zones. Many others were arrested along with armed insurgents and often disappeared. And when the regime targeted the armed insurgents' urban strongholds, it hit nonmilitary targets and killed noncombatants, especially in Misrata and Ajdabiya.[81]

But the Libyan leadership, caught off guard by the uprisings, did not issue shoot-to-kill orders right away. Its security forces refrained at first from aiming at protestors' chests and heads, and also used water cannons and tear gas to disperse them. Soon, though, the scale of the revolt overwhelmed the police and the army. From Bayda and Benghazi in the east to Tripoli and Zintan in the west, crowds attacked security forces, commandeered government buildings, stormed military encampments, threw gasoline bombs, seized weapons, and set vehicles, banks, hospitals, and police stations ablaze.[82] By February 21 the regime had effectively lost control of the east: rebels controlled Tobruk, Benghazi, Bayda, and Ajdabiya. That is when Gaddafi counterattacked in force.

No evidence suggests that his troops purposely killed civilians with heavy weapons and air attacks when retaking towns. As Alan Kuperman has shown by piecing together casualty figures and taking into account the proportion of women and children killed, which would have been high had the regime resorted to unrestrained violence, the numbers reported by the opposition, human rights groups, and the Western press were vastly inflated.[83] The fight—a civil war—played out between the regime and an armed opposition that had taken over many of Libya's major cities, not between the state's security forces and the civilian population.

The alliance touted its commitment to save civilians but abandoned that principle in Sirte, a Gaddafi stronghold on Libya's central coast. NATO aircraft bombed the city while rebel forces pounded it with artillery, tanks, and rockets.[84] To the anti-Gaddafi fighters firing the heavy weapons, the safety of Sirte's trapped civilians, many of whom lacked the bare necessities for survival, was an afterthought. Once they entered the city they shot bound prisoners, tortured others, and looted freely.[85] This was not an isolated instance. Even prior to NATO's intervention, regime supporters, soldiers, and their relatives were shot or hanged—notably in Benghazi, Bayda, and Derna—and others were abducted.[86] According to a State Department report, which also detailed the regime's various abuses, these incidents became more frequent as the conflict intensified.[87]

As in Kosovo, air strikes ratcheted up and prolonged the conflict; many more civilians died as a result. Once NATO's military campaign began, the regime concluded that it was fighting for survival, and the opposition, especially once it started receiving weaponry and training from abroad, believed it could win what it wanted on the battlefield and had no need for the bargaining table. Once the UN-sanctioned intervention machinery started turning, the anti-Gaddafi insurgents had no reason to compromise; political solutions fell by the wayside, and the R2P concept of a graduated continuum with diplomatic measures at one end and military force at the other collapsed quickly. The interveners showed no qualms about turning to the last resort first, which delighted the insurgents.

R2P's critics, particularly China and Russia, have learned from the Libyan campaign that the intermediate nonmilitary steps the doctrine specifies can easily be skipped, the continuum ignored, and the military element operationalized rapidly and expansively so that it sidelines everything else. Writing with NATO's Kosovo campaign in mind, the late Iris Marion Young observed that "arguments for the right to override the claims of state sovereignty for the sake of defending human rights often move too quickly to the position that the means of intervention should be war."[88] The danger, in her view, was that less drastic measures, including the use of military force on a smaller scale to protect noncombatants, get short shrift. Given the consequences of war in terms of casualties and the destruction of institutions and economic assets, she warned, those who insist on it must demonstrate that all other reasonable means have been tried and found wanting. She did not think that the case had been made in Kosovo.

Young's point carries over to Libya, and is especially important given, as we shall see in the next chapter, how destructive the war has proved for its society and future. Resolution 1973 mandated the pursuit of a political solution, but the bombing began within two days of its adoption; the United States, Britain, and France had already demanded that Gaddafi relinquish power, which, as a precondition, certainly precluded a deal. Once Security Council Resolution 1970 (paragraphs 4 and 6) referred the Libyan conflict to the International Criminal Court (ICC) on the grounds that the regime may have committed "crimes against humanity" and violated international humanitarian law, the prospects for a settlement—perhaps involving exile for Gaddafi and his closest associates in another country—were virtually nil.[89] The AU understood this, which is why it announced at its July summit—shortly after the ICC issued warrants for Gaddafi, his son, Saif ul-Islam, and Libyan military intelligence chief Abdullah al-Sanussi—that it would not assist the Court in making the arrests.[90] The ICC's move effectively scotched whatever chances remained for a deal involving Gaddafi's departure and the formation of an interim government: the Rome Statute's numerous signatories would have been obligated to hand him over to the Court for trial, and none of the countries that had not joined the Court rushed forward to offer him safe haven. With all avenues except continued war blocked, and with his back to the wall, Gaddafi fought on. The war stretched out; the body count increased.

Inconvenient Details

The postbellum paeans to NATO's Libya campaign have obscured some additional details that reveal the gulf between the interveners' ideals and actions. Few will mourn Gaddafi's vicious regime, but the decision to topple it in 2011 speaks to not a little hypocrisy on the part of an alliance that presented itself as motivated by human rights principles.

European and American leaders had known about the evils of Gaddafi's forty-two-year reign long before NATO's 2011 intervention. A State Department report documented the regime's repressive nature even before the uprising; so had similar reports by Western governments and human rights groups.[91] Gaddafi had been ostracized for supporting terrorism; conniving at the December 1988 bombing of Pan Am Flight 103 over Lockerbie, Scotland; and running a covert nuclear weapons program.

Critical to Gaddafi's political rehabilitation was his decision, in April 1999, to surrender two Libyans suspected of involvement in the

Lockerbie bombing. In 2003 he went further, agreeing to pay $1.5 billion in compensation to the relatives of those who had died and to abandon his weapons of mass destruction (WMD) program. Moussa Koussa, his intelligence chief (who would defect once the 2011 rebellion against Gaddafi began), liaised with senior American and British intelligence on counterterrorism. Prime Minister Tony Blair would present Gaddafi as an ally in the war against terrorism. Given the extensive post-9/11 collaboration between MI-6, the CIA, and Libyan intelligence services, it is easy to see why. As part of the partnership, the British and American intelligence agencies forcibly "rendered" into Gaddafi's hands members of the Libyan Islamic Fighting Group captured in Afghanistan. Rendition violated human rights laws and international treaties governing human rights. No matter—the detainees dumped in Libya were tortured and imprisoned for years without charge or trial.[92] (Washington and London sought assurance that the captives would not be tortured, but as Human Rights Watch observes, given the regime's routine use of torture, any promises provided would have been meaningless.[93])

Koussa also offered lucrative opportunities for Western companies, especially oil producers, as enticements.[94] In 2003 the UN lifted the economic sanctions imposed on Libya in the aftermath of Lockerbie, and in response to Gaddafi's new political course, the United States and Europe followed suit the next year. In those days, the leaders of the same European countries that would later spearhead the intervention were eager to meet with Gaddafi, invest in Libya, and even sell him arms worth substantial sums. Blair visited Gaddafi in 2004. He later announced that the Anglo-Dutch oil giant Shell had, as the *New York Times* reported, "won a $200 million contract worth up to $1 billion in the long term" and that British defense and aerospace contractor BAE Systems was nearing a deal on the sale of passenger jets to Libya.[95] After Blair left office, he traveled to Libya for six separate meetings with Gaddafi over three years. On two of those occasions, he flew on a private jet chartered by the Libyan government.[96] President Sarkozy welcomed Gaddafi to Paris in 2007. That visit produced a €10 billion agreement on the sale of Airbus commercial jets to Libya and cooperation on civilian nuclear projects. Gaddafi visited Italy twice, in 2009 and 2010. The first time, Prime Minister Silvio Berlusconi fawned over him at the G-8 summit, where the Libyan leader met a variety of Western leaders. Berlusconi and Gaddafi embraced during the visit, and Gaddafi addressed a group of Italian senators.[97] As bilateral relations warmed up, the Libyan government acquired shares in the Italian oil giant ENI, which had long been a major investor in Libya, as well as in Italy's biggest bank.[98] Gaddafi and Berlusconi became personal friends, which probably did not hurt the bank accounts of Gaddafi and his close associates, who had extensive financial connections in Italy. The EU countries also sold Libya $1 billion worth of weapons between 2005 and 2009, with Italy, Britain, and France accounting for 73 percent.[99] In 2009, Gaddafi, then serving as the AU's president, addressed the United Nations, demanding a permanent seat on the Security Council for Africa.[100]

The academic community also contributed to the reinvention of Gaddafi. The London School of Economics (LSE) conducted an embarrassing courtship with the Libyan strongman and accepted a large gift from his son, Saif ul-Islam. Leading scholars such as Anthony Giddens and David Held opined about Saif's reformist bent, as well as the regime's progressive potential. Held praised his dedication to democracy and liberalism. Giddens declared that Gaddafi was "genuinely popular" and that Libya "was not especially repressive" by the standards of single-party regimes. He praised Gaddafi's commitment to reform and projected a possible future for Libya as "the Norway of North Africa."[101] The Monitor Group, a slick, well-funded US public relations firm, arranged for big-name American and British intellectuals to travel to Libya—with all expenses covered, plus honorariums—for meetings with Gaddafi and his circle.[102] The Libyan strongman was no doubt pleased to be presented by Harvard professor Joseph Nye, in an essay written for the *New Republic*, as a leader who was open to new ideas and attempting to change his ways.[103]

Western leaders' courtship of Gaddafi did provoke criticism in Europe. (For instance, the Italian address was relocated from the senate chamber following protests, and an investigation by the British jurist Lord Woolf took the LSE to task for its link to the regime.) But the European governments argued that despite his terrible human rights record, Gaddafi's repudiation of terrorism and abandonment of a nuclear program augured well for further positive change, which they wished to encourage. To them, his sordid past either did not matter or was easy to rationalize. For instance, the June 1996 killing of 1,200 inmates of Tripoli's Abu Salim prison did not matter to these leaders, who were busy wooing Gaddafi. But they would later turn around and seek his removal on the grounds that he had trampled human rights.[104]

With Gaddafi's gruesome murder in October 2011, the interveners again discarded the values they invoked before and during their rescue mission. Gaddafi was fleeing Sirte with an entourage when he was captured, beaten, tortured, and shot to death by rebels.[105] His son, Muttasim, and others traveling with him were also killed, as were sixty-six additional Gaddafi loyalists in the vicinity. Fifty-five rotting bodies, apparently those of regime loyalists who had been shot, some with their hands tied, were discovered in a Sirte hotel located in a neighborhood controlled by the anti-Gaddafi militia from Misrata.[106] Western governments neither condemned these murders nor accused the perpetrators of war crimes—which these acts surely were, regardless of the victims' many faults. "We came, we saw, he died," Secretary of State Clinton announced, blending triumphalism and gallows humor upon learning of Gaddafi's murder.[107]

There is a final detail about the intervention, one both ironic as well as revealing as regards the gap between the human rights principles proclaimed by the interveners and their practices. Among the states that played a major role in arming and training the anti-Gaddafi fighters was none other than the Sudan of Omar al-Bashir, which Western governments and the human rights community had long denounced for committing mass atrocities and expulsions in Darfur.[108]

Bashir had no use for Gaddafi, who had earned his ire by harboring and supporting Darfuri guerrilla groups, in particular the Justice and Equality Movement (JEM). (Bashir, in turn, provided refuge and training to Gaddafi's opponents.) When the Libyan uprising began Bashir was quick to provide support, in particular to the Islamist groups he favored. Moreover, he ordered his army into Kufra, in southeastern Libya, both to secure a key supply route that Sudan and other supporters could use to send arms to the Libyan opposition as well as to fight the forces of the JEM. Sudan's army eventually took control of Kufra, and Sudanese military and intelligence officers, including Special Forces, trained rebels in various parts of Libya and improved their capacity to coordinate operations. More significantly, given the focus of this book, Bashir permitted NATO to use Sudanese airspace and, according to the NTC and Sudanese sources, supplied the alliance on-the-ground intelligence that improved the effectiveness with which its aircraft could strike sites crucial to Gaddafi's capacity to keep fighting.

Quite apart from his animus for Gaddafi and interest in shaping Libya's future, Bashir was eager to reduce his political isolation (a comical demonstration of that desire was Sudan's introduction, on behalf of the G-77 bloc, of an R2P-inspired resolution on "conflict prevention in Africa" during the 2009 UN General Assembly session in which the doctrine was discussed).[109] He doubtless saw cooperation with NATO (and the Arab states arrayed against Gaddafi) as a means to that end. Though it's impossible to ascertain how much Sudan's 2011 role in Libya accounts for it, following Gaddafi's fall there were signs that Bashir was making some headway with the West following the intervention. Alex de Waal noted in the wake of the February 2015 visit to Washington by Bashir's top aide and Sudan's foreign minister that "Khartoum's message that it is a force for stability in the Middle East is clearly getting a listen. Just as the ICC's prosecutor suspended further action on the Darfur file [in December 2014], the US is quietly shelving plans for further isolating Sudan."[110] Bashir has kept the gambit of presenting himself as an asset to the West going. As the Saudi-led air strikes in Yemen began in March 2015, he offered Saudi Arabia military aircraft, volunteered 6,000 troops, and provided military advisers. These moves distanced Bashir from Iran, one of Sudan's major arms suppliers, and were doubtless designed to get the attention of the Saudis as well as of the United States and to further his efforts to progress from pariah to partner.[111]

The Calculus of Intervention

Moral outrage prompted the war against Gaddafi, but it hasn't moved Western governments to act in Syria, where the civil war has claimed the lives of many more noncombatants. The United Nations offers what it considers a conservative estimate of the death toll: 191,369 killed between the start of the war in March 2011 and April 2014.[112] The Syrian Observatory for Human Rights (SOHR), a widely cited source, put the number killed during the same period at 150,344.[113] SOHR estimates noncombatant deaths at about a third of the total. Four million Syrians, 75 percent of them women and children, have fled to neighboring countries and Europe. More than four million others have been internally displaced.[114] The war is not over; more people will die and more will be driven from their homes. Whatever the precise numbers, Gaddafi's 2011 violence doesn't compare to what is happening in Syria: in 2013 the Libyan government revised its early estimate of the number of rebels and civilians killed from 50,000 down to 4,700, with 2,100 missing.[115] These lives should not be ignored, but the divergence in the West's treatment of Libya and Syria should be sobering to the humanitarian community. Among major powers that have declared support for universal human rights, none has proposed intervention to stop the carnage in Syria or sought UN authorization for such a mission.

It's not hard to explain this lack of enthusiasm. War-weary Westerners don't want to see their soldiers fighting on the ground on missions of mercy, but Syria is not a candidate for a no-fly zone or casualty-free intervention by air strikes. Unlike Gaddafi, Bashar al-Assad has reliable arms suppliers in Russia and Iran, from whom he has acquired the military capacity to raise the cost of an aerial intervention à la Bosnia, Kosovo, and Libya. But Western governments are not even willing to seriously arm the Syrian opposition's most democratic groups, whose agenda they applaud, in part because their citizens fear that arming Assad's foes will lead to deeper involvement and eventual entrapment in a quagmire. Critics also worry that arms sent to anti-Assad Syrian moderates might fall into the hands of radical Islamists fighting Assad.

The US did commence air strikes in Syria in September 2014, but that step was not prompted by outrage over civilian deaths or the refugee crisis. The catalyst was the rise of the Islamic State (IS), a radical Sunni movement, which by then had occupied large areas of northern and eastern Syria and extended its sway over Iraq's Sunni majority regions in the north and center.[116] Americans and Europeans feared that Western IS recruits would one day return home and engage in acts of terrorism and that an IS-run quasi-state in parts of Iraq and Syria would become a center for terrorist plots against the West, as Afghanistan had been for Al-Qaeda prior to the 9/11 attacks.

The United States, with support from a few Sunni Arab states and Turkey, started launching air strikes against IS redoubts in Syria and Iraq and, joined by Britain, France, and Germany, also began arming and training the Kurdish *peshmerga* and the Iraqi army to fight the ground war against IS. The accompanying efforts to equip and train moderate anti-Assad groups, including Syrian Kurdish fighters, aimed to put more military pressure on IS, not on Assad, whose forces and strongholds were not targeted by American aircraft.[117] Meanwhile, on the diplomatic front, Washington has subtly shifted away from its insistence that Assad relinquish power and not participate in any transitional government resulting from an agreement to end the war.[118]

Syrians understand that Western leaders are not acting out of conscience but are instead making hardboiled strategic calculations.[119] As the *Economist* put it, by the end of September 2014,

> [By the fall of 2014] Syria's civil war had been running for 1,288 days; it had claimed 200,000 lives and forced 9.5m people, more than a third of the population, from their homes. Given all that, asked sceptical Syrians, why was America acting directly only now, and only against the Islamic State and other jihadists about whom it has particular concerns? For all its brutality, one Syrian NGO reckons IS has killed 830 Syrian civilians, compared with the regime's 125,000. Its crimes are hideous but are they worse than Bashar Assad's ...?[120]

What Makes the Difference?

The answer to the question raised by the venerable British magazine is that in states' calculations about intervention, the magnitude of the atrocities does not matter most. Four other considerations count for more. The first is the likely ease of the operation, itself a function of the perpetrator's power. Seen thus, using force against, say, China or Russia becomes unimaginable even if either were to massacre many civilians, as Russia did in Chechnya in the 1990s. The second is whether powerful countries have important interests at stake. In Rwanda, they did not; in the Balkans during the 1990s they did. A third is whether the regime committing the atrocities has allies willing to block UN resolutions proposing intervention or to dilute those calling for sanctions or peacekeeping forces. For example, thanks to backing from China and Russia, the Sudanese government of President Omar al-Bashir has been able to shape the size, composition, and mandate of the AU/UN Darfur peacekeeping force to suit his needs and to rest assured that his friends would block any UN resolution on military intervention (not that any Western state has called for such a step, let alone threatened to take it). Gaddafi was not so lucky.

Finally, would-be interveners will desist when a conflict's complexity and scale of violence produce a sense of futility or fears of being sucked into a vortex in a country that the states capable of intervening do not regard as strategically critical. A case in point is the war that commenced in eastern Congo in 1994 after Hutu militants, who had fled from Rwanda after the genocide, ensconced themselves there, igniting a war that pitted them against Congolese Tutsis backed by Rwanda and Uganda. By 2008 between 2.7 and 5.4 million people had perished from the direct and indirect ravages of war. This horrific number makes the killing in Libya, and even Syria, pale in comparison.[121] Yet the UN's peacekeeping efforts proved pitifully feeble, certainly for most of the conflict. The organization dispatched 5,537 peacekeepers to the Congo in 2000—with a weak mandate and six years after the violence began. The deployment increased to 10,800 in 2003, to 16,431 in 2004 (half the increment requested by the Secretary General), and to 17,000 in 2005. By early 2015 19,815 UN soldiers and 1,441 police were in place.[122] By the end of 2005, the Congo peacekeeping mission had become the UN's largest. But for much of the conflict, the scale of the UN's intervention resembled a gnat biting an elephant. Eastern Congo's inhabitants were trapped in a long, vicious war featuring Hutu militias (who had fled there following the 1994 genocide), their Tutsi adversaries (supported by the Rwandan government), Rwandan and Ugandan troops, and a no-holds-barred rivalry among the warring parties for the region's bountiful natural resources. For a time UN forces themselves made life worse for the refugees by subjecting them to sexual abuse.[123]

A Weak Defense

Faced with evidence that state interests often sideline ethics, theorists of the new dawn of human rights offer a muddled defense, which ends up validating the very state-centric, national interest–driven policies that they abhor.

Here is a typical example. After discussing Australia's ties with Suharto and the 1989 accord, Nicholas Wheeler and Tim Dunne conclude, "Being a good international citizen does not require a state to sacrifice its vital security interests by imposing negative sanctions (supposing these were deemed to be most effective) on an illiberal regime to increase compliance with human rights standards."[124] Yet they criticize British Prime Minister Tony Blair's Labour government for selling arms to Suharto to advance "selfish economic interests." Why were Britain's economic interests more selfish than Australia's?

Compounding the confusion, Dunne and Wheeler drift toward realist shores in order to justify the Blair government's willingness to deal with China despite its dreadful human rights record. Among their defenses is that Blair and Foreign Secretary Robin Cook engaged Chinese leaders in a "dialogue" on human rights. Echoing Cook, they argue that such engagement yields substantial and positive results. They offer as proof minimal and cosmetic concessions made by Beijing, including the release of one dissident and the invitation to China of UN Commissioner for Human Rights Mary Robinson—in short, the typical token gestures Chinese leaders make to placate foreign critics of their human rights record.

Wheeler and Dunne further contend that a tougher stance toward Beijing would not have yielded Blair better results. This, too, resembles an official press release from No. 10 Downing Street and is not far removed from Richard Nixon's and Henry Kissinger's defense that calling Yahya Khan to account in 1971 would only have made him more intransigent, worsening the massacres in East Pakistan. Governments habitually tout the efficacy of quiet, behind-the-scenes diplomacy when they decide that it's too costly to back their human rights rhetoric with action.

Then comes the ultimate justification: Britain, Wheeler and Dunne argue, faced the "constraints" created by its "vital security interests" in East Asia, which it could not pursue successfully absent China's cooperation.[125] They are entirely right in pointing out the ineluctable, ubiquitous tension in politics between morality and practical interests. However, such explanations do not comport with the assertion that universal democratic norms have gained unprecedented and significant influence over the foreign policies of Western democracies.

Human rights principles and liberal norms can certainly shape foreign policy when governments deem the costs tolerable. But, as we have seen, they don't when leaders conclude that the price is too steep. When states push human rights principles to the side, the acolytes of "good international citizenship" plead exigent circumstances. Besides, they say, their theory does not deny the reality of power and interest or require that moral principles be applied mechanically. But realists, whom they castigate for their disregard for human rights, make the same argument. The realists' defense cannot be their defense. If governments set aside norms in favor of practical interests so regularly, then norms cannot exert all that powerful an influence over policy.

Outrage sparked by atrocities and the ethical imperative of saving strangers may well play a part in triggering humanitarian intervention, though it is impossible to say what their contribution is relative to other conditions that may account for the outcome. On occasion, the ethical imperative may even serve as the primary motivation and purpose. Yet the prevailing pattern has been, and will remain, the following: States contemplating intervention to stop atrocities will weigh their interests—prospective gains, risks, and costs, as best as these can be assayed—against their ethical obligations to noncitizens. Sometimes interests and ethics may complement each other. When they don't, the former prevail. The magnitude of the suffering and death will not change the calculus of prospective interveners if their interests are not significantly at stake but the risks are evident and substantial. What matters, and will continue to do so, is not how many are people being killed, but where they are being killed and by whom. The contention that the Cold War's passing has liberated democracies, finally enabling them to get serious about international human rights, amounts to a fiction—the product of end-of-history fantasies about the worldwide proliferation of democratic principles and the consequent change in states' long-standing patterns of behavior.

7

WAR AND POSTWAR

The initiators of wars often express confidence about how their military campaigns will evolve and end. But even meticulous plans encounter what Clausewitz called "friction"—the "countless minor incidents, the kind you can never really foresee."[1]

Napoleon's troops were poorly provisioned for France's war against Russia in 1812, which began in June; the emperor expected victory before winter. Instead he became embroiled in a war that lasted nearly six months and ended in a debacle in which the Grand Armée lost nearly 400,000 soldiers. Hitler would make a strikingly similar blunder 129 years later. "You will be home before the leaves have fallen from the trees," Kaiser Wilhelm told his army as it went to battle in August 1914. He might have specified which year he had in mind. When Russia dispatched the Red Army to Afghanistan in December 1979, the Kremlin expected to make quick work of the ragtag Afghan mujahideen menacing Afghanistan's wobbly Marxist government. The Soviets fought the Afghans for twice as long as they had the Nazis, but were forced to withdraw in defeat. President Johnson bet that a relentless American bombing campaign would crush the North Vietnamese. In his May 1, 2003, "Mission Accomplished" speech, President George W. Bush boasted, "Major combat operations in Iraq have ended" and "the United States and its allies have prevailed."[2]

This pattern of overconfidence in wartime appears throughout history, and humanitarian campaigners display it as well, as we shall see. They believe they know a lot about what will happen once the guns start blazing and, once the fighting stops, about how to build a just postwar order. But the supremely confident are precisely the ones most likely to experience hubris and its consequences.[3]

Kill More, Kill Faster

NATO's 1995 decision to bombard Bosnian Serb forces had the unforeseen result of altering the political balance in another part of the former Yugoslavia: Kosovo, where the Kosovar Albanian majority had long been chafing under Serb domination. Ibrahim Rugova, the "Balkan Gandhi," who had been seeking Kosovo's independence through nonviolent resistance, including building governing institutions that bypassed those of the Serbian state, was soon overshadowed by the Kosovo Liberation Army (KLA), which believed that the Serbs would understand only the language of violence.

The Dayton deal on Bosnia enabled by NATO's humanitarian intervention skirted Kosovo, confirming many Kosovars' conviction that the world took no interest in what they saw as an oppressive Serbian occupation that denied their right to self-determination.[4] After Dayton the KLA, convinced that NATO's intervention in response to the persistent violence in Bosnia had proved decisive, increased their attacks. Though the KLA targeted Serb soldiers and policemen, it also kidnapped and killed Serb civilians. It aimed not merely to seize and hold territory, but also to provoke the Serbs to scale up their offensive and to draw NATO into the conflict. The KLA understood that despite its commitment to fighting the Serbs, it lacked the power to defeat them singlehandedly.

The KLA's plan worked. Serbia, hoping to deprive the guerillas of support, sanctuary, recruits, and resources, directed its iron-fisted response at Kosovar civilians.[5] The Serbs shelled villages; abducted, tortured, and raped; and expelled people from their homes. As a result, Kosovo made Western headlines as never before—just as the KLA calculated. In Western capitals, intellectuals, politicians, and human rights groups called on their governments to do something.

They too understood that the KLA was no match for Serb forces; only an external military intervention would alter the pitiless arithmetic of the battlefield and end the carnage.

Bosnia greased the wheels for intervention in Kosovo. The Bosnia campaign brought a halt to violence, but NATO waited three years before acting. As a result, interventionists had an easy sell: air strikes worked before; why hold off this time? Surely Bosnia taught the lesson that delaying action would get even more Kosovars killed. So on March 24, 1999, NATO began dropping bombs on Serb targets, initially in Kosovo. For a time, this only accelerated the killing and evictions. Serbian President Slobodan Milošević hoped to finish off the KLA before the Serb army was battered by NATO's airpower and ramped up his offensive. As Ivo Daalder and Michael O'Hanlon, prominent American defenders of the intervention, concede, "The levels of violence in Kosovo before March 24, 1999, were modest by the standards of civil conflict and compared to what ensued during NATO's bombing campaign. The violence had caused the deaths of 2,000 people in the previous year. This was not an attempted genocide of the ethnic Albanian people."[6]

NATO ruled out a ground campaign at the outset, limiting itself to air strikes. The alliance's caution played into Milošević's hands. Given the Serb's extensive antiaircraft missile network, NATO restricted pilots to safe altitudes, at least for "many weeks in the initial stages of the war," according to Human Rights Watch, a conclusion confirmed by a Defense Department report to Congress.[7] And strike sorties were called off if cloud cover—frequent, given the season—precluded high-altitude bombing. The alliance withheld armed helicopters, such as the Apache AH-64, "because of Pentagon fears about US casualties."[8]

This method of warfare—"post-heroic," the military strategist Edward Luttwak calls it—limited NATO's speed and effectiveness, permitting Serb forces to kill and expel many more Kosovars from their homes.[9] In fewer than three months after the bombing commenced Serb troops killed as many as 10,000 Kosovars, five times the number killed before that date.[10] Another 1.4 million—about 90 percent of Kosovo's population—were forced from their homes. Some fled to other parts of Kosovo, others to neighboring countries, especially Albania and Macedonia. NATO's leaders failed to anticipate this brutal response—even though the presidents of Slovenia and Macedonia warned that it would happen—and made no change in their battle plan so as to stop the slaughter.[11]

The alliance displayed the limits of its widely touted humanitarian ideals. Its strategy included keeping NATO casualties to a minimum, no matter the horrific consequences for the people it had vowed to protect. The air campaign also used cluster bombs, which, because they disperse bomblets across a wide area, cannot discriminate between combatants and civilians. This lack of differentiation contradicts both just war theory and international humanitarian law.[12]

Milošević surrendered in June not only because Russia failed to offer him tangible support, but also because NATO's bombing extended to Serbia itself. The targets struck included nonmilitary installations. The alliance bombed the state television and radio center, a bridge, and a heating plant, as well as the city's electricity grid, thereby disrupting the supply of water and power across the country.[13] In Serbia and Kosovo, about 500 Serb noncombatants, hardly responsible for Milošević's brutality, perished because of NATO's bombing. Human Rights Watch, though taking care not to posit a moral equivalency between NATO's actions and Milošević's, criticized the bombing of these nonmilitary sites, whose destruction jeopardized and punished civilians without securing decisive military advantages or disrupting Serb military operations.[14] Indeed, when the war ended, Serb armored units left Kosovo mostly intact. As Grant Hammond of the Air War College summed it up, "The application of airpower for 78 days over 37,000 sorties without loss of life in combat and only the loss of two planes ... was truly remarkable. But we failed to destroy much of the fielded forces in Kosovo and instead destroyed civilian infrastructure in Serbia."[15] The inability of the world's mightiest military alliance, which then had a combined military budget of almost half a trillion dollars, to overcome "a small impoverished Balkan country with a defense budget of scarcely $1.5 billion" amounted, in Timothy Garton Ash's words, to "the humbling of high-tech hubris."[16]

Defenders of NATO's decision to go to war claim that Milošević would eventually have ratcheted up the killing and expulsions, and that delaying the air attacks in order to ascertain the Serb government's intentions in Kosovo would have been irresponsible. Did the

Serb government plan all along to do what it did, or did it plan to implement its assault on the Kosovars in the event that the negotiations between Serbia and the Western powers failed and war seemed inevitable? There is no definitive answer. A more relevant line of inquiry questions whether, given that its declared mission was to stop the slaughter and expulsion of Kosovars, NATO acted responsibly in limiting itself to air strikes once results of the Serbs' offensive became evident. The answer is no, if responsibility involves doing what is needed, including risking casualties, in order to protect civilians. But the alliance finely calibrated its military strategy to the political realities in Europe and America, where public opinion would not have supported a rescue operation that required sacrificing soldiers' lives.

The interveners failed in another respect. After the war ordinary Albanians and the KLA abducted, beat, and killed Serb civilians. Thousands of Serbs and Roma fled (some anticipating revenge attacks, but many following such incidents, or because they were evicted from their homes), even as NATO troops were moving in to police Kosovo.[17] These abuses should not have been surprising to the alliance given the KLA's anti-Serb nationalism and unsavory leadership. Among the KLA's senior leaders was Agim Çeku. Çeku, who served as an officer in the Yugoslav military, had signed up with the Croatian army, which the United States would arm and train, to fight Serbia, and commanded forces involved in the 1993 attack on Medak village that killed Serb civilians and in the 1995 expulsion of 200,000 Serbs from Croatia's Krajina region.[18] Both acts occurred right under NATO's nose.

Even before the Kosovo war, Western governments were aware of the KLA's ties to the underworld and involvement in gun-running and drug trafficking. Indeed, in February 1998, a senior American diplomat, Robert Gelbard, President Clinton's Special Envoy to the Balkans, stated that the organization was "without question a terrorist group."[19] As the violence in Kosovo intensified the KLA reportedly operated detention centers in Albania, which held several hundred Serbs and other minorities, plus Albanians suspected of complicity with the Serb authorities. They killed some and tortured others. In certain instances, prisoners' organs were removed and sold to criminal networks involving high-ranking KLA officials. In areas of Kosovo outside the control of Serb forces, criminal clans, in which KLA leaders also participated, reportedly commandeered factories, raw materials, and other resources, foreshadowing the corruption and criminality that mark Kosovo today.[20] The Manichaean morality of humanitarian intervention, however, invariably draws a clear line between heroes and villains.

KLA members also participated in the violence and expulsions that prompted Kosovo's Serb and Roma population to flee by the thousands.[21] But because of NATO's determination to stick to an air campaign it had no forces in place to deter these reprisal attacks, which frequently accompany violent ethnic conflicts and should therefore have been foreseen, particularly in light of the KLA's past.

Libya: Risk Aversion Redux

In Libya, NATO again mounted an intervention based on air and missile strikes so as to keep the casualties on its side as close to zero as possible. The world's mightiest alliance required seven months (from March to October 2011) to defeat a besieged dictator and his third-rate army of 50,000, which he distrusted because it had supported tribal rebellions and attempted several coups.[22] (His suspicions were well founded: during the revolt, troops defected to the opposition and refused to fire on protestors.) As the war dragged on, defying NATO's expectations, European coalition members ran out of munitions, necessitating American supplies; the unity of the alliance frayed; and the United States became exasperated with NATO states that refused to participate.[23] Even the governments that had backed the intervention fervently started wondering whether the opposition was up to the job of toppling Gaddafi, and there was talk of a deal.[24] As in Kosovo, so in Libya, NATO's preoccupation with avoiding casualties on its side and the consequent prolongation of the fighting between Gaddafi's forces and their adversaries increased the number of civilians maimed or killed. An estimated 1,200 to 2,000 Libyans perished prior to NATO's intervention; many more died in the seven months following it.[25]

NATO's risk aversion mirrored Western public opinion. A Gallup poll conducted soon after NATO's air campaign commenced showed that less than half of Americans backed the intervention, though more did than did not.[26] Other polls showed that a plurality or majority supported the imposition of the UN-authorized no-fly zone and the demolition of Libya air defenses.[27] But by June the mood had shifted: a Gallup survey revealed a plurality of Americans opposed to intervention, with two-thirds of those opposed opining that the United States should not be involved in the Libyan conflict.[28] Support for the war fell further when people were asked whether they supported more forceful (read: dangerous) action, including strikes on Libyan forces, even if these attacks were not required to maintain the no-fly zone. Throughout the war one constant endured: the public solidly opposed sending American troops to fight.[29]

Americans were not alone in becoming weary of the Libya war; the same was true in France and Britain, European NATO's foremost military powers. By June a plurality of the French, whose support for intervention had been strongest, opposed it.[30] British opinion was starkly divided even at the outset, with polls finding levels of support as high as 45 percent and as low as 35 percent. Downing Street, too, could not count on a strong, sustained popular mandate.[31] As in the United States, only a minority of Europeans favored dispatching ground troops to fight Gaddafi. In the EU as a whole less than a third did so, and the only countries in which more than 50 percent would support a ground war were France and the Netherlands.[32]

Jus Post Bellum

Scholars have written copiously about the conditions making war permissible (*jus ad bellum*) and about what is permitted, and not, during war (*jus in bello*). The duties that follow once the fighting ends (*jus post bellum*) have by comparison received less attention, though there has been a fair amount of discussion in recent years.[33] There is, however, no consensus, beyond generalities, on the obligations that fall to interveners following humanitarian wars.

Jus post bellum theorists argue that in any war, victors must eschew conquest and open-ended occupation. Under most circumstances, they must not remake the defeated country's political institutions wholesale, refashion its culture, plunder its economy, or mistreat civilians or prisoners. In addition, victors incur positive duties, which include bringing perpetrators of war crimes or crimes against humanity to justice through fair procedures; creating postwar political stability; promoting economic reconstruction; and meeting basic economic needs in war-ravaged societies. This school of thought sends the message that victors' conduct matters no less than their reasons for making war and the means by which they do so. The rules of *jus post bellum* imply that states cannot ethically fight humanitarian wars and then neglect the welfare of those who have been rescued.

This sounds both reasonable and enlightened. However, many *jus post bellum* discussions fail to reckon realistically with the cost of fulfilling the most ambitious positive duties; the degree to which citizens at home will support long-term, expensive commitments; and the myriad difficulties in achieving the desired outcomes. Enumerating postwar duties is one thing, discharging them quite another, particularly because countries that become venues for intervention have often already experienced prolonged internal war and violence or rule by repressive, corrupt regimes. Moreover, interventions can push all manner of simmering animosities to the surface. Individuals and groups seek vengeance and political advantage. They stake privileged claims to scarce resources and top posts, the latter often serving as a means to acquire the former. This scramble for dominance encourages violence, which in turn hastens the disintegration of state institutions, already weakened or discredited during the conflict. To make matters worse, the military and police forces, tainted by their association with the ancien régime, can unravel or even be dismantled. Armed groups may fill the vacuum and act with impunity to seize the upper hand in postwar power struggles. The economic destruction caused by war can exacerbate joblessness and poverty, creating additional sources of conflict. And elections, which in theory are supposed to create legitimate governments, often end up spawning violence because of divergent views about the future stemming from regional, religious, or ethnic divisions, accusations of voting fraud by the leaders of parties that lost, and fears about how those who win will treat their adversaries.[34]

Intervening countries invariably are poorly positioned to cope with these problems. Their leaders may have little knowledge about the countries into which they have projected their military power. Worse, they may, whether from ignorance or arrogance, be unaware of the inadequacy of their limited or false knowledge. Moreover, they tend to underestimate the time and money required to create and maintain order in politically divided, economically devastated societies as well as the perils (political and physical) accompanying a prolonged post-bellum presence. Both their own citizens and those now in their care tire of what appears to be an endless stewardship. That supporters of postintervention nation-building remain optimistic in spite of these hazards speaks to their faith in social engineering, discussed in the first chapter.

Economic reconstruction presents no less of a challenge than does the creation of order in post-bellum societies. It is a safe bet that humanitarian wars will not be fought in prosperous countries with well-run economies, but rather in poor places that have long been governed by crooked, incompetent leaders. Postintervention reconstruction projects incur high costs and curtailing corruption, by locals as well as the constellation of foreign contractors and consultants who arrive at the scene, presents significant challenges, especially when violence thwarts systematic monitoring. These difficulties cannot be surmounted with solemn statements about obligations or platitudes about the practical complexities of post-bellum operations.

Though some advocates of humanitarian intervention do under-score the importance of *jus post bellum*, their ideas have not transformed states' policy or won public support. Instead, once the military aspects of intervention have ceased, the humanitarians have a tendency to congratulate themselves and walk away, as in Libya. And when interveners do try to rebuild, à la Afghanistan and Iraq, the physical risks and economic costs of occupation and investment can become unbearable.

Lessons from Bosnia

Proponents of humanitarian intervention point to Bosnia to support their claim that the pitfalls of *jus post bellum* are avoidable.[35] True, NATO's intervention stopped the carnage in Bosnia and enabled refugees to return home. NATO's postwar presence (and later, that of EU troops and police) produced the stability needed for the establishment of democratic political institutions.

However, this narrative elides the importance of the shift in the balance of power on the ground in concluding the war in Bosnia and in easing the task of managing the country thereafter. The Bosnian Serbs faced enemies other than NATO. The US-trained Croatian army complemented NATO's air war and made major advances in May and August 1995 in Croatia—expelling Croatian Serbs en masse from the Krajina region in the process—and western Bosnia.[36] Absent the ground war waged by the Croats (and the Bosnians, who by then had received weapons from abroad), which took a heavy toll on Serb forces, NATO's *jus post bellum* project in Bosnia would have faced higher costs, greater risks, and an increased challenge of mobilizing and maintaining public support in the United States and Europe. These local conditions paved the way for the *jus post bellum* phase in Bosnia; interveners cannot always count on such advantages.

Moreover, NATO deployed tens of thousands of troops and thousands of police officers to Bosnia after the peace agreement had been reached.[37] Bosnia's small population, 3.5 million in 1995, enabled a high troop-to-population ratio—nineteen per thousand. This cannot be replicated in larger, less stable, and more war-torn societies, such as Afghanistan and Iraq. Afghanistan's population is eight times Bosnia's, Iraq's eighteen times. Both remain unstable, violent places despite a prolonged foreign military presence, and, in any event, Western citizens would not have supported investing the money and stationing soldiers required to match the resources employed per capita in Bosnia. In the event, the United States and its allies invested less in this respect in Afghanistan and Iraq than in Bosnia. Hence the prospects for post bellum success depend on the size of the country, the state of its economy, and on whether rival groups can easily resume the fighting.

In addition to the substantial military presence, post-Dayton Bosnia has been overseen by European Union "high representatives," of which there have so far been seven. These viceroys have wielded near-unchecked power to pass and rescind laws and to hire and fire functionaries. This accorded the Western powers a degree of control that they cannot realistically hope to replicate in other post bellum societies, not least because people tend not to tolerate being ruled by foreigners possessing unlimited powers.

Despite the substantial international efforts in postwar Bosnia, persistent political tensions among the country's major ethnic communities have necessitated the deployment of foreign troops for twenty years and counting. These frictions result in part from the peculiar polity produced by the agreements that ended the war. In post-1995 Bosnia, Serbs retain much of the territory they conquered and from which they expelled Bosnian Muslims. This Republika Srpska occupies nearly 50 percent of Bosnia's land, far larger than the proportion of Bosnia's population accounted for by Serbs. Together with the Federation of Bosnia Herzegovina, composed of Bosniaks and Croats, it constitutes the Bosnian state. The unity is illusory. Bosnia is a precarious ensemble of ethnicities—Bosniaks, Serbs, and Croats—whose members lead separate lives. Most Serbs in Republika Srpska wish to join Serbia or want an independent country. Croats in the Federation of Bosnia and Herzegovina identify with Croatia and resent what they consider Bosniak domination. Moreover, the cantons in the federation tend to have Croat or Bosniak majorities, thereby inhibiting integration. Bosnian Croats would prefer to have a separate ethnic unit within what would be a tripartite federation. Consequently, only a minority of Serbs and Croats share Bosniaks' loyalty to the post-Dayton state.[38]

The political system designed by the Dayton Accords entrenches ethnic divisions through its institutions: a two-part federation organized along ethnic lines and an anemic central government in which the most powerful positions are allocated on the basis of nationality. Add to the mix politicians who thrive on deepening ethnic divisions and mass media that both reflect and exacerbate ethnic animosities, and it is little wonder that in Bosnia there is scant contact among people across national lines, that the rate of intermarriage has plummeted compared to the prewar era, and that Sarajevo, once home to Yugoslavia various nationalities, has become a Bosniak bastion. The intervention stopped the slaughter, and the peace has held; regardless of these achievements, divisions among Bosniaks, Croats, and Serbs have grown. The peace remains tenuous.[39]

To hold up this creaky construct, NATO deployed the 70,000-troop Implementation Force (IFOR) in December 1995. A year later, IFOR was succeeded by the smaller Stabilization Force (SFOR)—32,000 troops, also mainly from NATO. SFOR shrank in 2002 and remained until 2004, when it was replaced by EUFOR, which still stations 7,000 EU troops in Bosnia. This military presence reflects an impressive commitment. But in how many places can such a prolonged deployment of international military forces be replicated in the name of creating a just postintervention polity, or, at minimum, preventing renewed bloodshed?

Furthermore, economic reconstruction has a high cost. Bosnia has received more than $15 billion ($2 billion of it from the United States) in international aid since Dayton. According to Patrice McMahon and Jon Western, "By the end of 1996, 17 different foreign governments, 18 UN agencies, 27 intergovernmental organizations, and about 200 nongovernmental organizations—not to mention tens of thousands of troops from across the globe—were involved in reconstruction efforts. On a per capita basis, the reconstruction of Bosnia—with less than four million citizens—made the post–World War II rebuilding of Germany and Japan look modest."[40] Yet in 2013, Bosnia's unemployment rate of 45 percent ranked 193rd out of 203, globally; and as late as mid-2014, it was 43.7 percent. Youth unemployment approached 60 percent, among the highest in the world, and has contributed to the exodus of young, well-educated Bosnians.[41]

In 2014 an International Crisis Group report summed up the country's situation as follows: "Bosnia . . . poses little risk of deadly conflict, but after billions of dollars in foreign aid and intrusive international administration and despite a supportive European neighbourhood, it is slowly spiraling toward disintegration."[42] In light of prolonged international tutelage (coming up on twenty years), persistent ethnic polarization, and massive sums of economic aid, the report lamented, "There is so much effort, so little to show for it. The same problems come up repeatedly."[43]

Libya: Just Postbellum Botched

Libya's postintervention history has proven far more violent and chaotic than Bosnia's. It reveals a *jus post bellum* challenge more fundamental and more formidable: averting anarchy amid rampant violence by myriad armed groups. Given the characteristics of countries in which humanitarian intervention is likely to be conducted, Libya's postwar setting may offer a better example than Bosnia's.

After Gaddafi's regime collapsed, Libya shattered into local fiefdoms controlled by freewheeling militias and militant religious groups, some wedded to terrorism. Having bled and died for the revolution, the militias' loyalties were to their leaders and localities, not to the new government, which they ignored. They took the law into their own hands, arresting, torturing, and killing rivals. They ran protection rackets, seized oil fields, and fought turf wars while Libya's official postwar leadership watched helplessly, even paying some militias to control others. The authorities' dependence on mercenaries further marginalized and demoralized the already-feeble military and police forces, which were also riven by the same divisions that are rupturing the rest of the country.

Libya faces problems other than militias. The historic east–west tensions between Tripolitania in the northwest and Cyrenaica in the east resurfaced and worsened, raising the possibility that the country would fracture into multiple states, especially because the southern province of Fezzan has also been racked by fighting among tribes, smuggling rings, and terrorist groups, including Al-Qaeda in the Maghreb.[44] The danger of fragmentation increased in the latter part of 2014, when two separate governments, each claiming to be Libya's legitimate authority, emerged.[45] One, based in Tripoli and known as Libyan Dawn, drew its support from Islamist groups, some members of parliament, the powerful Misrata militia, and various tribes. The other, Libyan Dignity, arose following the June 2014 parliamentary elections, which it won. But its rival refused to accept it as Libya's rightful government. The fighting that followed forced the elected government to decamp from Tripoli, the capital, to the east. Part of it set up shop in Bayda, from which the prime minister sought to control state institutions in Tripoli. Another segment based its operations in Tobruk, where the parliament (save those members who defected to the Tripoli-based opposition) operates to little effect. The eastern group enjoys the support of Gaddafi loyalists, regional tribes, and a clutch of militias that includes fighters from Zintan, who have been locked in a deadly struggle with their foes from Misrata.[46]

Particularly in the east, the pandemonium has opened the door to millenarian, violent Islamist groups such as Ansar al-Shari'a, which stormed the American consulate in Benghazi on September 11, 2012. They intimidate and attack Libyans whose lifestyles, politics, and religious beliefs they reject.

The groups arrayed against the radical Islamists include defectors from the Libyan army and fight under the command of Khalifa Hifter, the main source of Libyan Dignity's muscle. A onetime Gaddafi general and ally, Hifter fought the Libyan strongman's war against Chad in the 1980s, but after he was taken prisoner in Chad, Gaddafi, seeking to deny Libya's military intervention, abandoned him. Hifter then broke with Gaddafi, eventually finding refuge in the United States, possibly with the help of American intelligence, which was then keen to recruit anti-Gaddafi elements.[47] Having returned from exile following the revolution, Hifter has ambitions of his own and operates outside of the official Libyan government's control. His soldiers come from eastern tribes and urban militias—especially from Zintan, Misrata's archrival. And he has an external patron: the military-dominated Egyptian government of Abdel Fattah el-Sisi.[48]

To make matters worse, the two main blocs vying for control of Libya—one in Tripoli, the other in the east—lack unity. The fractiousness aggravates the chaos and violence, making dialogue, to say nothing of a lasting political settlement, between them harder still because neither grouping can achieve an internal consensus on the terms of reconciliation and power-sharing.

The upheaval that has engulfed post-Gaddafi Libya should surprise no one. The opposition to Gaddafi's regime was divided from the rebellion's outset. American commentaries on Libya's civil war rested on a simplistic view of Gaddafi as a reviled, isolated ruler. Yet he could not have fought the world's most powerful alliance for seven months without support from segments of Libyan society. The civil war that erupted following Gaddafi's ouster grew out of the deep tensions that had been kept in check through oppression: between Tripolitania and Cyrenaica, among pro- and anti-Gaddafi tribes and cities, and between the Arab-dominated state and the non-Arab Amazigh (Berber) minority. NATO's intervention papered over these fissures: militarily, by promoting battlefield coordination among disparate fighting forces, and politically, through the Western-backed National Transitional Council, which contained many émigrés and lacked deep support among Libyans.

Libya's civil war is especially dangerous—and not just for Libyans—because there is a cornucopia of weapons with which to wage it. According to a 2014 Rand Corporation study, written before the governmental split, because of the looting of Gaddafi's armories and the arms supplied by outside countries backing the rebellions, "the country is awash in weapons." The government "has no security forces of its own" and in the aftermath of Gaddafi's ouster "was unable to control the streets of Tripoli and was constantly subject to the whims of whatever groups were willing to brandish weapons and threaten officials."[49] As a result, armed takeovers of ministries, assassinations, bombings, suicide attacks, and kidnappings (including of the prime minister in October 2013) became standard fare. The main cities, Tripoli, Benghazi, and Tobruk, have turned into war zones, terrorist targets, and redoubts for rivalrous radical Islamist groups. The Libyan economy has been battered by the turmoil and uncertainty created by the rampant violence, the absence of an effective state, and militias' seizure of oil fields and export terminals.[50] The fighting has claimed at least 2,500 lives since mid-2014 alone.[51]

To make matters worse, Libya's internal war has created an arena for international rivalries, which were evident even during NATO's intervention but accelerated once the state collapsed and Libya drifted into chaos. Egypt, Saudi Arabia, and the United Arab Emirates back what might be called the official government, which operates from Bayda and Tobruk; Qatar, Sudan, and Turkey stand behind its Tripoli-based rival.[52] These foreign benefactors provide additional money and arms to fuel the fighting. Prominent Libyan politicians operating from exile in the UAE and Qatar are also mobilizing outside support for their respective sides. Misrata and Zintan have become deadly enemies backed by foreign sponsors. As Libya's disarray and violence increased, so did the scale of foreign military intervention and rivalry. In 2014, UAE pilots flying from Egyptian air bases launched air strikes on radical Islamist groups in Tripoli.[53] By early 2015, evidence mounted that the Islamic State had established itself in Libya's western, eastern, and southern regions. After its members beheaded

21 Egyptian Coptic Christians who had gone to Libya in search of work, Egyptian jets bombed the group's bastions in the eastern city of Derna.[54] Foreign influence also complicates a potential settlement because a durable deal among Libya's warring parties will require the cooperation of states with conflicting interests.

Libya's anarchy threatens not only its own people but also the security of Egypt and the entire Maghreb and Sahel. This wider effect manifested itself in Mali, which was destabilized as a direct consequence of Gaddafi's overthrow. Once Gaddafi's fate seemed sealed, ethnic Tuaregs, some of whom had served him as mercenaries, feared for their lives: many Libyans viewed them as outsiders, but also as Gaddafi's henchmen. Seeking safety, some 3,000 well-armed Tuaregs crossed into northern Mali, aggravating a long-running conflict between the Tuaregs of that region and Mali's central government. Tuareg fighters chased the Malian army from the north and, amid the blame game between it and the civilian leadership, the military overthrew the democratically elected Malian government. Then the nationalist Tuaregs (the National Movement for the Liberation of Azawad) and Islamists (Ansar Dine), once allies, turned on one another, their enmity exacerbated by the influx of Libyan Tuaregs. The victor, Ansar Dine, which is aligned with Al-Qaeda in the Islamic Maghreb, erected a mini state that it ran with extreme cruelty. Those who dared defy its draconian definitions of shari'a suffered horrendous punishments, including stoning and amputations. Eventually, the threat the Islamists posed to the rest of Mali, as evidenced by their expansion southward toward Bamako, the capital, prompted a French military intervention in January 2013. French troops evicted Ansar from major northern towns, but that merely prepared the ground for a new war. One side consists of Ansar and various non-Malian jihadist allies, the other of the shaky Malian army, supported by Chadian soldiers, some members of the Economic Community of West African States (ECOWAS), and anti-Ansar Tuareg nationalists.

The Malian, Chadian, and ECOWAS soldiers, joined by UN peacekeepers, assumed responsibility for security as France began withdrawing troops in April 2013. The UN force, which numbers 9,000, has a near-impossible assignment. Its soldiers have come under armed attack in northern Mali, where the vast majority is stationed, while also being condemned by the rival groups fighting there, sometimes for being partisan, at other times for being ineffectual.[55] Meanwhile, by mid-2015, 100,000 people had been displaced in Mali's north.[56]

Although the French intervention stabilized Mali for a time, the Maghreb and the Sahel will likely witness more insurgencies and terrorism as a result of spillover from Libya. Radical movements will find a hospitable habitat in the region as well as support from Libya's radical Islamists. The Algerian government, which already faced a major terrorist attack on its In Amenas gas plant in January 2013 by a group that appeared to have come across the Libyan border, had no particular liking for Gaddafi. But Algeria's leaders now fear that a volatile, violent Libya threatens to destabilize their state and neighborhood. Tunisia and Niger share this well-founded apprehension, the former already having been hit in 2015 by two major terrorist attacks traced to militant Islamist, and possibly IS-run, training camps in Libya.[57] Though Algeria has sought to stabilize Mali and safeguard the region by mediating a peace agreement, success remains a distant prospect.

The civil war in Libya and the crumbling of Gaddafi's state also proved a boon for radical Islamists and terrorist organizations. Once anti-Gaddafi fighters began raiding state armories amid Libya's mounting chaos, Al-Qaeda in the Islamic Maghreb (AQIM) grabbed weapons, including antiaircraft missiles, and gained recruits, starting in the uprising's early phases. That windfall made AQIM a much larger and militarily more powerful group, and its capacity to wreak havoc in the Maghreb grew substantially, especially once it moved arms from Libya to redoubts in adjoining areas.[58] As for IS, its effort to ensconce itself in Libya was helped by the return to eastern Libya of men who had slipped out to join the war against Bashar al-Assad's regime. IS made its presence known by detonating car bombs; attacking embassies, oil fields, and hotels; and committing atrocities.[59] The radical Islamists are a divided lot, but the battles among them, particularly those pitting IS and its followers against Al-Qaeda and its acolytes, will worsen Libya's violence and mayhem.

This dismal dénouement vindicated the warnings of Chad's president, Idris Déby, that Libya's civil war, which NATO and the Arab states that intervened framed as a democratic uprising against tyranny, would eventually spill over into its neighbors and threaten their stability.[60]

Some of the most prominent advocates of humanitarian intervention hailed the Arab-NATO campaign in Libya as a model and as a "textbook example" of R2P's application, arguing that it stopped atrocities and delivered Libyans freedom and self-determination.[61] But in the aftermath of the intervention Libya has become a venue for pervasive upheaval and violence, which together have created serious, long-term problems for the neighborhood and indeed for the West. None of this, it would appear, has inspired soul-searching among those enthusiastic about armed humanitarianism. Instead, they complain that R2P has wrongly been equated with military intervention, even as they hail Gaddafi's ouster as an exemplary application of their doctrine.

Postwar Libya validates John Stuart Mill's view that authentic self-determination must be worked out from within, not delivered or accelerated from without, just as it does Clausewitz's warning about "friction."[62]

Iraq: Postbellum Violence, Waste, Corruption

Post-Saddam Iraq offers additional lessons about the pitfalls of *jus post bellum*, ones worth considering even though the 2003 Iraq war isn't typically categorized as a humanitarian intervention. For one thing, some prominent intellectuals—such as Christopher Hitchens, Michael Ignatieff, and Fernando Tesón—supported the war on the grounds that it would free Iraqis from a tyrant's grip. Prime Minister Tony Blair and President George W. Bush repeatedly used that same argument, even though they primarily justified the war by purporting to rid Iraq of weapons of mass destruction. The downfall-of-the-dictator rationale became much more prominent once it turned out that Iraq had neither a nuclear arms program nor chemical weapons. Given the intervention's many failures, its supporters and architects tend to invoke the humanitarian defense that it deposed a cruel dictator, no matter the bedlam and killing that pervades post-Saddam Iraq. Finally, regardless of the motivations behind the intervention, Iraq reveals some of the problems that any state embarking on a prolonged effort to create order and promote economic reconstruction in a post-war society will encounter.

Like Libya, post-Saddam Iraq rapidly descended into sectarian bloodletting. The Kurds and the Shi'a bore the brunt of Saddam's savage repression and welcomed the American-led intervention that ended his dictatorship. But Iraq's long-dominant Sunnis soon came to fear—and rightly so—that the armed forces and police established with American assistance were becoming Shi'a-dominated organizations. They worried not only that they would be excluded from the new security services, but also that they would become targets. These apprehensions were aggravated by the marginalization of the Sunnis as the drafting of the new constitution commenced. The alienation deepened to the point that the Sunnis boycotted the January 2005 parliamentary election.[63]

In March 2010, an opportunity arose to bridge the divide. In the parliamentary election, the Iraqiya coalition, led by Iyad Allawi, a secular Shiite, attracted Sunni political parties and swept the Sunni areas. It gained a plurality of votes and parliamentary seats. But Iraqiya failed to agree with Prime Minister Nouri al-Maliki's State of Law bloc on a national unity government, the deadlock depriving Iraq of a government for nearly eight months. Once Maliki managed to form one, he continued to sideline the Sunnis.

The failure to seek reconciliation through political inclusiveness deepened the sectarian divide. Maliki was slow to provide jobs to the Iraqi Awakening, the Sunni fighters who broke with Al-Qaeda in 2006, abandoned their insurgency in return for American economic and military aid, and agreed to join Iraqi institutions. The Sunni fighters' defection was critical in taking wind out of the insurgency's sails, tamping down the violence between Sunni and Shi'a militias, and isolating Al-Qaeda. But by mid-2010, only 41,000 of the 94,000 former Sunni insurgents had received jobs in Iraq's civilian or military bureaucracy.[64] Eventually, frustrated Sunnis started to rejoin the battle, and Al-Qaeda in Iraq enticed them with attractive pay. By the time Maliki's political support ran out in 2014, Sunni disaffection with the Shi'a-run government provided an opening to the IS, which extended its sway from northern and eastern Syria to Sunni regions in north and central Iraq. IS gained a foothold despite its ruthless methods. As for the Iraqi army—built through massive American expenditures—it often shrank from IS instead of fighting it.[65] Meanwhile, Shi'a and Sunni death squads continue their killing sprees, while the Kurds remain within Iraq only because they have far-reaching autonomy and understand that the United States, Europe, and especially Turkey, would oppose their secession. For its part, Iran has become the most influential foreign power in Iraq.

Amid the widening sectarian schism, the United States poured money into Iraq.[66] Postwar reconstruction enriched private contractors, companies, and consultants from the intervening countries. Waste and fraud inflated the cost still further. Local power brokers had no commitment to clean, democratic government but proved adept at employing their influence to profit from foreign assistance programs or to extract payment in exchange for cooperation. James Risen, other journalists, and the reports of the Special Inspector General for Iraq Reconstruction have shown the extent of the problem: by September 2012, waste and corruption had squandered $8 billion of the $53.26 billion the United States spent for economic and security assistance.[67]

Thus, after more than a decade, during which the United States deployed tens of thousands of troops and spent tens of billions of dollars in military and economic assistance, Iraq remains a violent and divided place; a precarious assemblage of Shi'as, Sunnis, and Kurds, none of whom trust the other; home to an IS proto-state whose rise was enabled by Sunni disaffection; and a place where Iran's influence has been strengthened beyond anything its leaders could have imagined. Postintervention Iraq, more so than postwar Bosnia and Libya, reveals the numerous difficulties an outside power, even a superpower, encounters when it tries to create trust among rival ethnic and religious communities in war-shattered societies. Absent that indispensable sentiment, which violence eviscerates, the grandiose nation-building projects of foreigners will amount to fantasies.

These snapshots of postintervention Bosnia, Libya, and Iraq raise some basic questions about the aftermath of humanitarian intervention: How many such nation-building ventures can Americans and Europeans stomach? How many years of nation-building—and at what price in blood and treasure—can Western governments and citizens tolerate? The countries conducting interventions may be powerful, but they are not all-powerful. Their well equipped, disciplined, and technologically advanced militaries are good at fighting, especially against the weak states that intervention usually targets. But *jus post bellum* presents a much harder challenge, and the consequences of the failure to achieve it prove far-reaching and long-lasting.

THE "INTERNATIONAL COMMUNITY"

Proponents of humanitarian intervention aver that there is such a thing as an "international community," and they consider it neither a cliché nor a vacuous diplomatic buzzword. As they see it, part of what makes for a global community is the increasing consensus on fundamental human rights, which in turn includes an ethical commitment to end mass atrocities, as exemplified by the influence of R2P and the creation of an International Criminal Court (ICC) to hold perpetrators accountable.

Yet the horrors that occurred during the violence that erupted within countries since the mid-1970s and the largely ineffectual responses—and even nonresponses—to them raise a basic question: Is the international community anything more than a platitude trotted out by leaders or their media panjandrums when a mass killing occurs and they are pressed to respond? "I am confident that the international community will not tolerate this outrage and will do its duty," they often say, saying nothing.

Material Versus Normative Community

An international community certainly exists in the material sense: a space, planetary in scale and intricately interconnected, inhabited by states, international organizations, NGOs, multinational corporations, transnational movements, and social media enthusiasts. Information, goods, money, and people course through it in volumes and at velocities hitherto unimaginable. "Globalization" and "global village" have long since become household words. Events "there" affect life "here," and vice versa—and with unprecedented speed. Consider, for example, economic crises, the spread of diseases far beyond their places of origin, the worldwide flows of refugees and illegal narcotics, and the near-instantaneous transmission of news across continents, thanks to the Internet.[1] None of these phenomena is new but the rapidity with which their ripple effects register worldwide has novel and profound consequences.

But "community" connotes more than the material transactions and information flows that connect people, whether through the global reach of trade, investment, or the Internet. It suggests, as well, the recognition of shared responsibility among members of a collectivity, which, in turn, involves the predisposition to feel at one with, and to assist, fellow members when they are in need of help or protection and to regard security (in the broad sense) as a common concern. Affective bonds, not merely material ones, make for community. Yet the rosy rhetoric about global values and norms notwithstanding, an international community in this sense exists, at best, in anemic form: consider the barriers to reaching agreement on the principles and procedures required to act in concert against atrocities. Asserting that human rights norms have redefined sovereignty and that governments that violate them wholesale will face justice as a result does not amount to proving that this has in fact happened, or even that a significant number of states want it to happen.[2] The latter case has not been made persuasively.

Hedley Bull and the English School of International Relations of which he was part are known for their thesis that there does exist an "international society" constituted by the balance-of-power system, international law, institutions, diplomacy, convergent interests among the major powers, and "rules of order." This interpretation, which reminds us that world politics does not play out in a Hobbesian state of nature, bears some resemblance to reality and provides a useful corrective to crude realpolitik-based analyses.[3] The same cannot be said about the more extravagant claim—made even by some scholars associated with the English School—that a normative international community has in fact emerged and that its characteristics include like-mindedness on human rights and on procedures and institutions for enforcing them when egregious violations, such as mass atrocities, occur.

Reinhold Niebuhr pointed out many decades ago that a global community based on connectivity—flows of trade, finance, and information—would not become an international community of moral responsibility as well. "A technological civilization," he observed, "has created an international community, so interdependent as to require, even if not powerful or astute enough to achieve, ultimate social harmony. While there are halting efforts to create an international mind and conscience ... modern man has progressed only a little beyond his fathers in extending his ethical attitudes beyond the group to which he is organic and which possesses symbols, vivid enough to excite his social sympathies."[4] Furthermore, "While the rapid means of communication have increased the breadth of knowledge about world affairs among citizens of various nations, and the general advance of education has ostensibly promoted the capacity to think rationally and justly ... there is nevertheless little hope of arriving at a perceptible increase of international morality through the growth of intelligence and the perfection of the means of communication."[5] "Our problem," he observed, "is that technics have established a rudimentary world community but have not integrated it morally or politically. They have created a community of mutual dependence but not of mutual trust and respect."[6] As Niebuhr saw it, principles that appear to be universal and are presented as such by their originators invariably reflect the underlying realities of power and serve particular rather than general ends. Far from restraining states or proving the moral progression of the international community, they enable the most powerful to clothe their narrow interests in the alluring garb of collective, disinterested morality. Moreover, states, particularly the mightiest, will always be determined to ensure that the interpretation and implementation of normative principles comport with their interests—and even then with the proviso that they can claim exemptions as needed.[7] Niebuhr's interpretation remains apposite.[8]

Yet today prominent individuals have taken a different view, insisting that we are at a different stage now, one in which an international community has arisen—in the normative, not merely instrumental, sense. Former United Nations Secretary General Kofi Annan, for example, celebrates "a shared vision of a better world" expressed in the UN Charter, in treaties, in laws, and in conventions. "The skeptics," he declares, "are wrong. The international community does exist. It has an address. It has achievements to its credit. And more and more, it is developing a conscience."[9] This assessment aligns with the mainstream writing on human rights in general and R2P in particular.

Annan's bold claim lacks factual support. A community coheres in part because of what Adam Smith, in his *Theory of Moral Sentiments*, called "fellow-feeling." But to what extent does the international community contain this sentiment? Consider the gap between rhetoric and action when it comes to a particularly pitiable segment of humanity: refugees. The 1954 Convention Relating to the Status of Refugees has been signed by 145 states (as of 2015), but their record in helping displaced people turns out to be both unimpressive and uninspiring. Sadako Ogata, UN High Commissioner for Refugees from 1999 to 2000, recalled the difficulty of persuading states to act on the commitment they had made: "I sought to enlist governments and the global public for support in my efforts, insisting that borders be kept open, asking that asylum seekers' claims be fairly examined, and soliciting funds to cover victims' needs." She "faced great difficulties seeking to ensure that states lived up to the provisions of the convention, even regarding the acceptance of people in desperate flight." "The international community," she lamented, "did not seem to exist even in the face of human tragedies." It was, she concluded, "a virtual community."[10]

Others involved in refugee relief have shared Ogata's sobering experience. Recall from Chapter 2 the dismay of Jan Egelund, head of the Norwegian Refugee Council and a former senior UN official, upon witnessing the Syrian refugee camps. Egelund's reaction illuminates the mismatch between the international community's efforts, whether in providing economic assistance to relief programs or admitting refugees, and the magnitude of the humanitarian crisis created by the war in Syria. In 2012 the UNHCR appealed for funds to care for Syrian refugees; a month later it had received but a fifth of the $84 million requested, and only eight of the thirty-four agencies, including the UNHCR, organized under the Syria Regional Response Plan, had received contributions.[11] The pattern persisted. In January 2013, the organization sought $1.1 billion in additional funding to manage the massive increase in refugees from Syria; about a month later it had received less than a fifth of that amount.[12] In December 2014, the UN's World Food Program (WFP) ran out of money to feed Syrian refugees (just as had happened previously in Kenya, Somalia, and Sudan) and announced that 1 million Syrian and Iraqi refugees and internally displaced persons (IDPs) would be deprived of basic necessities as a result. WFP encountered the same problem in 2015 and announced that it would be unable to provide food vouchers to a third of the Syrian refugees living in various Middle Eastern countries, the overwhelming majority in Jordan, Lebanon, and Turkey. Since the beginning of that year it had already cut the number of eligible voucher recipients from 2.1 million to 1.4 million, while also reducing the value of each voucher.[13] Meanwhile, as the UNHCR planned for 2015, it was still contending with the gap between resources and the requirements created by existing and incoming Syrian refugees.[14]

By early 2015 about four million Syrian refugees—not counting 6.5 million IDPs—had fled to neighboring countries and over 50,000 Syrians were seeking asylum, with the number increasing sharply as the year wore on. The countries adjacent to Syria, above all Jordan, Lebanon, and Turkey, were struggling to cope and had begun to impose entry restrictions.[15] Ogata's successor, António Gutteres, urged wealthy countries to admit 130,000 Syrian refugees and asylum seekers over two years, but the combined offers fell short by a third.[16] Even the number of offers received represented an undercount because they included pledges made in previous years. The upshot was that the countries bordering Syria were left to provide succor to 95 percent of its refugees. By contrast, the West, Aron Lund notes, has been willing to take in "less than one percent of the total, or about two weeks of new arrivals to the UNHCR refugee camps."[17]

Some countries did respond generously, notably Germany and Sweden.[18] And as the number of Syrian refugees making their way to Europe soared in 2015, several other European countries agreed to take in more.[19] But that was scarcely the norm in wealthy countries; and even in Europe the generosity of West European states contrasted sharply with the prevailing sentiment in east-central Europe, which was to shut and lock the gates and resist proposals for EU-wide refugee quotas.[20] The east-west division in Europe over who should admit refugees and in what number became acrimonious. The United States, having admitted only 1,500 Syrian refugees and asylum seekers since the Syrian war began in 2011, was expected to take in 1,000 to 2,000 in 2015, but dogged resistance from members of Congress warning of security threats left the actual number uncertain. By the fall of 2015, only 260 Syrian refugees had qualified for resettlement in Britain since 2011, and Prime Minister Cameron reassured the public that there would be no steep increase, even as he maneuvered to coordinate with his fellow EU leaders to help manage the massive increase in the number of refugees arriving in Europe.[21] A leading British newspaper called the London government's response to asylum and refugee resettlement request "shaming," adding that "if 10 times as many of the most vulnerable people from Syria were admitted [to the United Kingdom] as are at present, that would still be only a thousand a year."[22]

According to an extensive December 2014 Amnesty International report on the international response to the Syrian refugees crisis, none of the oil-rich Persian Gulf countries had offered any Syrian refugees asylum or resettlement; nor had China, Japan, and Russia. And leaving aside Germany and Sweden, exceptional in their openness, prior to the swell in refugee flows to Europe in 2015, the remaining twenty-six EU countries had "pledged a total of 6,305 places, which amounts to just 0.17% of the refugees currently living in the main host countries."[23] Germany and Sweden aside, Aron Lund observed, "the other 26 EU members seem more concerned with shutting their borders than with offering refuge to Syrian citizens." Britain and France's lukewarm promises to receive refugees, he adds, contrasts with their enthusiasm for "sending arms, bombing, and trying to get the EU militarily engaged" in Syria.[24]

Are There Ties That Bind?

Though multiple reasons account for the lackluster response to Syrian refugees, the general lassitude demonstrates that the sense of international community and obligation remains weak, no matter the dense network of connections drawing countries closer together.

To understand why, compare a functional national political community—by which I mean a polity that keeps order and governs, and even if it is not democratic, eschews large-scale, systematic violence against its citizens—to its international counterpart.[25] Sentiments of belonging that reflect, among other things, shared historical experiences and customs and a sense of common destiny help unite such national communities. Societies change; new groups emerge, empowered; they challenge established national narratives, and even transform them. The elemental question of who qualifies as a rightful member and who does not evolves through continuing negotiations as well as struggles, some of them violent. The stories shaping nationalism do not lack for humbug and hypocrisy. Traditions and tales that create cohesion often turn out to be invented, embellished, or downright false.[26] Maudlin expressions of solidarity and patriotism notwithstanding, the people constituting a national community do not feel as one because they encounter one another in the quotidian ways that inhabitants of a neighborhood do. Most will remain strangers to one another, and Benedict Anderson has aptly characterized the nation as an "imagined community."[27]

Still, the national communities that endure create boundaries—territorial, political, psychological, economic, and cultural—that distinguish "us" from "them," a dichotomy critical to group solidarity, and not just during wartime. Stable national communities cohere despite their ethnic, cultural, and religious pluralism—territories governed by modern states rarely tend toward homogeneity—because ties, sufficient in number and strength, both instrumental and affective, exist to create a sense of belonging, a "we-ness." These connections are supplemented by shared institutions and laws, which, if they work well, enable disputes to be worked out through political and legal process rather than violence.

People make extraordinary sacrifices on behalf of their nation. Marxists in particular have long been vexed by nationalism's capacity to inspire passions that trump class allegiance. Likewise, nationalism has frustrated proponents of universalism, who view people's common humanity as the fundamental, and higher, connection among them.

Reifying the nation is a harmless error, deifying a dangerous blunder: at its worst nationalism can incubate jingoism and bellicosity. But to regard it as just another social construct ignores its power and the anchoring it provides to people.[28]

The international community, by contrast, lacks clear delineation. It comprises a crazy quilt of contrasts: economic, political, cultural, and religious. The diversity of national political communities cannot compare to that of their international analogue. The international community, vastly larger, also lacks a "them" in relation to whom a sense of "us" can be articulated and a compelling narrative of solidarity and shared obligation created. All of this exists in theory, but has not yet come to fruition.

Order and Protection: The Institutional Deficit

The difference between national communities and the international community does not turn on sentiment and the degree of solidarity alone. The two collectivities also contrast starkly with respect to the coherence and power of their institutions. This difference matters when it comes to the possibilities for delivering justice.[29] National communities are governed by bureaucracies—collectively, the state. Ideally, these structures maintain order, provide physical security, bring lawbreakers to justice when prevention fails, enforce obligations, and collect the revenue required to provide various services to society. In practice, of course, not all members benefit equally; not every institution works as it should. Nor is the state a neutral arbiter; its choices and operations reflect the uneven distribution of power among classes and social groups.

Still, whatever the imperfections of national political communities, global institutions lack comparable power and legitimacy. The United Nations and its affiliated organizations resemble national institutions only in form. The UN, by design, cannot mobilize collective action effectively and reliably. Lacking powers of taxation, it depends on voluntary, though specified, contributions from its members, and when, as often happens, they are delinquent in their dues, the UN can do nothing other than plead and be patient. Nor does the UN have a standing army or police forces. It can appeal to its members for troops, but the Security Council must approve the deployment of an international force, whether for peacekeeping or peace enforcement, and any one of the permanent members (the P-5) can cast a blocking veto and even prevent lesser measures intended to punish, or even castigate, states perpetrating atrocities. High-minded recommendations that the Council's permanent members should agree not to veto resolutions that propose interventions to stop mass killings, especially those approved by the General Assembly with a two-thirds majority, have come to naught.[30] Great powers seldom, if ever, surrender their privileges voluntarily for the greater good.

Even when agreement within the Security Council permits the assemblage of a UN peacekeeping force, it is the P-5 that determines how large and powerful it will be, what it can and cannot do; and their decisions reflect their own interests much more than the larger interest.[31] Moreover, UN peacekeeping forces tend to be assembled from disparate countries whose soldiers have most likely never trained, let alone fought, together. These troops vary in preparedness and material capacity, particularly because many hail from poor countries that regard peacekeeping operations as a source of income. Yet the New York–based superiors of those who command such motley forces expect them to do a lot with little. Recall poor General Dallaire in Rwanda.

Stopping violence within states, keeping the peace, and preventing atrocities require resources. The UN has problems on that front as well. Given the focus of this book, the UN's Department of Peacekeeping Operations offers a pertinent example. It has run sixty-nine "field operations" since 1948—on a shoestring budget of $54 billion. In 2014 the Department oversaw the missions of 89,607 soldiers (plus 12,436 police and 1,775 military observers) attached to sixteen operations. It did so with an authorized budget of $7.06 billion, of which $1.8 had yet to be received as of the end of 2014.[32] By comparison, the 2014 budget for New York City's police department was $4.7 billion and for its fire department $1.7 billion.[33] In other words, the NYPD and FDNY, which serve a city of 8.4 million people, had only 25 percent less money to work with than did the UN peacekeeping department, which serves a world of seven billion.

Justice Versus Exceptionalism

International judicial institutions have proven even feebler than those responsible for providing order and security. The International Court of Justice (ICJ) has compulsory jurisdiction only when states agree to provide it and to abide by its ruling (seventy-one have done so).[34] It also lacks independent means of enforcement.

The judicial institution more relevant to this book's concerns is the ICC (which, recall, was created by the 1988 Rome Statute that became operative in 2002, following its ratification by 60 countries).[35] The ICC is no less encumbered than the ICJ. It does not have a police force to investigate, track, and apprehend suspects and must therefore rely on member states' goodwill. The world's most powerful country, the United States, has refused to join the Court. President Clinton authorized his lead negotiator, David Scheffer, to sign the Rome Statute only at the tail end of his presidency. But Clinton did not send the treaty to the Senate for ratification and advised his successor not to do so unless US soldiers and officials were guaranteed immunity from the Court's decisions. In May 2002, President Bush ended the drama by informing the UN Secretary General that the United States would no longer be party to the Statute. President Obama, despite his kind words for the Court and the assistance his administration has provided to help it bring perpetrators in other countries to justice, has not changed course.

The United States lacked enthusiasm for the ICC from the outset—and for several reasons. Washington worried that American troops and officials who happened to be on the territory of countries that are "state parties" to the ICC could be charged with crimes, past or present, and remanded to the Court. Moreover, it did not want a court that would answer to member states rather than to the Security Council, as the ad hoc tribunals for the former Yugoslavia and Rwanda had, especially because the ICC's prosecutors have wide investigatory powers that even member states cannot curb.

The United States threatened to veto the extension of the UN peacekeeping force in Bosnia unless American troops were guaranteed across-the-board immunity from ICC prosecution. The Bush administration pressured countries that had ratified the Statute to pledge, through "Article 98 Bilateral Immunity Agreements," that they would not turn over Americans on their territory to the Court's jurisdiction. By the end of President Bush's second term 100 countries had complied.[36] For good measure, Washington warned some governments that rebuffing its request would jeopardize their relationship with the United States and disrupt flows of aid and military assistance. More pointedly, the August 2002 American Service-Members' Protection Act (ASPA) forbade military aid to countries that would not agree to exempt US troops from the ICC's reach and blocked American participation in peacekeeping operations absent an assurance of immunity. ASPA went further, authorizing the president "to use all means necessary and appropriate" to free US troops or officials "being detained by, on behalf of, or at the request of the International Criminal Court."[37]

In short, the United States demanded a unique status.[38] American soldiers and leaders, regardless of their conduct, cannot be investigated or tried by the ICC. While trumpeting its commitment to universal human rights, backing the ICC's efforts to bring perpetrators of atrocities to justice, and proclaiming the need for global leadership, the US insisted on standing outside and above the Court—a symbol, in the eyes of its advocates, of the power of transnational human rights norms. Universalism, in Washington's eyes, applies to everyone save itself.

Like the United States, Russia and China attempted to have the ICC subordinated to the Security Council. And they too refused to sign the Rome Statute, in part because their militaries also operate internationally, potentially within countries that have joined the Court, but also because they do not look kindly on international judicial interventions into countries' internal affairs. For its part, India, not a Security Council member, rejected the entire concept of the ICC as an infringement of sovereignty. Even Great Britain, which overcame its misgivings and eventually joined the Court, sought immunity for its soldiers serving in Afghanistan as part of the International Security Assistance Force. Its position recalled NATO's during and after the Kosovo war. The alliance, though happy to supply the International Criminal Tribunal for the Former Yugoslavia (ICTY) with abundant intelligence to help indict and prosecute Serbs accused of war crimes, refused to provide any information that might enable it to investigate civilian deaths caused by NATO air strikes, effectively making any such inquiry impossible.[39]

Weak Court, Willful States

The ICC cannot do the job it has been assigned without the financial support, intelligence, and investigative services provided by its member states, particularly the major democratic powers. This includes the United States, which, though not a state party, assists the Court. Little wonder, then, that the ICC has been forced to accede to the wishes of states, especially the most powerful, and to overlook their misdeeds, such as the use of torture and rendition by the United States and some of its allies in Afghanistan and Iraq. ICC prosecutor Luis Moreno Ocampo assured Washington that an investigation into those misdeeds wasn't on his to-do list.[40]

Though the major powers have been selective and self-interested in their cooperation with the ICC and other tribunals dealing with atrocities and war crimes, so have other states. Following Rwanda's genocide, its president, Paul Kagame, pressed the International Criminal Tribunal for Rwanda (ICTR) to go after Hutu officials and militia leaders, but he ruled out investigations aimed at ascertaining whether the Rwandan Patriotic Front, which he had commanded, had also committed atrocities in 1994.[41]

Ugandan president Yoweri Museveni, too, manipulated the ICC for his political purposes.[42] Seeking to pressure the notorious Lord's Resistance Army (LRA), he referred it to the ICC in 2004. But when Uganda's negotiations with the LRA—which began in 2006 but ultimately collapsed—looked promising for a time, he refused to implement the arrest warrants the Court had issued in 2005 for the LRA's head, Joseph Kony, and four of his senior commanders. Having used the Court as a stick against the LRA, Museveni turned it into a carrot. So much for international justice.

The Ugandan government went further. In exchange for its help in finding Kony and his henchmen and building a case against them, it insisted that the ICC not investigate the deaths and displacement of the Acholi people during the army's massive counterinsurgency war, which began in 1996.[43] Museveni got his way. The Court made quite a concession given what the Ugandan army did in Acholiland. Adam Branch describes it as "a government-directed campaign of murder, intimidation, bombing, and burning of entire villages" and estimates that by 2002 "almost a million [people], encompassing nearly the entire rural population of the Acholi subregion," had been corralled into camps.[44] The abysmal living conditions contributed to "a massive humanitarian crisis with excess mortality levels of approximately 1,000 per week."[45]

The leaders of the Democratic Republic of Congo, the Côte d'Ivoire, and Libya have also referred opponents to the ICC while insisting that the Court could not cast its net wider and investigate allegations against groups and individuals that they favor. In post-Gaddafi Libya, for example, the ICC, while it has focused on the misdeeds of the ancien régime, has not seen fit to investigate the conduct of the armed opposition, their allies from the Persian Gulf States, or NATO. Likewise, the permanent members of the Security Council shield allied and friendly governments, as witness China's and Russia's blocking of attempts to refer the members of the Assad regime in Syria to the ICC.[46]

In short, the presentation of the ICC as a neutral organization—above politics, guided only by law and the pursuit of justice—does not withstand scrutiny.[47]

Judging the Court

Lack of money cannot explain the ICC's shortcomings.[48] Its annual budget has been around $140 million, which totals $1.6 billion since it started operating in 2002, and a staff of 700 supports its thirty-four judges. Yet in all this time the ICC has taken custody of only three people, militia commanders charged with recruiting child soldiers during Congo's civil war: Thomas Lubanga, Germain Katanga, and Bosco Ntaganda.[49] Lubanga and Katanga were convicted and sentenced: the former for fourteen years, minus the eight he spent in the Court's custody, the latter for twelve years, also with consideration for the six he served while awaiting trial. The Court has not, however, investigated the DRC's armed forces and police, both of which have been implicated in war crimes. The omission was hardly coincidental: it was the DRC government that handed over Lubanga, Katanga, and Ntaganda. Now, it could be said that that $1.6 billion amounts to a small sum for justice, which in any event should not carry a price, even if the result has been that only two militia leaders have been convicted. But that constitutes rhetoric, not reasoned argument, especially given the political considerations shaping the Court's activities and the extent to which it has been manipulated and politicized by states.

Moreover, the ICC has yet to bring to justice any top leaders connected to atrocities. It did issue an arrest warrant for Sudanese President Omar al-Bashir in March 2009, charging him with crimes against humanity and war crimes in Darfur. (The Security Council had referred the Darfur conflict to the ICC in March 2005.) In July 2010, the Court issued a second warrant against Bashir, this time for genocide.[50] He responded to the first by evicting from Sudan aid agencies that had provided a lifeline to 1 million Darfuri refugees and also blocked ICC investigators from entering Darfur to collect evidence.

To keep the Court at bay, and doubtless in response to the Security Council's referral of the Darfur crisis to the ICC, the Sudanese government created the Special Criminal Court for the Events in Darfur (SCCED) in June 2005. But this tribunal has not charged a single person with committing atrocities in Darfur. Moreover, Bashir has refused to apprehend two other Sudanese whom the ICC has sought to arrest: Ahmad Mohammed Harun (minister of state for humanitarian affairs when the warrant was issued in 2007 and later North Kordofan province's governor) and Ali Muhammad Ali Abd al-Rahman ("Ali Kushayb"), a top Janjaweed commander. (Sudan in this respect followed the example of Indonesia, which refused to extradite people for whom the UN Special Panels for Serious Crimes in East Timor, created in 2000, issued arrest warrants and established its own Ad Hoc Human Rights Court to investigate the atrocities. The Indonesian tribunal, recall, exonerated all of the senior military and intelligence officers implicated in the killings of Timorese.)

Rather than rally to the Court's defense, Bashir's fellow African leaders defended him and bashed the ICC. Despite the provisions on human rights and humanitarian intervention contained in its

Constitutive Act, in July 2008 the African Union, invoking Article 16 of the Rome Treaty, called on the UN Security Council to stop the Court's investigation of Bashir. At its July 2009 summit in Sirte, Libya, the AU went further. Invoking its duty to protect "the dignity, sovereignty and integrity of the continent," it voted not to cooperate with the ICC on "the arrest and surrender" of Bashir.[51]

The Arab states (most of which backed the intervention against Gaddafi in 2011) have been no less supportive of Bashir. Shortly after the first indictment against him, the Arab League countries convened for their summit in Doha, Qatar, in March 2009 and excoriated the Court's efforts to "undermine the sovereignty, unity and stability of Sudan." Bashir, who was assured in advance of the gathering that the ICC's warrant would not be enforced, received "red carpet treatment" and an "effusive embrace." The League's secretary general, Amr Moussa, declared that the organization would "continue our efforts to halt the implementation of the warrant."[52] ICC Chief Prosecutor Luis Moreno Ocampo called for Bashir to be arrested once his plane exited Qatar's airspace, but Moreno Ocampo's words were wasted; none of the leaders assembled in Qatar took the slightest notice.[53]

Since the ICC issued its arrest warrant, Bashir has not been able to shop in New York, Paris, or Berlin, or to attend Davos conferences, and some African and Arab countries have refused to receive him. But many others, some on multiple occasions, have welcomed him as a legitimate head of state, permitted him to visit for medical treatment, or, in Saudi Arabia's case, allowed him to participate in the hajj.[54] Most importantly from Bashir's vantage point, he continues to rule Sudan. Meanwhile, in December 2014, the ICC's chief prosecutor, Fatou Bensouda, announced the shelving of the investigation into human rights crimes in Darfur, a decision Bashir duly touted as a triumph. For good measure, he blasted the Court as a "tool to humiliate and subjugate" his country, a sentiment echoed by Ugandan president Museveni, who called on African countries to withdraw from the Court.[55]

The bloodletting in Darfur drags on, and the Sudanese government and the state-supported Janjaweed paramilitaries have exercised no pity nor shown any fear of the ICC. In 2014 alone, the UN and the African Union reported that as many as 500,000 people fled for their lives. The situation was as grim as in 2013, when some 460,000 were displaced by the violence. More than two million Darfuris have become refugees since the African Union/UN peacekeeping force was deployed in their homeland in 2008.[56] With 14,500 troops in a country the size of Spain, the joint force cannot possibly provide effective protection. Some 300,000 Darfuris have been killed since the war began in 2003, and the number continues to increase.

Bashir has not been the only president the ICC has targeted. In 2012 the Court indicted another sitting head of state, Kenyan president Uhuru Kenyatta, on charges of fomenting violence in 2007 and 2008 following a disputed presidential election.[57] As they did Bashir's case, several African governments rose to Kenyatta's defense, even though it was a Kenyan commission charged with investigating the postelection violence that referred the matter to the ICC in 2009. Various African leaders castigated the Court for targeting African leaders. Ugandan president Museveni, once a big supporter of the Court who had even barred Bashir from visiting Uganda for the 2010 AU summit, called upon the organization, thirty-four of whose members are members of the Court, to withdraw from the Rome Treaty.[58] In the event, the Court's case against Kenyatta collapsed in 2014: some witnesses refused to testify out of fear; others appeared to have been bought off. During his 2013 election campaign, Kenyatta, taking a page from Bashir's playbook, parlayed the ICC indictment to his advantage, portraying the Court as a colonial creature that preys on Africans.

Referring leaders thought to be guilty of committing atrocities to the Court while the conflicts in which they are embroiled are still underway and a political settlement remains possible may not be wise. As we have seen, the charges made against Gaddafi early on in Libya's civil war relied on statistics about casualties that were thrown about precipitously and recklessly, by the opposition and Western supporters of intervention, with the express purpose of enabling a military operation aimed at regime change. More importantly, the Security Council's decision to refer the Libyan conflict to the ICC on the basis of such information did not reduce the violence, let alone create conditions for a negotiated settlement, one that may in the end have even involved Gaddafi's exile.

The Deterrence Myth

Contrary to the claims of its champions, the Court's existence does not deter rulers determined to use violence to preserve their power or dissuade insurgencies and unofficial militias from killing people for political ends.[59] Following the LRA's indictment by the ICC, and the counterinsurgency campaign that the Ugandan government launched against it, the movement extended its war to parts of Uganda beyond Acholiland and also infiltrated northeastern Congo (exacerbating the already massive violence there), the Central African Republic, and South Sudan. Despite the Court's existence, the LRA has not abandoned the brutal practices that have made it infamous.[60] Likewise, the horrific violence in Darfur, South Sudan, Libya, Syria, Myanmar, eastern Congo, Sri Lanka, and the Central African Republic—to take a few examples—refutes ICC enthusiasts' claim that the Court deters mass killings or even reduces their severity.

Take the Central African Republic (CAR), which has not been discussed in this book. By the end of 2014, the violence that erupted in December 2013 between the CAR's Muslim minority and its Christian majority had claimed more than 5,000 lives, most of them Muslim. On top of that, by 2015 over 400,000 people had been forced from their homes to other parts of the country, and another 400,000 had fled to neighboring countries.[61] The AU dispatched 6,200 peacekeepers, and the UN brought in 1,800 more in September 2014, taking control of the mission. Supplementing these forces were 2,000 French troops, who were deployed once the violence began. These deployments, while commendable, amounted to 10,000 soldiers and police for keeping peace in a country of 5.3 million people.

In eastern Congo, which we have considered, despite the ICC's indictment of Lubanga, Katanga, and Ntaganda, the abduction, rape, and killing of civilians continue.[62]

And then there is South Sudan, which gained its independence from Sudan in 2011 following a horrific civil war that stretched back to 1955 and had killed 1.5 million people by the time the 2005 peace accord, which paved the way for independence, was signed. In December 2013, fighting erupted in the young country between the followers—divided along tribal lines—of president Salva Kiir and his former deputy, Riek Machar. The bloodletting that followed and the spillover from Sudan's wars in its Blue Nile and South Kordofan provinces, which are adjacent to South Sudan, had killed 50,000 by January 2015, according to the International Crisis Group. In addition, over 1.5 million people in South Sudan (which has a population of 11.3 million) fled to other parts of the country and 500,000 others to Ethiopia, Kenya, Sudan, and Uganda.[63] To create order, in May 2014, the UN Security Council authorized the stationing in South Sudan of 12,500 soldiers and as many as 1,232 police.[64] The peacekeepers face a daunting challenge: South Sudan, at 239,283 square miles, is comparable in size to France.

These conflicts show that the UN remains overstretched and underfunded despite the paeans to universal human rights norms and the international community's commitment to ending mass killing. They demonstrate, as well, that the fear of being dragged before the ICC doesn't dissuade those determined to kill.

Deterrence works best when such states, groups, or individuals conclude that they are certain to face serious consequences. But the chances that the leaders of states or the senior commanders of armies, insurgencies, and private militias will be apprehended and handed over to the ICC or ad hoc tribunals remain too slim to produce the fear required to safeguard people facing slaughter. The record of the ICTR is telling in this regard. Over a seven-year period, the Tribunal tried 26 individuals (another 26 trials are in progress), but the Rwandan government's estimates that 130,000 individuals committed atrocities in 1994. If so, the ICTR tried .002 percent of the likely offenders. And even if all the trials yet to be completed yield convictions, its success rate will be .004 percent.[65] Consider the ICC's capacity for deterrence in this light, bearing in mind that unlike the ad hoc tribunals it has a global writ.

Regimes that commit atrocities don't do so in a fit of irrationality or mindless sadism. They kill as part of a calculated effort to maintain power or to defeat adversaries; unofficial armed groups do so for the latter purpose as well as to gain compliance from the people inhabiting the territories under their control.[66] The conflicts to which they are party involve high stakes, which include political, even personal, survival. Add to that the long odds of ending up in the ICC's dock and it would be surprising were those prepared to employ mass killing as a political means to be daunted by the fear of an investigation or even an indictment by the Court.[67] Regimes and movements that murder en masse aren't run by individuals who lie awake at night fretting about their international reputation and legacy. If they conclude that mass killings will help preserve their grip on power, they will resort to them. And even assuming that they take into account the possibility of being apprehended and shipped off to the Court someday, they know that the Court's punishment cannot compare to the violence their victorious enemies are capable of visiting on them.[68] Unsurprisingly, most studies of the ICC's effectiveness in deterring atrocities conclude that it has been limited at best.[69] Even those who insist that the Court's existence has made a difference offer modest claims—largely unpersuasive ones at that.[70]

A number of countries have ratified the Rome Statute and have then signed additional agreements with the Court that obligate them to assist its work and to accord it jurisdiction when their own legal systems are unable to prosecute those accused of war crimes or crimes against humanity. But these countries are the ones least likely to perpetrate atrocities to begin with. Conversely, the countries that have spurned the Rome Statute are those most likely to do so. In short, the states that least need to be deterred are already part of the ICC; those that most need to be deterred are outside its jurisdiction, and only a referral by the Security Council can subject them to the Court's authority. The members of P-5, let us recall, have been known to protect their friends at the expense of justice.

The Upshot

To be successful to the degree its promoters desire, humanitarian intervention requires a robust, not "virtual," international community—one with shared norms and states committed to enforcing them, a strong spirit of common responsibility and obligation, and institutions that have the authority and resources required for protecting vulnerable people and punishing their tormentors and killers. The present international system lacks these attributes in sufficient strength. States, which remain the most consequential units in international politics, have divergent conceptions of justice and sovereignty, little desire to create institutions capable of holding them accountable, and no hesitation in subverting such treaties and institutions as do exist to stop atrocities. Humanitarian interventionists are convinced that a substantive international community exists already and that, occasional setbacks notwithstanding, it is becoming progressively stronger and more hospitable to their program. This amounts to a triumph of hope over reality.

CONCLUSION

In discussions with advocates of humanitarian interventionism I invariably encounter two questions. First, what do I propose other than standing by, arms akimbo, when ruthless regimes slaughter innocent people and show no inclination to cease, or when ethnic or religious strife within a country destroys countless lives, and the leadership, though unable to stop it, refuses outside help?

While we would all like to see an end to atrocities, I don't believe that a conclusive, comprehensive solution—applicable worldwide, based on universal agreement—is possible. R2P's architects certainly seek to offer one, but it won't work; nor will any others, present or prospective. Reaching global consensus on the when, how, and by whom of humanitarian intervention will prove impossible given the deep disagreements among countries on the political, legal, and ethical aspects of the doctrine.

True to the spirit of the Enlightenment, humanitarian interventionists, undaunted, assume that time, effort, and human ingenuity will overcome even the most intractable of problems. This optimism has been vindicated to an impressive extent in the realms of science and technology, and though history is in many respects a saga of progress, some age-old phenomena—the perpetration of mass atrocities among them—won't go the way of the horse and buggy. On the basis of copious statistics Steven Pinker assures us that the incidence of all forms of violence has fallen over the past several centuries.[1] Yet the fact remains that wars and atrocities persist and will not disappear.[2]

States may intervene to save people in other countries when they regard the hazards as bearable, and especially if intervention aligns with their practical aims. But they will not do so when leaders consider the costs and risks excessive or conclude that intervention would harm important national interests; they will watch people perish instead. This is the lesson of East Pakistan, Cambodia, Rwanda, Darfur, and Syria, which are not exceptions. Neither among citizens nor leaders, even in democracies, is fellow feeling, cosmopolitan sentiment, or ethical commitment sufficient to make the body count the criterion for intervention.

The second question supporters of humanitarian intervention ask concerns consistency. They believe I am misguided in criticizing the policy for lacking this quality. Even if there cannot be an intervention against every atrocity, they contend, states must be prepared to intervene and save lives when the circumstances permit.

Quite apart from the fact that I do not measure the humanitarian project's success using the yardstick of complete consistency, this defense in effect concedes that strategic realities will necessarily make interventions selective. Now, this pragmatism is certainly understandable, even desirable; the alternative, after all, is total recklessness. But it cannot be squared with the universalistic commitment to human rights that advocates of humanitarian intervention proudly point to as the quality that lends their project nobility and appeal.

What becomes of ethical principles and altruism when, in practice, intervention is hostage to many caveats, constraints, and exceptions? Nuclear-armed countries, non-nuclear states possessing substantial military power, states with powerful friends and allies, and countries ravaged by violence so messy that outsiders consider them quagmires are all off limits for intervention. Either interveners act with enough consistency to warrant the claim of universality, or there are so many contingent circumstances they must yield to that we revert to the retrograde realm of "reasons of state"—realism, if you will.[3] The latter outcome, however, would distress humanitarian interventionists deeply: realism represents the mode of thinking they most vehemently reject, seeing it as amoral at best, immoral at worst. At its core, theirs is an ethical enterprise, not one dominated by strategic calculations.

Humanitarian intervention faces another challenge: it generates mistrust, even cynicism in many parts of the world, in part because liberal democracies, the project's most ardent advocates, have not always honored the basic universal human rights norms that they themselves tout—and use to judge other countries. The United States violated the Convention on Torture after 9/11. Under presidents Bush and Obama, it imprisoned terrorism suspects without formally charging them or trying them in open courts. Even people cleared of terrorism charges remained in custody. The American "rendition" program forcibly transferred suspected terrorists to brutal regimes that were notorious for using torture. Other Western democracies also held terrorism suspects in the CIA's network of black sites or rendered them to regimes that practice torture. Yet none of these Western democracies has faced an investigation by an international body for violating human rights principles and treaties. Washington readily recognizes the International Criminal Court's authority over other countries, but steadfastly refuses to submit itself to the Court's jurisdiction and has even pressured states into guaranteeing that American soldiers or officials on their territory would never be remanded to the Court.

Washington's embrace of drones, particularly under President Obama, as the weapon of choice in the post-9/11 war against terrorism has also raised human rights questions, not least because these devices have been used for preventive (as opposed to preemptive) strikes, many, and according to some the majority, of which have been "signature strikes"—based on the behavior patterns of individuals rather than evidence tying them to terror attacks, past or planned.[4]

Finally, as we have seen, the democratic great powers most committed to stopping atrocities have been prepared, for strategic reasons, to support and do business (in the broad sense) with regimes that have done—and still do—a great many atrocious things.

At first blush, democracies' violations of human rights norms may appear to have no bearing on international attitudes toward humanitarian intervention. But because the project rests, ultimately, on an ethical foundation and the belief that in today's world all states are expected to respect human rights, its legitimacy suffers and cynicism thrives when the states that sanctify universal human rights and are expected to lead by example treat the most basic ones as expendable depending on the circumstances.

Humanitarian interventionists insist that their normative values have a strong appeal in democratic societies, indeed in the world at large.[5] That may be true in the abstract; no one would be surprised if democratic citizens were to tell a pollster that human beings everywhere have the fundamental right not to be killed arbitrarily. Yet as we have seen, it is a different matter when they are asked to opine on deploying their country's ground troops to save foreigners from massacre. It turns out that they don't have much enthusiasm for sending their soldiers off to die for missions of mercy. And leaders in democratic countries know that they won't lose much political capital if they refuse to authorize such interventions and may even increase their popularity at home.

Americans have a particular distaste for risky humanitarian interventions. That's why Clinton and Obama announced from the start that they would not send ground troops to Kosovo and Libya, respectively.

Michael Walzer, among others, finds this aversion to risking soldiers' lives disturbing and ethically problematic. When leaders contemplate intervention, Walzer notes, "They are not focused on the costs . . . to the men and women whose danger or suffering poses the question, but only on the costs to their own soldiers and to themselves, that is, to their political standing at home."[6] "Humanitarian interventions and peacekeeping operations," he adds, "are first of all military acts directed against people who are already using force, breaking the peace. They will be ineffective unless there is a willingness to accept the risks that naturally attach to military acts—to shed blood, to lose soldiers . . . Soldiers are not like Peace Corps volunteers or Fulbright scholars or USIA [US Information Agency] musicians and lecturers . . . Soldiers are destined for dangerous places, and they should know that (if they don't, they should be told)."[7] Walzer argues, convincingly, that interventions that rule out ground troops and rely on aircraft flying at high altitudes and missiles based far away prompt perpetrators to accelerate the killing and provide them more time to do so.

Similarly, Nicholas Wheeler asserts that "NATO should have been prepared to launch a ground intervention to rescue Kosovars rather than rely on an air campaign that posed low risks to NATO aircrew."[8] Wheeler sympathizes with leaders who must make "godlike consequentialist calculations" about how many of their soldiers can be sacrificed to protect foreigners and emphasizes that the likelihood of success and the proportionality between means and ends must be considered prior to an intervention.[9] In the end, however, he and Walzer reach the same conclusion. Both insist that the lives of soldiers from country X can and must sometimes be sacrificed to rescue people in country Y. As Wheeler, echoing Walzer, puts it, "When soldiers join the military, they accept an obligation to serve wherever they are sent by the government" and "governments should not be inhibited from undertaking humanitarian intervention because soldiers have not explicitly volunteered for such actions."[10]

It's easy to agree with Walzer and Wheeler if one has never held a gun, much less been shot at. But the moral requirement that soldiers' lives be risked during humanitarian interventions has far more serious implications for those sent to the battlefield than for the intellectuals who demand their deployment on ethical grounds. What's more, in countries such as the United States, where military service is not compulsory, soldiers tend to come from modest circumstances, not the ranks of the rich and privileged. This obliges those of us who will not be ordered to fight and die in wars to reflect on our secure status before devising ethical frameworks that could contribute to others' getting killed for principles we deem dear. Yes, soldiers enlist knowing that they may one day have to fight wars and possibly die doing so. But typically they reckon with this risk not for benevolent purposes or to enforce universal, rights-based principles but to defend their country, or simply because they need a job.

Thinkers such as Walzer and Wheeler seem to forget that only the United States has the capacity to mount and sustain distant military operations regularly and will therefore carry a particularly heavy burden if ground troops are used in humanitarian missions. As we have seen, even in Libya, where the United States handed off the air campaign to its NATO allies after conducting the initial series of strikes against Gaddafi's air defense network, the Europeans could not sustain their air and missile attacks without substantial US assistance, including such basics as aerial refueling and the replenishment of munitions.

This imbalance in military capacity within the alliance has a back-story and is not about to disappear. Despite American pressure on its NATO allies to increase defense spending to meet the alliance's benchmark of 2 percent of gross domestic product (GDP), the disparity in expenditures between them and the United States continues. In 2007 the United States devoted over 4 percent of its GDP to the military and in 2014 it allocated 3.7 percent. In 2007 only four of the other twenty-seven NATO members (Britain, Bulgaria, Greece, and France) had defense budgets that exceeded 2 percent of GDP, and only one (Greece) did so in 2014.[11] In 2007 twelve non-US NATO countries spent less than 1 percent of GDP on defense; in 2014 nineteen spent less than 1 percent. The United States covered 73 percent of the costs of keeping NATO running in 2014—an increase of five percentage points since 2007.[12] Moreover, Europeans are even charier about using military force than are Americans.[13]

The upshot is that—barring dramatic, and unlikely, changes in European defense expenditure patterns—American soldiers will have to make the biggest sacrifices if drawn-out air campaigns are dispensed with during humanitarian interventions and ground forces are deployed to hasten victory.

If we are serious about risking soldiers' lives to save people regardless of who they are and where they live, there are three possible ways to go about it. We could reinstitute the draft and make it clear to those in uniform that they may be dispatched to die not only for causes connected to the national interest but universal moral principles as well. The national debate provoked by such an enlistment policy would reveal just how much death citizens are prepared to accept in the name of universal norms.

The second choice is to create two classes of enlistees: those who serve to protect national interests—as defined by a given government—and those who fight to stop atrocities. Such a system would encounter practical problems yet would not be impossible to establish. And we would learn who truly believes in the intervention project.

Daniele Archibugi, a prominent representative of the cosmopolitan stream in philosophy, which has influenced thinking on various justice-related international issues, including humanitarian intervention, offers a third model.[14] It involves the creation of a central authority comprising representatives from all over the world that would determine the criteria for intervention.[15] This body would reach consensus on basic principles for interventions so that the missions would not be twisted to suit the practical interests of powerful states, or attacked by weak ones as window dressing for old-fashioned power politics. It would oversee "a permanent Rescue Army" trained for humanitarian interventions and civilians with expertise in postwar economic reconstruction, political reconciliation, and other necessary tasks. So as to create a truly international force, the Army's personnel would be drawn from different parts of the world. A global parliament chosen from an international "council of experts" and influential human rights NGOs would decide, on a case-by-case basis, the appropriateness and necessity of intervention; and the missions would be conducted with the understanding that soldiers' lives may be imperiled. The parliament would prohibit unilateral intervention. The UN Security Council, given its susceptibility to paralysis-by-veto, would be excluded from decisions on interventions, as would individual states, lest they shape, even subvert, missions to serve their selfish ends.

Archibugi's plan, while creative, is unworkable given the nature of present-day international politics. States will not surrender decision-making authority, especially on military matters, to a supranational organization to the degree his plan envisages. The Security Council's P-5 will not let a conclave of human rights activists and experts control humanitarian intervention; nor will the great powers relinquish the prerogative they now have to authorize, and to block, interventions. Few, if any, governments would agree to place their soldiers under the permanent command of international institutions dedicated to humanitarian intervention, and American leaders would certainly reject any proposal envisaging such an arrangement.

In essence, the sovereign states' proclivities and Archibugi's plan are irreconcilable. As William Smith concludes in a sympathetic evaluation of blueprints like Archibugi's, they "tend to focus more on the ways in which interventions would take place in a more cosmopolitan future than on the difficult normative questions posed by interventions in our non-cosmopolitan present."[16] For cosmopolitan humanitarian interventions to be feasible, the world must first become cosmopolitan. That is a distant prospect at best.

The humanitarian intervention project has identified a serious problem: the slaughter of innocent people, often by their own governments. But its solutions, most prominently the Responsibility to Protect, rest on untenable assumptions. The preponderance of evidence establishes that governments are unwilling to undertake concrete obligations to stop atrocities, that their interventions are highly selective, and that they are unwilling to risk their soldiers' lives to save outsiders.

Yet interventionists assure us that a normative consensus is gaining ground worldwide, that we are witnessing the rise of an international community constituted by shared normative values, not just the connections created by the flows of trade and finance and communications. This community, they tell us, is committed to ending mass atrocities and to constructing institutions capable of bringing perpetrators to book. But these sentiments, bonds, and institutions are not nearly as strong or consequential as we are led to believe.

Humanitarian interventionists are intoxicated by the grandeur and moralism of their transformative program. The resulting certitude, even hubris, makes them unmindful of the extent to which their doctrine arouses distrust in many parts of the world. They appear unmoved by the fact that many states are fearful of capricious interventions and that the great powers are unwilling to assume serious obligations to stop atrocities. They do not face up to the limited public support their enterprise garners even within democracies. Worse, they do not learn from the unintended consequences created by interventions. They are blithe about the costs of creating a stable postintervention order, cavalier about the complexities of remaking societies about which they often know little. They believe that history's moral progression, which their plan supposedly exemplifies, will eradicate one of the worst, yet durable, features of human behavior.

It is for these reasons that I speak of the conceit of humanitarian intervention.

NOTES

INTRODUCTION

1. Indeed, that is true for the entire twentith century. Benjamin Valentino, citing the studies of Rudolph Rummel and other scholars, notes that atrocities within states claimed between 50 and 150 million lives during that period while wars among states claimed 68 million. Valentino, "Final Solutions: The Causes of Mass Killing and Genocide," *Security Studies*, Vol. 3, No. 9 (2000), 1–2.
2. Katherine Hille and John Reed, "Moscow to Deploy 2,000 in Syria Air Base Mission's First Phase," *Financial Times*, September 21, 2015, www.ft.com/intl/cms/s/0/95971a4e-607d-11e5-a28b-50226830d644.html#axzz3mZdokVTm.
3. For details, see Samantha Power, *"A Problem from Hell": America in the Age of Genocide* (New York: HarperCollins, 2002), 171–226.

CHAPTER ONE

1. See Roberto Belloni, "The Problem with Humanitarianism," *Review of International Studies*, Vol. 33, No. 3 (July 2007), 451–455, on this point.
2. Michael Barnett, *Empire of Humanity: A History of Humanitarianism* (Ithaca, NY: Cornell University Press, 2011), 11.
3. I should specify here that although armed humanitarian intervention is a variant of humanitarian intervention, for the sake of brevity, I use the latter term to encompass the former.
4. Adam Smith, *Theory of Moral Sentiments* (New York: Penguin, 2009), 13–14.
5. Alasdair MacIntyre, "Is Patriotism a Virtue?" in Thomas Pogge and Keith Horton, eds., *Global Ethics: Seminal Essays*, Vol. II: Global Ethics (St. Paul, MN: Paragon House, 2008), 119–138. Originally published in 1984 as "Is Patriotism a Virtue?" The Lyndley Lecture at the University of Kansas by the University of Kansas Press.

6. Alasdair MacIntyre, "Is Patriotism a Virtue?" In a somewhat different vein, see Thomas Hurka, "The Justification of National Partiality," in Pogge and Horton, eds., *Global Ethics*, 379–403. Originally published in Robert McKim and Jeff McMahan, *The Morality of Nationalism* (New York: Oxford University Press, 1997), 139–157. For a nuanced defense of nationalism and its positive role in providing identity and community, see David Miller, *On Nationality* (Oxford: Oxford University Press, 1995).

7. Benjamin Barber, "Constitutional Faith," in Joshua Cohen, ed., *For Love of Country* (Boston, MA: Beacon Press, 1996), 30, 33–35.

8. A cogent survey of this debate, within the context of duties to the poor, can be found in Richard Miller, *Globalizing Justice: The Ethics of Poverty and Power* (New York: Oxford University Press), esp. Introduction and Chs. 1 and 2; Samuel Scheffler, "Families, Nations and Strangers," The Lindley Lecture, Department of Philosophy, University of Kansas, October 17, 1994, http://kuscholarworks.ku.edu/bitstream/handle/1808/12407/Families,%20Nations%20and%20Strangers-1994.pdf?sequence=1. On relationships among people and the obligations arising therefrom, see Samuel Scheffler, "Relations and Responsibilities," *Philosophy and Public Affairs*, Vo. 26, No. 2, (Summer 1997), 189–209.

9. For an insightful defense of cosmopolitanism in the context of human rights, see Toni Erskine, *Embedded Cosmopolitanism: Duties to Enemies and Strangers in a World of "Dislocated Communities"* (New York: Oxford University Press, for the British Academy, 2008).

10. Samuel Moyn, *The Last Utopia: Human Rights in History* (Cambridge, MA: Harvard University Press, 2010). Moyn has been criticized, even by those largely convinced by his thesis, for shortchanging earlier thinkers, novelists, and movements that contributed to the modern human rights movement and, in particular, for overlooking its Latin American antecedents. But his larger point—that it is hard to find a prior period in history in which human rights had the worldwide scope, transnational networks, and methods of organization that it acquired from the 1970s onward—still stands, in my opinion. For a sympathetic review of Moyn that makes the aforementioned criticisms, see Robin Blackburn, "Reclaiming Human Rights," *New Left Review*, Vol. 69 (May–June 2011), 126–138. For Moyn's response to such criticisms, see his "Of Deserts and Promised Lands: The Dream of Global Justice," *The Nation*, March 19, 2012, a review of Jenny Martinez, *The Slave Trade and the Origins of International Human Rights Law*, and Kathryn Sikkink, *The Justice Cascade: How Human Rights Prosecutions Are Changing World Politics.*

11. I am concerned here with the "classical realist" position rather than "neorealist" perspective. Neorealism reduces states' behavior to the constraints, vulnerabilities, opportunities, and predispositions that stem from their competition for relative advantages in power—using war as one means—in an anarchic international system, that is, one in which there is no central authority that is comparable to the state in national politics. There are no international institutions capable of maintaining order, enforcing laws, and protecting the weak from the strong. For two versions of neorealism, see Kenneth N. Waltz, *Theory of International Politics* (New York: McGraw-Hill, 1979) and John J. Mearsheimer, *The Tragedy of Great Power Politics*, Updated Edition (New York: Norton, 2014). Classical realism and neorealism reach compatible conclusions, though through different routes.

12. Reinhold Niebuhr, *Moral Man and Immoral Society* (New York: Scribner, 1960), esp. Introduction and Ch. 1; Niebuhr, *The Children of Light and the Children of*

Darkness (New York: Scribner, 1944), esp. Ch. 5; Hans Morgenthau, *Politics Among Nations: The Struggle for Power and Peace* (New York: Knopf, 1948); George F. Kennan, "Morality and Foreign Policy," *Foreign Affairs*, Vol. 64, No. 2 (Winter 1985/1986), 205–218.

13. On the normative dimension in realist thinking, see Richard Ned Lebow, *The Tragic Vision of Politics* (Cambridge: Cambridge University Press, 2003), esp. Ch. 6, "Hans J. Morgenthau," and Ch. 7, "The Wisdom of Classical Realism"; Udi Greenberg, *The Weimar Century: German Émigrés and the Ideological Foundations of the Cold War* (Princeton, NJ: Princeton University Press, 2014), Ch. 5, "From the League of Nations to Vietnam: Hans J. Morgenthau and the Realist Reform of International Relations." The charge of sidelining of moral considerations is more tenable when leveled against neorealists, such as Kenneth Waltz and John Mearsheimer.

14. E. H. Carr, *The Twenty Years' Crisis, 1919–1939: An Introduction to the Study of International Relations* (New York: Harper and Row, 1964), 91, 93.

15. Reinhold Niebuhr, "Ideology and the Scientific Method," in Robert McAfee Brown, ed., *The Essential Reinhold Niebuhr: Selected Essays and Addresses* (New Haven, CT: Yale University Press, 1986), Ch. 4, on the limits of knowledge, whether based on social science or ideologies.

16. Hans Morgenthau, *In Defense of the National Interest* (New York: Knopf, 1951), 35.

17. Kennan, "Morality and Foreign Policy," 206.

18. For the Melian Dialogue, see Robert B. Strassler, ed., *The Landmark Thucydides: A Comprehensive Guide to the Peloponnesian War* (New York: Free Press, 1996), 350–357.

19. Fernando Tesón, *Humanitarian Intervention* (Ardsley, NY: Transnational Publishers, 2005), 113–121, 223–225; Tesón, "Humanitarian Intervention: Loose Ends," *Journal of Military Ethics*, Vol. 10, No. 3 (2011), 199–206.

20. Thomas G. Weiss, *Humanitarian Intervention*, Second Edition (Cambridge: Polity Press, 2012), 8. The spread of norms related to the "Responsibility to Protect," is discussed in Michael Doyle, "International Ethics and the Responsibility to Protect," *International Studies Review*, Vol. 13, No. 1 (March 2011), 72–84. On ethical case for humanitarian intervention, see Terry Nardin, "The Moral Basis of Humanitarian Intervention," in Joel Rosenthal and Christian Barry, eds., *Ethics and International Affairs: A Reader* (Washington, DC: Georgetown University Press, 2009), 85–101.

21. Nardin, "The Moral Basis of Humanitarian Intervention," 90; Fernando Tesón, "Hugo Grotius on War and the State," The Liberty Fund, March 2014, http://oll. libertyfund.org/pages/lm-grotius; R. J. Vincent. "Grotius, Human Rights, and Intervention," in Hedley Bull, Benedict Kingsbury, and Adam Roberts, eds., *Hugo Grotius and International Relations* (Oxford: Oxford University Press, 1990), 241–256.

22. Martha Finnemore, *The Purpose of Intervention: Changing Beliefs About the Use of Force* (Ithaca, NY: Cornell University Press, 2003); Nicholas J. Wheeler, *Saving Strangers: Humanitarian Intervention and International Society* (Oxford: Oxford University Press, 2000), 4–11; Wheeler, "The Humanitarian Responsibilities of Sovereignty: Explaining the Development of a New Norm of Military Intervention in International Society," in Jennifer M. Welsh, *Humanitarian Intervention and International Relations* (Oxford: Oxford University Press, 2004), Ch. 3, esp. 29–41.

23. For a critique of the Melian model of politics and of realism more generally, see Michael Walzer, *Just and Unjust Wars: A Moral Argument With Historical Illustrations*, Second Edition (New York: Basic Books, 1977), Ch. 1. For an extended realist response

to Walzer, see David Hendrickson, "In Defense of Realism: A Commentary on Just and Unjust Wars," *Ethics and International Affairs*, Vol. 11, No. 1 (March 1997), 19–53. Wheeler, *Saving Strangers*, 27–33, responds to realist critiques of humanitarian intervention.

24. Tesón, *Humanitarian Intervention*, 61–95.

25. On the gap between the principle of sovereignty and the practices of states, see Stephen D. Krasner, *Sovereignty: Organized Hypocrisy* (Princeton, NJ: Princeton University Press, 1999).

26. Belloni, "The Trouble with Humanitarianism," 453. Emphasis in the original.

27. Allen Buchanan, "The Internal Legitimacy of Humanitarian Intervention," *Journal of Political Philosophy*, Vol. 7, No. 1 (March 1999), 71–87.

28. Jon Western and Joshua Goldstein, "Humanitarian Intervention Comes of Age: Lessons from Somalia to Libya," *Foreign Affairs*, Vol. 90, No. 6 (November/December 2011), 54.

29. German Marshall Fund of the United States, *Transatlantic Trends 2012* (Washington, DC: German Marshall Fund, 2012), 35.

30. Pew Research Center for People and the Press, "Public Wary of Military Intervention in Libya," March 14, 2011, www.people-press.org/2011/03/14/public-wary-of-military-intervention-in-libya/.

31. The public mood in the United States shifted in 2014, with a majority favoring the use of military force in Syria—but only against the Islamic State, which by then had created a state-within-a-state in parts of Syria and Iraq. Peter Moore, "One Year Later, Americans Back Military Action in Syria," YouGov.com, August 29, 2014, https://today.yougov.com/news/2014/08/29/military-action-syria/. In short, the change occurred not because of Assad's continued brutality or use of chemical weapons but because of the rise in Syria of an extremist movement that Americans deemed a threat to their safety. On the Syrian regime's use of chemical munitions, see Alice Ross and Shiv Malik, "Syrian Doctors to Show US Evidence of Assad's Use of Chemical Weapons," *Guardian*, June 16, 2015, www.theguardian.com/world/2015/jun/16/syria-assad-regime-is-weaponising-chlorine-us-congress-to-hear.

32. Herbert Butterfield, *The Whig Interpretation of History* (New York: Norton, 1965). As E. H. Carr pointed out, the degree to which historians see history as linear progress depends on the immediate circumstances of the society in which they reside and work; in crisis or decline, let alone disintegration, their propensity to see history as progress recedes. E. H. Carr, *What Is History?* (London: Penguin, 1961), 39–43 and Ch. 5.

33. Gareth Evans, *The Responsibility to Protect: Ending Mass Atrocity Crimes Once and for All* (Washington, DC: Brookings Institution Press, 2008).

34. Niebuhr, *Children of Light*, 7–17, 162–163; Michael Oakeshott, *Rationalism in Politics and Other Essays*, Expanded Edition (Indianapolis: Liberty Fund, 1991), Ch. 1.

35. John Gray, *The Silence of Animals: On Progress and Other Modern Myths* (New York: Farrar, Straus and Giroux, 2013), 75.

36. See, for example, Philip Rieff, *Freud: The Mind of a Moralist*, Third Edition (Chicago: University of Chicago Press, 1979), for instance, 248–250.

37. For a sampling of the evaluations made by some of the major architects of the war on its tenth anniversary, see "10 Years Later: The Architects of the Iraq War," MSNBC, March 13, 2013, www.msnbc.com/msnbc/10-years-later-the-architects-the-iraq-wa.

38. Thomas G. Weiss, "The Sunset of Humanitarian Intervention: The Responsibility to Protect in a Unipolar Era," *Security Dialogue*, Vol. 35, No. 2 (June 2004), 135–153.
39. Langdon Gilkey, *On Niebuhr: A Theological Study* (Chicago: University of Chicago Press, 2001), 105–109 (quote on 105). Niebuhr's warning about the perils of pride applied to its secular as well as its religious and moral manifestations. See, for example, Niebuhr, "The Christian Church in a Secular Age," in Brown, *The Essential Niebuhr*, Ch. 4.
40. This negative effect is noted by Eric A. Heinze, *Waging Humanitarian War: The Ethics, Law, and Politics of Humanitarian Intervention* (Albany: State University of New York Press, 2009), 124–125.
41. See, on this point, Tzvetan Todorov, "The Responsibility to Protect and the War in Libya," in Don E. Scheid, ed., *The Ethics of Armed Humanitarian Intervention* (Cambridge: Cambridge University Press, 2015), 46–58.

CHAPTER TWO

1. One of the most influential advocates for providing assistance without regard to boundaries—and to the point where giving more would impose significant hardship—is the philosopher Peter Singer, notably in "Famine, Affluence, and Morality," *Philosophy and Public Affairs*, Vol. 1, No. 3 (Spring 1972), 229–243. See also Larry S. Temkin, "Thinking About the Needy, Justice, and International Organizations," *Journal of Ethics*, Vol. 8, No. 4 (2004), 349–395.
2. Organization for Economic Cooperation and Development (OECD), "Official Development Assistance 2013," www.compareyourcountry.org/chart.php?project=oda&page=0&cr=oecd&lg=en; See also Anup Shah, "Foreign Aid for Development Assistance," *Global Issues*, www.globalissues.org/article/35/foreign-aid-development-assistance#ForeignAidNumbersinChartsandGraphs (page last updated on April 8, 2012).
3. Catherine Rampell, "Which Americans Are Most Generous, and to Whom?" *New York Times*, October 18, 2011, http://economix.blogs.nytimes.com/2011/10/18/which-americans-are-most-generous-and-to-whom/?_php=true&_type=blogs&_r=0; "Tax Deductions for American Charitable Donations Abroad," *The Becker-Posner Blog*, http://economix.blogs.nytimes.com/2011/10/18/which-americans-are-most-generous-and-to-whom/?_php=true&_type=blogs&_r=0; Shah, "Foreign Aid."
4. On the lack of strong public support in the United States for increasing foreign aid, see Kevin Robillard, "Poll: Most Only Want Foreign Aid Cuts," *Politico*, February 22, 2013, www.politico.com/story/2013/02/poll-most-only-want-foreign-aid-cuts-087948. For the argument that support for aid nevertheless remains high and that increases are opposed by the public chiefly because of an erroneous belief that it may constitute 10, or even close to 30, percent of federal spending as opposed to the actual figure, less than 1 percent in 2015, see Steven Kull, "Preserving American Support for Foreign Aid," *Brookings Blum Roundtable Policy Briefs*, Brookings Institution, September 2011, www.brookings.edu/~/media/research/files/reports/2011/9/global%20development/2011_blum_foreign_aid_kull.pdf. Even so, it turns out that once provided with the correct share of foreign aid in the national budget, only 28 percent of those polled in 2013 (by the Kaiser Family Foundation) favored an increase. (Americans under thirty years of age are markedly more inclined to support foreign aid increases than those

over fifty.) See Ezra Klein, "The Budget Myth That Just Won't Die: Americans Think That 28 Percent of the Budget Goes to Foreign Aid," *Washington Post*, November 7, 2013, www.washingtonpost.com/news/wonkblog/wp/2013/11/07/the-budget-myth-that-just-wont-die-americans-still-think-28-percent-of-the-budget-goes-to-foreign-aid/. This same tendency to overestimate, and by a large margin, official spending on aid is also evident in Europe and Australia; and support for it tends to correlate with public perceptions of whether economic inequality at home is increasing or decreasing. See Bina Fernandez, "The Politics of Foreign Aid for a Post-2015 Development Agenda: Political Parties and Public Opinion," *Global Policy Journal*, July 26, 2013, www.globalpolicyjournal.com/blog/26/07/2013/politics-foreign-aid-post-2015-development-agenda-political-parties-and-public-opini. Within the EU support for foreign aid is strong, though there are variations among countries. See European Commission, *Making a Difference in the World: Europeans and the Future of Development Aid* (Brussels: European Commission, September 2011), 8–12. The variations and nuances in public support for aid is separate from my argument here, which is that political leaders in wealthy countries do not emphasize increased spending for foreign aid in their political campaigns and do not suffer politically for failing to support increases in spending.

5. On this point, see William Easterly, *The Tyranny of Experts: Economists, Dictators, and the Forgotten Rights of the Poor* (New York: Basic Books, 2013).

6. Thomas Pogge, *World Poverty and Human Rights* (New York: Polity Press, 2008); Center for Global Development, "Commitment to Development Index 2013," www.cgdev.org/sites/default/files/CDI2013/cdi-brief-2013.html; Hans Peter Lankes, "Market Access for Developing Countries," *Finance and Development*, Vol. 39, No. 3 (2002), www.imf.org/external/pubs/ft/fandd/2002/09/lankes.htm; David Miller, *Globalizing Justice: The Ethics of Poverty and Power* (New York: Oxford University Press, 2010), 77–78; Organization for Economic Cooperation and Development (OECD), "The Doha Development Agenda: Tariffs and Trade," Policy Brief (August 2003), www.oecd.org/trade/tradedev/8920463.pdf; Claire Provost, "Foreign Aid Reaches Record High," *Guardian*, April 8, 2014, www.theguardian.com/global-development/2014/apr/08/foreign-aid-spending-developing-countries.

7. UNICEF, *Levels and Trends in Child Mortality: Report 2013* (New York: UNICEF: 2013), 1, 9–14; UNICEF, *State of the World's Children 2010* (New York: UNICEF, 2009), 17–19, www.unicef.org/rightsite/sowc/pdfs/SOWC_Spec%20Ed_CRC_Main%20Report_EN_090409.pdf; UNICEF, *State of the World's Children 2014* (New York: UNICEF, 2014), 8, www.unicef.org/sowc2014/numbers/documents/english/SOWC2014_In%20Numbers_28%20Jan.pdf. The 2010 report provides a figure of 25,000 for 2009.

8. On this limitation when it comes to theories and movements identified with universal human rights, see W. Spike Peterson, "Whose Rights: A Critique of Givens in Human Rights Discourse," *Alternatives*, Vol. 15, No. 3 (Summer 1990), 310–311. There are of course notable exceptions, as exemplified by the work of, for example, Henry Shue, Thomas Pogge, Amartya Sen, Larry Temkin, Martha Nussbaum, and Peter Singer.

9. On the tendency to forget the wider context and backdrop and the part played by the countries acting as rescuers and by international organizations such as the World Bank and IMF (through their austerity programs) in contributing to the upheavals that end in mass violence, see Anne Orford, *Reading Humanitarian Intervention: Human Rights and the Use of Force in International Law* (Cambridge: Cambridge

University Press, 2003), Ch. 3; Catherine Lu, *Just and Unjust Humanitarian Interventions in World Politics: Public and Private* (Basingstoke, UK: Palgrave Macmillan, 2006), 155–156.

10. Jack Goldsmith, "Liberal Democracy and Cosmopolitan Duty," *Stanford Law Review*, Vol. 55, No. 5 (May 2003), 1680–1682; Jack Goldsmith and Eric Posner, *The Limits of International Law* (New York: Oxford University Press, 2005), 213–215.

11. German Marshall Fund, Transatlantic Trends, "Survey: US, European, and Turkish Publics Oppose Intervention in Syrian Conflict, Favor Democracy Over Stability in MENA Region," http://trends.gmfus.org/survey-u-s-european-and-turkish-publics-oppose-intervention-in-syrian-conflict-favor-democracy-over-stability-in-mena-region/. The poll was conducted between June and July 2013. German Marshall Fund of the United States, *Transatlantic Trends 2013: Key Findings* (Washington, DC: German Marshall Fund, 2013), 31–32, http://trends.gmfus.org/files/2013/09/TT-Key-Findings-Report.pdf

12. "Poll: Public Supports Strikes in Iraq, Syria, Obama's Ratings Hover Near His All-Time Lows," *Washington Post*, September 9, 2014, www.washingtonpost.com/politics/poll-public-supports-strikes-in-iraq-syria-obamas-ratings-hover-near-his-all-time-lows/2014/09/08/69c164d8-3789-11e4-8601-97ba88884ffd_story.html; "Obama Authorizes Air Strikes in Syria," *Financial Times*, August 3, 2015, www.ft.com/cms/s/0/9eb93c54-3992-11e5-bbd1-b37bc06f590c.html#axzz3mCscPmGO.

13. Jan Egelund, "Where Is the Outrage on Syria?" *Guardian*, February 14, 2014, www.theguardian.com/commentisfree/2014/feb/14/syria-public-outrage-horrors.

14. For the poll results, see www.nytimes.com/interactive/2013/09/10/world/middleeast/poll-results-document.html?ref=middleeast. For a discussion of additional polls pointing to a similar opposition to taking military action in Syria, see Marc Lynch, "The Problem with #With Syria," *Washington Post*, March 14, 2014, www.washingtonpost.com/blogs/monkey-cage/wp/2014/03/14/the-problem-with-with-syria/.

15. See, for example, "Two Senators Say U.S. Should Arm Syrian Rebels," *New York Times*, February 19, 2012, and "Statement by Senators John McCain and Lindsey Graham on President Obama's Remarks on Syria," August 31, 2013, www.mccain.senate.gov/public/index.cfm/press-releases?ID=6b468513-b6c4-4d60-90c1-77112c75011b.

16. Samantha Power, *"A Problem from Hell": America and the Age of Genocide* (New York: HarperCollins: 2002), 85. See pp. 79–85 for her account of Proxmire's efforts.

17. For the text, see https://treaties.un.org/doc/Publication/UNTS/Volume%2078/volume-78-I-1021-English.pdf.

18. David Scheffer, "Lessons from the Rwandan Genocide," *Georgetown Journal of International Affairs* (Summer/Fall 2004), 125–132, www.hks.harvard.edu/~hepg/index.php/content/download/70274/1253906/version/1/file/LessonsFromRwandaGencoide.pdf.

19. The declassified text, obtained under a Freedom of Information Act filed by the National Security Archive, is available at www2.gwu.edu/~nsarchiv/NSAEBB/NSAEBB356/rw050194.pdf.

20. Luke Glanville, "The Responsibility to Protect Beyond Borders," *Human Rights Law Review*, Vol. 12, No. 1 (March 2012), 8.

21. "US Chose to Ignore Rwandan Genocide, *Guardian*," March 31, 2004. For the declassified original documents, see William Ferroggiaro, ed., "The US and the Genocide

in Rwanda 1994," National Security Archive, August 20, 2001, Documents 14, 15, and 16, www2.gwu.edu/~nsarchiv/NSAEBB/NSAEBB53/.

22. Alan J. Kuperman, "Rwanda in Retrospect," *Foreign Affairs*, Vol. 79, No. 1 (January/February 2000), 94–118. For a spirited rebuttal of Kuperman's thesis and a reply by him, see Alison L. Des Forges, "Alas We Knew [With Reply]," *Foreign Affairs*, Vol. 79, No. 3 (May/June 2000), 141–144.

23. Madeleine Albright, *Madam Secretary: A Memoir* (New York: Miramax Books, 2003), 190.

24. Bill Clinton, *My Life* (New York: Vintage, 2004), 593.

25. Albright, *Madam Secretary*, 191.

26. Albright, *Madam Secretary*, 194.

27. The text of the resolution (H.Con.Res 467), adopted on July 22, 2004, is available at www.congress.gov/bill/108th-congress/house-concurrent-resolution/467. The Senate did not pass the resolution.

28. Rebecca Hamilton, *Fighting for Darfur: Public Action and the Struggle to Stop Genocide* (New York: Palgrave Macmillan, 2011); Hamilton, "Inside Colin Powell's Decision to Declare Genocide in Darfur," *Atlantic*, August 17, 2011, www.theatlantic.com/international/archive/2011/08/inside-colin-powells-decision-to-declare-genocide-in-darfur/243560/. For the text of Taft's June 25, 2004 memo, see National Security Archive, www2.gwu.edu/~nsarchiv/NSAEBB/NSAEBB356/20040625_darfur.PDF. Article I of the Genocide states that genocide "is a crime under international law which they [the signatories] undertake to prevent and punish." For the text, see "Convention on the Prevention and Punishment of the Crime of Genocide," www.preventgenocide.org/law/convention/text.htm. The Convention was adopted by the UN General Assembly on December 9, 1948, and took effect on January 12, 1951.

29. Hamilton, *Fighting for Darfur*, 39, notes that while human rights groups hailed Powell's move, "Little did they know how insulated Powell's decision had been from the rest of the U.S. government."

30. "Bolton Voices Opposition to UN Proposals," *Washington Post*, September 1, 2005, www.washingtonpost.com/wp-dyn/content/article/2005/08/31/AR2005083102309.html; Luke Glanville, "The Responsibility to Protect Beyond Borders," *Human Rights Law Review*, Vol. 12, No. 1 (March 2012), 12–13.

31. For the text, see www.humanrightsvoices.org/assets/attachments/documents/bolton_responsibility_to_protect.pdf.

CHAPTER THREE

1. For details, see, for example, Gary J. Bass, *The Blood Telegram: Nixon, Kissinger, and a Forgotten Genocide* (New York: Knopf, 2013); Srinath Raghavan, *1971: A Global History of the Creation of Bangladesh* (Cambridge, MA: Harvard University Press, 2013); and Rounaq Jahan, "Genocide in Bangladesh," in Samuel Totten and William S. Parsons, eds., *Genocide: Essays and Eyewitness Accounts*, Fourth Edition (New York: Routledge, 2013), 249–78. As for the number of deaths, the official Pakistani estimate is 26,000, the Indian government's one million. Jahan, 249, puts the figure at three million, which is also the one officially claimed by Bangladesh. Bass, 350–351 (fn. 6), deems the official Indian and Bangladeshi estimates to be "inflated" and cites other studies whose estimates range from 269,000 to 500,000. My formulation of the death toll reflects the lack of agreement on the precise number of people who

were killed and the desire to avoid the lowest and highest estimates and to settle on the most commonly accepted figure, and then too as an approximation.

2. Nicholas Wheeler, *Saving Strangers: Humanitarian Intervention in International Society* (Oxford: Oxford University Press, 2000), 58.

3. Bass, *Blood Telegram*, 291–295, 306–316.

4. On the policies of the Khmer Rouge that led to the deaths of so many Cambodians and the regime's assault against ethnic and religious minorities (Vietnamese, the Muslim Cham, and Buddhist monks), see Ben Kiernan, *Blood and Soil: A World History of Genocide and Extermination from Sparta to Darfur* (New Haven, CT: Yale University Press, 2007), 540–554, and Kiernan, "Documentation Delayed: The Historiography of the Cambodian Genocide," in Dan Stone, ed., *The Historiography of Genocide* (New York: Palgrave Macmillan, 2010), esp. 474–479.

5. After 1982, the Khmer Rouge occupied the UN seat as part of a coalition with two noncommunist parties, but held the dominant hand, politically and militarily, their partners being smaller and weaker. This arrangement produced the "Coalition of Democratic Kampuchea," but as the renowned historian of Cambodia Ben Kiernan put it, "it was neither a real coalition, nor a government, nor democratic, nor in Cambodia!" Ben Kiernan, "Cambodia's Twisted Path to Justice," *The History Place: Points of View*, 1992, www.historyplace.com/pointsofview/kiernan.htm. The coalition was largely a cosmetic change engineered by the United States and China amid the growing criticism of their continued support for the Khmer Rouge. See John Pilger, "How Thatcher Gave Pol Pot a Hand," *New Statesman*, April 17, 2000, www.newstatesman.com/politics/politics/2014/04/how-thatcher-gave-pol-pot-hand.

6. Stephen Erlanger, "Khmer Rouge Get More China Arms," *New York Times*, January 1, 1991; Robert Pear, "US Says China Sent Large Arms to Khmer Rouge," *New York Times*, May 1, 1990; Puangthong Rungswasdisab, "Thailand's Response to the Cambodian Genocide," Cambodian Genocide Program, Yale University, 2010, www.yale.edu/cgp/thailand_response.html; On Brzezinski's revelations to Becker, see Elizabeth Becker, *When the War Was Over: Cambodia and the Khmer Rouge Revolution*, Revised Edition (New York: PublicAffairs, 1998), 435.

7. Pilger, "How Thatcher Gave Pol Pot a Hand"; "Butcher of Cambodia Set to Expose Thatcher's Role," *Guardian*, January 8, 2000, www.theguardian.com/world/2000/jan/09/cambodia.

8. Mona Fixdal and Dan Smith, "Humanitarian Intervention and Just War," *Mershon International Studies Review*, Vol. 42, No. 2 (November 1998), 283–312: Gordon Graham, *Ethics and International Relations*, Second Edition (Malden, MA: Blackwell, 2008), 113–116.

9. Michael Walzer, *Just and Unjust Wars: A Moral Argument with Historical Illustrations*, Second Edition (New York: Basic Books, 1977).

10. Michael Walzer, "The Moral Standing of States: A Response to Four Critics," *Philosophy and Public Affairs*, Vol. 9, No. 2 (Winter, 1980), 212.

11. Walzer, *Just and Unjust Wars*, 87; John Stuart Mill, "A Few Words on Non-Intervention," *Fraser's Magazine* (December 1859), reprinted in *New England Review*, Vol. 27, No. 3 (2006), 252–264.

12. Walzer, *Just and Unjust Wars*, 89.

13. Walzer, "Moral Standing of States," 214.

14. Walzer, *Just and Unjust Wars*, 105–108; Walzer, "The Politics of Rescue," *Social Research*, Vol. 61, No. 1 (Spring 1995), 55–56; Walzer, "A Foreign Policy for the Left,"

Dissent (Spring 2014), www.dissentmagazine.org/article/a-foreign-policy-for-the-left; Briand Orend, *The Morality of War* (Peterborough, ON: Broadview Press, 2006), 90–96, offers a superb summary of Walzer's views on humanitarian intervention.

15. Walzer, "Politics of Rescue," 58–60.

16. Charles Krauthammer, "Immaculate Intervention," *Time*, July 26, 2003.

17. See John Langan, "The Elements of St. Augustine's Just War Theory," *Journal of Religious Ethics*, Vol. 12, No. 1 (Spring 1984), 19–38: Darrell Cole, "St. Thomas Aquinas on Virtuous Warfare," *Journal of Religious Ethics*, Vol. 27, No. 1 (Spring 1997), 57–80.

18. James D. Fearon, "Ethnic and Cultural Diversity by Country," *Journal of Economic Growth*, Vol. 8, No. 2 (June 2003), 205.

19. Walzer, *Just and Unjust Wars*, 90.

20. John Rawls, *The Law of Peoples* (Cambridge, MA: Harvard University Press, 1999), 82–85. Rawls and Walzer represent different political traditions, but on humanitarian intervention and the question of what counts when it comes to states' legitimacy, they share some common ground.

21. Rawls, *Law of Peoples*, 4, 80–81, 93. For a discussion of Rawls on this point, see Henry Shue, "Rawls and the Outlaws," *Politics Philosophy Economics*, Vol. I, No. 3 (October 2002), 307–323.

22. Rawls, *Law of Peoples*, 81.

23. Fernando Tesón, *A Philosophy of International Law* (Boulder, CO: Westview Press, 1998), 39, 40. See the second chapter, "Sovereignty and Intervention," for a full account of what Tesón labels his "Kantian" perspective on international law generally and humanitarian intervention specifically.

24. Thomas Pogge, "An Institutional Approach to Humanitarian Intervention," *Public Affairs Quarterly*, Vol. 6, No. 1 (January, 1992), 93–95.

25. David Luban, "Just War and Human Rights," *Philosophy and Public Affairs*, Vol. 9, No. 2 (Winter 1980), 165.

26. Gerald Doppelt, "Walzer's Theory of Morality in International Affairs," *Philosophy and Public Affairs*," Vol. 8, No. 1 (Autumn 1978), 10. Emphasis in the original.

27. Tesón, *A Philosophy*, 44.

28. For a nuanced reading of Walzer that takes account his distinction between the political community and the state but nevertheless concludes that he privileges the state by framing interventions in military terms, thus giving short shrift to other forms of external intervention that may be feasible and appropriate, see Catherine Lu, *Just and Unjust Interventions in World Politics* (Basingstoke, UK: Palgrave Macmillan, 2006),

29. Doppelt, "Walzer's Theory," 7.

30. Luban, "Just War," 174–175.

31. Luban, "Just War," 177.

32. Anne-Marie Slaughter, "A Liberal Theory of International Law," *Proceedings of the Annual Meeting (American Society of International Law)*, Vol. 94 (April 5–8, 2000), 240–253.

33. Slaughter, "Liberal Theory," 240.

34. Slaughter, "Liberal Theory," 240.

35. Slaughter, "Liberal Theory," 240.

36. See, for example, Geoffrey Robertson, *Crimes Against Humanity: The Struggle for Global Justice*, Fourth Edition (New York: New Press, 2012), 444–445, 412–418,

741–742; Ken Booth, "Human Wrongs and International Relations," *International Affairs*, Vol. 71, No. 1 (January 1995), 103–126; Andrew Linklater, "Citizenship and Sovereignty in the Post-Westphalian State," *European Journal of International Relations*, Vol. 2, No. 1 (March 1996), esp. 98–99; for a critical survey of the antisovereignty literature and a qualified defense of sovereignty, see Martti Koskenniemi, "What Use for Sovereignty Today?" *Asian Journal of International Law*, No. 1 (2011), 61–70, www.helsinki.fi/eci/Publications/What%20use%20for%20Sovereignty-.pdf.

37. Charles R. Beitz, Political Theory and International Relations (Princeton: Princeton University Press, 1979), 90.

38. Beitz, *Political Theory*, 90–91.

39. Aryeh Neier, *The International Human Rights Movement: A History* (Princeton, NJ: Princeton University Press, 2012), 312. Neier notes, "In that era, humanitarian grounds were not recognized as an acceptable basis for entering into a military conflict. The concept was particularly unwelcome in Africa, where many states were still ruled by elites that had taken part in the struggle to end colonial rule and who knew that their former masters had often justified their actions on humanitarian grounds." See also Anne Orford, "Moral Internationalism and the Responsibility to Protect," *European Journal of International Law*, Vol. 24, No. 1 (February 2013), 93–94.

40. Tanzanian president Julius Nyerere did call attention to Amin's brutalities, but Nyerere justified Tanzania's war not on the grounds that it was a humanitarian intervention but rather a defense against aggression. For details on the 1978–1979 war between Uganda and Tanzania and Nyerere's defense of Tanzania's actions, see Daniel G. Acheson-Brown, "The Tanzanian Invasion of Uganda: A Just War?" *International Third World Studies Journal and Review*, Vol. XII (2001), 1–11. See also Wheeler, *Saving Strangers*, Ch. 5, "Good or Bad Precedent? Tanzania's Intervention in Uganda"; Sean Murphy, *Humanitarian Intervention: The United Nations in an Evolving World Order* (Philadelphia: University of Pennsylvania Press, 1996), 105–107.

41. Terence Lyons, "Can Neighbors Help? Regional Actors and African Conflict Management," in Francis Deng and Terence Lyons, eds., *African Reckoning: The Quest for Good Governance* (Washington, DC: Brookings Institution, 1998), 74–75.

42. "OAU Charter," www.au.int/en/sites/default/files/OAU_Charter_1963_0.pdf.

43. This provision is contained in Article 4 (h) of the AU's Constitutive Act. The text of the Constitutive Act is available at www.au.int/en/sites/default/files/ConstitutiveAct_EN.pdf.

44. See Benjamin Valentino, *Final Solutions: Mass Killing and Genocide in the 20th Century* (Ithaca, NY: Cornell University Press, 2005). For a shorter and early version of his argument, see Valentino, "Final Solutions: The Causes of Mass Killing and Genocide," *Security Studies*, Vol. 9, No. 3 (Spring 2000), 1–59.

45. David Chandler, *From Kosovo to Kabul: Human Rights and International Intervention* (London: Pluto Press, 2005), 160–186, 193–198.

46. Chandler, *From Kosovo to Kabul*, 155.

CHAPTER FOUR

1. Katharina Remshardt, "Under What Circumstances Has the UN Been Able to Use Its Chapter VII Powers," *E-International Relations*, November 13, 2010, www.e-ir.info/2010/11/13/under-what-conditions-has-the-un-been-able-to-use-its-chapter-vii-powers/.

2. "Charter of the United Nations," www.un.org/en/documents/charter/. All citations to the Charter in this chapter are from this text.

3. On this point see Aidan Hehir, *Humanitarian Intervention After Kosovo: Iraq, Darfur, and the Record of Global Civil Society* (New York: Palgrave, 2008), 20. Hehir notes, "the inconsistency of application, the lack of explicit legal authorization and the reluctance to set a precedent militate when used militates [sic] against the provisions of Chapter VII constituting legal legitimacy for humanitarian intervention, but certainly does not prevent such designations."

4. Fernando Tesón, *A Philosophy of International Law* (Boulder, CO: Westview Press, 1998).

5. Philip Bobbitt, "A Premier League for Democracy?" *Prospect*, November 23, 2008, www.prospectmagazine.co.uk/magazine/apremierleaguefordemocracy/; Geoffrey Robertson, *Crimes Against Humanity: The Struggle for Global Justice* (New York: New Press, 1999), 447 (this prescription is absent from the subsequent editions of Robertson's book); Robert Kagan, "A Case for a League of Democracies," *Financial Times*, May 13, 2008, www.ft.com/intl/cms/s/0/f62a02ce-20eb-11dd-a0e6-000077b07658.html#axzz2zXCXd6xe; Ivo Daalder and James Lindsay, "Democracies of the World, Unite," *American Interest*, January 1, 2007, www.the-american-interest.com/articles/2007/01/01/democracies-of-the-world-unite/; John McCain, "An Enduring Peace Built on Freedom," speech at the Hoover Institution, Palo Alto, California, May 1, 2007, text available at http://media.hoover.org/sites/default/files/documents/McCain_05-01-07.pdf; G. John Ikenberry and Anne-Marie Slaughter, "Forging a World of Liberty Under Law," *Princeton Project Papers*, September 27, 2006, www.princeton.edu/~ppns/report/FinalReport.pdf.

6. Hitler's attempts to legitimize his expansionist agenda by claiming that Germans in Austria and Czechoslovakia deserved the democratic right of self-determination (which to him meant becoming part of Germany) were seen as a ruse; but the intent of those who drafted the UN Charter was to prevent this claim, even if spurious, from being used in the future to legitimize naked power plays.

7. Ian Brownlie, "Thoughts on Kind-Hearted Gunmen," in Richard B. Lilich, ed., *Humanitarian Intervention and the United Nations* (Charlottesville, VA: University of Virginia Press, 1973), 143.

8. Thomas Franck, "Interpretation and Change in the Law of Humanitarian Intervention," in J. L. Holzgrefe and Robert O. Keohane, eds., *Humanitarian Intervention: Ethical, Legal, and Political Dilemmas* (Cambridge: Cambridge University Press, 2003).

9. Mary Ellen O'Connell, "Regulating the Use of Force in the 21st Century: The Continuing Importance of State Autonomy," *Columbia Journal of Transnational* Law, Vol. 36, Nos. 1&2 (1998), 477.

10. Louis Henkin, "Kosovo and the Law of 'Humanitarian Intervention'," *American Journal of International Law*, Vol. 93, No. 4 (October 1999), 825–828.

11. Hehir, *Humanitarian Intervention After Kosovo*, 20–22, 24.

12. Michael Glennon, *Limits of Law, Prerogatives of Power: Interventionism After Kosovo* (New York: Palgrave, 2001), 19–35.

13. Anthony D'Amato, "The Invasion of Panama Was a Lawful Response to Tyranny," *American Journal of International Law*, Vol. 84, No. 2 (1990), 516–524.

14. See Anne-Sophie Massa, "Does Humanitarian Intervention Serve Human Rights?" *Amsterdam Law Forum*, Vol. 1, No. 2 (2009), 51–52, http://amsterdamlawforum.org/article/view/63/90.

15. For an extended defense of nonintervention and the principle's importance for international order and justice, which includes a discussion of ex-colonial states' concerns, see Hehir, *Humanitarian Intervention After Kosovo*, 25–32.

16. "Bush and Noriega: Examining their Ties," *New York Times*, September 28, 1988; "Manuel Noriega—From U.S. Friend to Foe," *Guardian*, April 27, 2010; "Noriega's Ties With the CIA," *Seattle Times*, January 7, 1990, http://community.seattletimes. nwsource.com/archive/?date=19900107&slug=1049476. For a comprehensive history of US relations with Panama that contains revealing details on Washington's dealing with Noriega, see Luis E. Murillo, *The Noriega Mess: The Drugs, The Canal, and Why the US Invaded* (Berkeley, CA: Video Books, 1995).

17. "The Contras, Cocaine, and Covert Operations," National Security Archive, "Electronic Briefing Book No. 2," www2.gwu.edu/~nsarchiv/NSAEBB/NSAEBB2/ nsaebb2.htm#3a.

18. Grenada, a former British colony, gained its independence in 1974. In March 1979, the leftist New Jewel Movement (NJM) led by Prime Minister Maurice Bishop seized power. The United States and the Bishop government got off to a rocky start. But the relationship deteriorated following Bishop's murder in October 1983 by a radical faction within the NJM led by Bernard Coard and Hudson Austin. The US government's explanations for the necessity of the 1983 invasion remain unconvincing. Neither the Grenadian government nor its Cuban advisers attempted to block the evacuation of the medical students. The school's administrators did not report that any threats had been made to harm or detain the students. Although much was made of the massive flow of Soviet and arms to Grenada, the weapons certainly existed but not the massive arsenal that Washington implied in its statements. And the White House's estimates of the number of Cuban troops and military advisers in Grenada in relation to Cubans who were involved in construction kept fluctuating. As for the 10,000-foot runway that the Soviets and Cubans were building for military purposes, American and British companies were involved in the project, which was funded by Algeria, Canada, Mexico, and Venezuela; and the World Bank had encouraged it, along with a new airport, to boost tourism to Grenada. Other Caribbean countries (including Aruba, Antigua, and Curacao) already possessed runways of comparable length. See Stephen Zunes, "US Invasion of Grenada: A 30 Year Retrospective," *Truthout*, October 23, 2013, www.truth-out.org/news/item/ 19551-us-invasion-of-grenada-a-30-year-retrospective#; "Briefing: Touching Down in Grenada," *New York Times*, March 26, 1983, www.nytimes.com/1983/03/26/us/briefing-058430.html; "The Reasons for Invading," *New York Times*, November 1, 1983, www.nytimes.com/1983/11/01/world/the-reason-for-invading.html.

19. W. Michael Reisman, "Unilateral Action and the Transformations of the World Constitutive Process: The Special Problem of Humanitarian Intervention," *European Journal of International Law*, Vol. 11, No. 1 (2000), 3–18.

20. Michael J. Glennon, "The New Interventionism: The Search for a Just International Law," *Foreign Affairs*, Vol. 78, No. 3 (May/June 1999), 2–7.

21. Reisman, "Unilateral Action," 13–17.

22. Glennon, "New Interventionism," 7.

23. Glennon, "New Interventionism," 7.

24. Simon Chesterman, *Just War or Just Peace? Humanitarian Intervention and International Law* (Oxford: Oxford University Press, 2001). The lack of universal consensus on humanitarian intervention over the ages, including currently, on occasions when it is conducted outside the UN, is a major theme in Chesterman's book.

25. Chesterman, *Just War*, 220.

26. Glennon, *Limits of Law*, 81. Emphasis in the original. On the barriers to arriving at a common understanding, based on principles presented as universal, on the legal bases for humanitarian intervention in a culturally and politically diverse world, see Alfred P. Rubin, "Humanitarian Intervention and International Law," in Aleksandar Jokic and Burleigh Williams, *Humanitarian Intervention: Moral and Philosophical Issues* (Peterborough, ON: Broadview Press, 2003), esp. 109–113.

27. Ryan Goodman, "Humanitarian Intervention and Pretexts for War," *American Journal of International Law*, Vol. 100, No. 1 (January 2006), 107–141. For a critical assessment of Goodman's argument, see Clemens E. Ziegler, "Humanitarian Intervention and Pretexts for War: A Critique of Ryan Goodman," *Hanse Law Review*, Vol. 5, No. 2 (2009), 177–194. www.hanselawreview.org/pdf8/Vol5No2Art03.pdf

28. For COW data see www.correlatesofwar.org/.

29. Tesón, *Humanitarian Intervention*, 108–113.

30. Tesón, *Humanitarian Intervention*, 111.

31. Tesón, *Humanitarian Intervention*, 112.

32. Tesón, *Humanitarian Intervention*, 127. Emphasis in the original.

33. Bruno Simma, "NATO, the UN and the Use of Force," *European Journal of International Law*, Vol. 10, No. 1 (1999), 1–22.

34. Jürgen Habermas, "Bestiality and Humanity: A War on the Border Between Legality and Morality," *Constellations*, Vol. 6, No. 3 (September 1999), 263–272. This essay was first published in German in *Die Zeit*, April 29, 1999, www.zeit.de/1999/18/199918.krieg_.xml; *The Kosovo Report: Conflict, International Response, Lessons Learned* (Oxford: Oxford University Press, 2000), 4, 164–165. On the distinction, informed by Hannah Arendt's *On Violence*, between what is justified (morally) and legitimate (legally), see Iris Marion Young, "Violence Against Power: Critical Thoughts on Military Intervention," in Deen K. Chatterjee and Don E. Scheid, eds., *Ethics and Foreign Intervention* (Cambridge: Cambridge University Press, 2003), 258–263.

35. Allen Buchanan, "From Nuremberg to Kosovo: The Morality of International Legal Reform," *Ethics*, Vol. 111, No. 4 (July 2001), 673–705.

36. Buchanan, "Nuremberg to Kosovo," 680–682.

37. Buchanan, "Nuremberg to Kosovo," 687–689.

38. Buchanan, "Nuremberg to Kosovo," 675, 680, 682–688; Tesón, *Humanitarian Intervention*, 12–18.

39. Thomas Franck, "Interpretation and Change in the Law of Humanitarian Intervention," in Holzgrefe and Keohane, *Humanitarian Intervention*, 205–213, 227–230.

40. Michael Byers and Simon Chesterman, "Changing the Rules About Rules: Humanitarian Intervention and the Future of International Law," in Holzgrefe and Keohane, *Humanitarian Intervention*, 187–194. I draw on their argument here.

41. China, India, and South Africa are G-77 members. See the G-77 "Ministerial Declaration" of September 24, 1999, paragraph 69, in which the group "rejected the so-called right of humanitarian intervention, which had no basis in the UN Charter or in international law." For the text, see www.g77.org/doc/Decl1999.html.

42. Byers and Chesterman, "Changing the Rules," 183–185, 190–191; Brian Lepard, *Rethinking Humanitarian Intervention: A Fresh Legal Approach Based on Fundamental Ethical Principles in International Law and World Religions* (University Park: Penn State University Press, 2002), 337–338, 340–341, 351–353; Glennon, *Limits of Law*,

157–162. The texts of these resolutions can be found at www.un.org/documents/resga.htm.

43. See, for example, Jack L. Goldsmith and Eric A. Posner, "A Theory of Customary International Law," *University of Chicago Law Review*, Vol. 66, No. 4 (Autumn 1999), 1113–1177; Detlev F. Vagts, "International Relations Looks at Customary Law: A Traditionalist's Defense," *European Journal of International Law*, Vol. 15, No. 5 (2004), 1031–1040; Mark A. Chinen, "Game Theory and Customary International Law: A Response to Professors Goldsmith and Posner," *Michigan Journal of International Law*, Vol. 23, No. 191 (Fall 2001), 143–189; Jack Goldsmith and Eric Posner, "Further Thoughts on Customary International Law," *Michigan Journal of International Law*, Vol. 23, No, 191 (Fall 2001), 191–200.

44. Goldsmith and Posner, "A Theory of Customary International Law," 1122–1128. They provide an additional motive: the desire, arising from the self-interest of states, to coordinate and to arrive at rules that provide for predictable behavior.

45. Goldsmith and Posner, "A Theory of Customary International Law," 1172–1176.

46. Ian Hurd, "Is Humanitarian Intervention Legal? The Rule of Law in an Incoherent World," *Ethics and International Affairs*, Vol. 29, No. 3 (2011), 307–311.

47. For the Russian government's invocation of R2P and a critique, see "Georgia-Russia Crisis and RtoP," International Coalition for the Responsibility to Protect, n.d., www.responsibilitytoprotect.org/index.php/crises/178-other-rtop-concerns/2749-the-crisis-in-georgia-russia.

CHAPTER FIVE

1. See, for example, Gary J. Bass, *Freedom's Battle: The Origins of Humanitarian Intervention* (New York: Vintage, 2008), and Martha Finnemore, *The Purpose of Intervention: Changing Beliefs About the Use of Force* (Ithaca, NY: Cornell University Press, 2003), esp. 58–66. For a critical appraisal of the effort to portray the European interventions as humanitarian, see Samuel Moyn's review of Bass's book: "Spectacular Wrongs," *Nation*, November 24, 2008.

2. Many excellent books discuss the rise and decline of the Empire, including Donald Quataert, *The Ottoman Empire, 1700–1922* (New York: Cambridge University Press, 2000), and Lord Kinross, *The Ottoman Centuries: The Rise and Fall of the Turkish Empire* (New York: Quill, 1977).

3. This process is well described by Ronald G. Suny in the course of presenting his nuanced account of the Armenian Genocide. See Suny, *"They Can Live in the Desert but Nowhere Else": A History of the Armenian Genocide* (Princeton, NJ: Princeton University Press, 2015), esp. Ch. 4, "Great Powers."

4. See the excellent account, from which I draw, of Matthias Schulz, "The Guarantees of Humanity: The Concert of Europe and the Origins of the Russo-Ottoman War of 1877," in Brendan Simms and D.J.B. Trimms, eds., *Humanitarian Intervention: A History* (Cambridge: Cambridge University Press, 2011), 184–204.

5. Schulz, "Guarantees of Humanity," 203–204.

6. See Davide Rodogno, *Against Massacre: Humanitarian Intervention in the Ottoman Empire 1815–1914* (Princeton, NJ: Princeton University Press, 2012), 65–66. On violence against Ottoman Muslims in the Empire's Balkan provinces and the resulting refugee exodus, see Suny, *"They Can Live in the Desert,"* 183–187. See also, Berna Pekesen, "Expulsion and Emigration of the Muslims from the Balkans," European

History Online, July 3, 2012, http://ieg-ego.eu/en/threads/europe-on-the-road/forced-ethnic-migration/berna-pekesen-expulsion-and-emigration-of-the-muslims-from-the-balkans. Finnemore, *Purpose* (58), writes in relation to the violence in Greece that "massacring Christians was a humanitarian disaster; massacring Muslims was not." She adds that "the European Powers were impressed only by the murder of Muslims …."(60). But she then fails to square this with her argument about the power of humanitarian norms and in fact concedes that there was a "circumscribed definition of who was 'human' in the nineteenth-century conception" (59).

7. Although the precise number of deaths and deportations that occurred during Russia's North Caucasus war is disputed and may never be known, Austin Jersild offers a careful estimate in *Orientalism and Empire: North Caucasus Mountain People and the Georgian Frontier* (Montreal: McGill-Queens University Press, 2003), 23–28. See also Walter Richmond, *The Circassian Genocide* (New Brunswick, NJ: Rutgers University Press, 2013), and Rutgers University (Newark), Center for the Study of Genocide and Human Rights, "The Mid-Nineteenth Century Genocidal 'Pacification' of the Circassians in the Russian Caucasus," n.d., www.ncas.rutgers.edu/center-study-genocide-conflict-resolution-and-human-rights/mid-nineteenth-century-genocidal-pacifica.

8. Finnemore, *Purpose*, 70–71, saves her thesis about the power of humanitarian norms in the use of military force by arguing that many colonizers believed they were bringing progress to backward people and indeed making them truly human, that that attitude later changed, and that colonized themselves eventually used liberal principles to demand freedom. But selective humanitarianism is an odd concept.

9. Adam Jones, *Genocide: A Comprehensive Introduction*, Second Edition (New York: Routledge, 2011), 70.

10. A vivid account of imperial Belgian rule in the Congo is provided by Adam Hochschild, *King Leopold's Ghost: A Story of Greed, Terror and Heroism in Africa* (Boston: Houghton Mifflin, 1998); Dominik Schaller, "Genocide and Mass Violence in the 'Heart of Darkness'," in Donald Bloxham and A. Dirk Moses, eds., *Oxford Handbook of Genocide Studies* (Oxford: Oxford University Press, 2010), 362. See also the report on the documentary "White King, Red Rubber, Black Death," in *BBC News*, "King Leopold's Legacy of DR Congo Violence," February 24, 2004, http://news.bbc.co.uk/2/hi/africa/3516965.stm. The documentary is available at www.youtube.com/watch?v=aUZLtkLAoVE. Finally, in 2002, Belgium's Museum of the Belgian Congo commissioned an inquiry by a panel of historians. Andrew Osborn, "Belgium Confronts Its Colonial Demons," *Guardian*, July 18, 2002, www.theguardian.com/world/2002/jul/18/congo.andrewosborn.

11. Rodogno, *Against Massacre*, 11–12. Also see 32–33 on this point.

12. Rodogno, *Against Massacre*, 21–22, 48–54.

13. On the spread of human rights norms, see Kathryn Sikkink, *The Justice Cascade: How Human Rights Prosecutions and Changing the World* (New York: Norton, 2011); Ruti Teitel, *Humanity's Law* (New York: Oxford University Press, 2011). Both books demonstrate compellingly a change in the lexicon, conceptions, and norms of justice. Sikkink, a political scientist, focuses on human rights generally, examining the effect of the norm shift she discerns with reference to the trials of individuals charged with human rights violations, especially in Latin America. Teitel, an international law scholar, dwells on "humanity law," as she chooses to call it, the product of a new legal "discourse" that, in her view, has transformed thinking about

in international law related to human rights and justice. "Humanity law" universalizes: a) protection (now available, in principle, to all people everywhere, and from harm done by governments as well as private groups and individuals, whether or not they were connected to the state, during conflicts); and b) jurisdiction (cases can be brought in one country's court against a person charged with committing the offense somewhere else). Focusing on crimes against humanity, Teitel considers, in particular, the International Criminal Court as well as the ad hoc tribunals created for the former Yugoslavia, Rwanda, and other postconflict societies. Both books underscore the waning influence of state-privileging conceptions of sovereignty, the diminishing value of "state-centric" interpretations of international politics and law, and the increasing effectiveness with which the new norms highlight the rights and protection of individuals rather than of states. Sikkink's and Teitel's books are impressive and rightly influential. But this much remains clear. First, these new norms cannot have the intended practical consequences without the cooperation of states; the ship of justice runs aground when states balk, which they do frequently. Second, the norms' efficacy hinges on the political and strategic circumstances at play in a given instance, which means that in practice the norms apply to certain states and not others (and that undercuts their legitimacy). The hierarchy of power still matters massively, as does the question of whether an accused state, group, or individual has powerful friends or allies. Third, states are masterful at manipulating the norms to serve their strategic interests, which generally have nothing to do with justice. There is, then, rather more universalism in the language, or, to use Teitel's words (7), "the grammar and syntax," of these norms than in their actual effect. For a critical assessment of Sikkink's book, see the review essay by Padraig McAuliffe, "The Roots of Transitional Accountability: Interrogating the Justice Cascade," *International Journal of Law in Context*, Vol. 9, No. 1 (March 2013), 106–123. For a critique of Teitel's volume, see Martti Koskenniemi, "Humanity's Law by Ruti Teitel," *Ethics in International Affairs*, September 13, 2013, www.ethicsandinternationalaffairs.org/2012/humanitys-law-by-ruti-g-teitel/. Teitel's response appears in *Ethics and International Affairs*, May 31, 2013, www.ethicsandinternationalaffairs.org/2013/a-response-to-martti-koskenniemis-review-of-humanitys-law/.

14. On humanitarian intervention as an emerging global norm, see Nicholas Wheeler, *Saving Strangers: Humanitarian Intervention in International Society* (Oxford: Oxford University Press, 2000) and Finnemore, *Purpose*.

15. A point well made in Stephen Hopgood, *The Endtimes of Human Rights* (Ithaca, NY: Cornell University Press, 2013), and anticipated in some respects by David Kennedy, *The Dark Side of Virtue: Reassessing International Humanitarianism* (Princeton, NJ: Princeton University Press, 2004), esp. 18–27.

16. See Shareen Hertel, "Re-Framing Human Rights: The Rise of Economic Rights," forthcoming in *Human Rights Futures*, edited by Jack Snyder, Leslie Vinjamuri, and Stephen Hopgood (unpublished manuscript). My thanks to Jack Snyder for allowing me to cite Hertel's chapter.

17. See James Ron and David Crow, "Who Trusts Local Human Rights Organizations? Evidence from Three World Regions," *Human Rights Quarterly*, Vol. 37, No. 1 (February 2015), 188–239. The authors devised polling questions following interviews with 233 individuals (from 66 countries) knowledgeable about human rights organizations and used the questions in opinion surveys in locales in Mexico, India, Colombia, and Morocco. They found that the people who most trust human rights

organizations are those knowledgeable about the underlying principles of human rights and familiar with human rights groups' work and personnel to begin with; that lower levels of trust in local institutions and political leaders correlates with higher levels of trust in local human rights organizations; that greater education, urbanization, and exposure to the world beyond does not reliably increase trust in local human rights groups; that, contrary to a common assumption, human rights groups do not necessarily encounter mistrust as a result of foreign funding; and that the middle class tends to place more trust in rights groups than the poor or the rich. But Ron and Crow end with skepticism about "broad generalizations" and stress the need for "contextual, country-specific explanations" (216).

18. Eric Posner, *The Twilight of Human Rights Law* (New York: Oxford University Press, 2014), Introduction and 92–115.

19. The use of torture by the United States in the post-9/11 "global war on terror" is detailed in the mammoth report of the Senate Select Committee on Intelligence, released in December 2014. For the text, see www.nytimes.com/interactive/2014/12/09/world/cia-torture-report-document.html?_r=0. For the contrast between professed ideals and the policies pursued in America's post-9/11 global war on terror, see Jane Mayer, *The Dark Side: The Inside Story of How the War on Terror Turned Into a War on American Ideals* (New York: Doubleday, 2008) and James Risen, *Pay Any Price: Greed, Power and Endless War* (Boston: Houghton Mifflin, 2014), 166–201.

20. Oona A. Hathaway, "The Promise and Limits of the International Law of Torture," in Sanford Levinson, ed., *Torture: A Collection* (New York: Oxford University Press, 2004), 204. Emphasis in original. More broadly, the evidence that states' human rights improve substantially after they sign human rights treaties is mixed and weak. For a review of the relevant literature, see Adam S. Chilton and Eric A. Posner, "The Influence of History on States' Compliance With Human Rights Obligations," University of Chicago, Coase-Sanders Institute for Law and Economic Research, Research Paper Number 719, May 5, 2015, http://papers.ssrn.com/sol3/Papers.cfm?abstract_id=2573330.

21. This argument is made at length in Posner, *Twilight of Human Rights*.

22. United Nations, General Assembly, "2005 World Summit Outcome," Resolution 60/1, 40 (Clause 139), www.un.org/womenwatch/ods/A-RES-60-1-E.pdf.

23. See the account of a speech by Gareth Evans at the Central European University on November 19, 2012, http://spp.ceu.hu/article/2012-11-19/gareth-evans-says-mass-atrocity-crimes-are-everyones-business. Also see Stewart Patrick, "Libya and the Future of Humanitarian Intervention: How Qaddafi's Fall Vindicated Obama and RtoP," *Foreign Affairs*, August 26, 2011, www.foreignaffairs.com/articles/68233/stewart-patrick/libya-and-the-future-of-humanitarian-intervention. On how the Libyan intervention will prove to be a setback for R2P, see David Rieff, "R2P, RIP," *New York Times*, November 7, 2011.

24. For an explanation of the estimates, see "Bosnia War Dead Figure Announced," *BBC News*, June 21, 2007, http://news.bbc.co.uk/2/hi/europe/6228152.stm.

25. Laura Silber and Allan Little, *Yugoslavia: Death of a Nation* (New York: Penguin Books, 1995), 265–275; Roger Cohen, *Hearts Grown Brutal: Sagas of Sarajevo* (New York: Random House, 1998), 260–262, 268–277, 342, 417–419.

26. For the events leading up to the wars in the former Yugoslavia, see Noel Malcolm, *Bosnia: A Short History*, Updated Edition (New York: New York University Press, 1996), Ch. 15, "Bosnia and the Death of Yugoslavia."

27. Malcolm, *Bosnia,* 230, Malcolm argues that the West could not have prevented Yugoslavia's violent implosion given the pace of events on the ground, the strength of Serbian and Croatian nationalism, Belgrade's systematic radicalization of Serb minorities in Croatia and Bosnia, and its willingness to wage (or promote) irredentist war. The West's rush to recognition and failure to press for a political solution to address the fears of the Serb minority in Bosnia and Croatia were mistakes nonetheless.

28. PBS, *Frontline,* "Rwanda: A Chronology," www.pbs.org/wgbh/pages/frontline/shows/rwanda/etc/cron.html; Linda Melvern, *A People Betrayed: The Role of the West in Rwanda's Genocide,* Updated Edition (New York: Zed Books, 2009), 168–195.

29. See the documents obtained under the Freedom of Information Act by the National Security Archive in Will Ferrogiaro, ed., "The US and the Genocide in Rwanda 1994: Evidence of Inaction," National Security Archive, August 20, 2001, http://nsarchive.gwu.edu/NSAEBB/NSAEBB53/.

30. Alan J. Kuperman, "Rwanda in Retrospect," *Foreign Affairs,* Vol. 79, No. 1 (January/February 2000), 94–118, for the argument that the killing could not have been prevented. Kuperman insists that it would have taken about 40 days to fully deploy a force of sufficient size (he puts the number at 15,000), but that is because advance units could have acted in the meantime, an intervention "could have spared 125,000 Tutsi from death, 25 percent of the ultimate toll." For a critique of Kuperman (and his response), see Alison Des Forges, "Shame: Rationalizing Western Apathy in Rwanda," *Foreign Affairs,* Vol. 79, No. 3 (May/June 2000), 141–144. For a passionate argument that the lack of political will was what prevented action, see Roméo Dallaire (the commander of UNAMIR), *Shake Hands With the Devil: The Failure of Humanity in Rwanda* (New York: Carroll and Graf, 2003), esp. 510–520. See also Taylor B. Seybolt, *Humanitarian Military Intervention: The Conditions for Success and Failure* (Oxford: Oxford University Press, 2007), 207–208, 214–215.

31. On France's role in Rwanda before and during the 1994 massacres, see Philip Gourevitch, *We Wish to Inform You That Tomorrow We Will Be Killed Along With Our Families: Stories from Rwanda* (New York: Picador, 1999), 154–157; Chris McGreal, "France's Shame?," *Guardian,* January 11, 2007, www.theguardian.com/world/2007/jan/11/rwanda.insideafrica.

32. See Andrew Wallis, *Silent Accomplice: The Untold Story of France's Role in the Rwandan Genocide* (London: IB Tauris, 2014), Ch. 7, "Operation Turquoise"; McGreal, "France's Shame."

33. French troops eventually arrived in Bisesero and provided safety and medical care to wounded Tutsi but also saw firsthand the extent of the killing, about which they had received reports, that had been going on, even after they had deployed to the area.

34. For a methodical account of the nature, evolution, and effects of Operation Turquoise and of France's motives as they evolved from June through July 1994, see Alison Des Forges, *"Leave No One to Tell the Story": Genocide in Rwanda* (New York: Human Rights Watch, 1999), 1013–1051.

35. Des Forges, *"Leave No One to Tell the Story,"* 1027.

36. Des Forges, *"Leave No One to Tell the Story,"* 1047.

37. Des Forges, *"Leave No One to Tell the Story,"* 1046.

38. Des Forges, *"Leave No One to Tell the Story,"* 1049.

39. Report of the International Commission on Intervention and State Sovereignty, *The Responsibility to Protect* (Ottawa: International Development Research Center, 2001).

Alex Bellamy provides a useful account of the ICISS in *Responsibility to Protect: The Global Effort to End Mass Atrocities* (Cambridge: Polity Press, 2009), Ch. 2.

40. On the similarities between Walzer's views on humanitarian intervention and R2P, see Anne Orford, "Moral Internationalism and the Responsibility to Protect," *European Journal of International Law*, Vol. 24, No. 1 (2013), 83–84, 86, 90, 98.

41. Francis M. Deng, Sadikiel Kimaro, Terence Lyons, Donald Rothchild, and I. William Zartman, *Sovereignty as Responsibility: Conflict Management in Africa* (Washington, DC: Brookings Institution, 1996). On the evolution of the idea that state sovereignty imposes the duty to protect citizens, the rethinking of traditionally understood sovereignty, and resistance to the new conceptualization, see Bellamy, *Responsibility to Protect*, Ch. 1 and the briefer survey in Bellamy, *Global Politics and the Responsibility to Protect: From Words to Deeds* (New York: Routledge, 2011), 9–13.

42. This point is made by Robert W. Murray, "Humanitarianism, Responsibility or Rationality? Evaluating Intervention As a State Strategy," in Aidan Hehir and Robert Murray, eds., *Libya: The Responsibility to Protect and the Future of Humanitarian Intervention* (Basingstoke, UK: Palgrave Macmillan, 2013), 25–26.

43. For a cogent summary on the background and intent of the November 1950 Uniting for Peace Resolution, see Christian Tomuschat, "Uniting for Peace: General Assembly Resolution 377 (V), New York, 3 November 1950," United Nations, Audio Visual Library of International Law, 2013, http://legal.un.org/avl/ha/ufp/ufp.html.

44. The most comprehensive explication of R2P remains Gareth Evans, *The Responsibility to Protect: Ending Mass Atrocity Crimes Once and for All* (Washington, DC: Brookings Institution, 2008).

45. See Emma Gilligan, *Terror in Chechnya: Russia and the Tragedy of Civilians in War* (Princeton, NJ: Princeton University Press, 2010), for the death estimate and Introduction and Chs. 1–3 for the various ways in which civilians have been killed. On the devastation created by the war, see Anatol Lieven, *Chechnya: Tombstone of Russian Power* (New Haven, CT: Yale University Press, 1998); Sebastian Smith, *Allah's Mountains: The Battle for Chechnya* (London: IB Tauris, 2005); Carlotta Gall and Thomas de Waal, *Chechnya: Calamity in the Caucasus* (New York: New York University Press, 1998); Anna Politkovskaya, *A Small Corner of Hell: Dispatches from Chechnya* (Chicago: University of Chicago Press, 2007); and Rajan Menon, "Russia's Quagmire," *Boston Review*, Vol. 29, Nos. 3&4 (Summer 2004), 26–32.

46. Monica Serrano, "The Responsibility to Protect and Its Critics: Explaining the Consensus," *Global Responsibility to Protect*, Vol. 4, No. 3 (2011), 1–13.

47. Bellamy, *Responsibility to Protect*, 83–90; Bellamy, *Global Politics*, 21–25.

48. See Anne Orford, *International Authority and the Responsibility to Protect* (Cambridge: Cambridge University Press, 2011), 133–134, 162–163, 168.

49. On this point see Orford, *International*, 187–188, 192–195.

50. Global Center for the Responsibility to Protect, "UN Resolutions Referencing R2P," October 17, 2012, www.globalr2p.org/resources/335.

51. On the debate, see United Nations, Meetings Coverage and Press Releases, July 23, 2009, "Delegates Seek to End Global Paralysis in the Face of Atrocities as General Assembly Holds Interactive Dialogue on Responsibility to Protect"; United Nations, Meetings Coverage and Press Releases, July 28, 2009, "Delegates Weigh Legal Merits of Responsibility to Protect Concept as General Assembly Concludes Debate," www.un.org/press/en/2009/ga10850.doc.htm. For the resolution on addressing conflict in

Africa and the debates over it, see United Nations, General Assembly, July 23, 2009, http://www.un.org/en/ga/search/view_doc.asp?symbol=A/63/PV.97; United Nations, Meetings Coverage and Press Releases, "Delegates Seek to End Global Paralysis in Face of Atrocities as General Assembly Holds Interactive Dialogue on Responsibility to Protect," July 23, 2009, www.un.org/press/en/2009/ga10847.doc.htm.

52. Bellamy, *Global Politics*, 25.

53. Robertson, *Crimes Against Humanity*, 762. Similarly, Aidan Hehir observes that "while the principle of 'the responsibility to protect' was formally incorporated into the *Outcome Document*, the provisions … constituted a significant diminution of the original proposals proffered by the ICISS." Hehir, *Humanitarian Intervention After Kosovo: Iraq, Darfur, and the Record of Global Civil Society* (New York: Palgrave, 2008), 147. Italics in the original.

54. United Nations, "Responsibility While Protecting: Elements for the Development and Promotion of a Concept," Annex to the Letter Dated November 9, 2011, from the Permanent Representative of Brazil to the United Nations Addressed to the Secretary General, A/66/551, S/211/701, November 11, 2011, http://cpdoc.fgv.br/sites/default/files/2011%2011%2011%20UN%20conceptual%20paper%20on%20RwP.pdf.

55. Oliver Stuenkel, "Emerging Powers Remain Divided on R2P and RWP," *Post Western World*, July 8, 2012, www.postwesternworld.com/2012/07/08/why-emerging-powers-are-divided-on-r2p-and-rwp/.

56. United Nations, 67th General Assembly, "General Assembly Adopts Text Condemning Violence in Syria, Demanding That All Sides End Hostilities," May 15, 2013, www.un.org/press/en/2013/ga11372.doc.htm.

57. "Libya No-Fly Resolution Reveals Global Split in UN," *Guardian*, March 18, 2011, www.theguardian.com/world/2011/mar/18/libya-no-fly-resolution-split.

CHAPTER SIX

1. See, for example, Frederic Wehrey, "The Forgotten Uprising in Eastern Saudi Arabia," Carnegie Endowment for International Peace, June 14, 2013, http://carnegieendowment.org/2013/06/14/forgotten-uprising-in-eastern-saudi-arabia; "Saudi Response to Increasing Violence in Eastern Province," Stratfor, January 17, 2012, https://stratfor.com/analysis/saudi-response-increasing-violence-eastern-province; "Saudi Policeman Killed During Raid in Oil-Rich Eastern Province," Reuters, April 6, 2015, www.reuters.com/article/2015/04/06/us-saudi-security-idUS KBN0MX06Y20150406.

2. See *Report of the Secretary-General's Panel of Experts on Accountability in Sri Lanka*, March 31, 2011, www.un.org/News/dh/infocus/Sri_Lanka/POE_Report_Full.pdf. See also "UN: Sri Lanka's Crushing of Tamil Tigers May Have Killed 40,000 Civilians," *Washington Post*, April 21, 2011, www.washingtonpost.com/world/un-sri-lankas-crushing-of-tamil-tigers-may-have-killed-40000-civilians/2011/04/21/AFU14hJE_story.html; and "Sri Lankan Forces Blamed for Most Civilian Deaths," *New York Times*, May 16, 2010, citing a report by the International Crisis Group.

3. "Growing China Ties Let Sri Lanka Rebuff US War Inquiry Push," Bloomberg Business, March 6, 2014, www.bloomberg.com/news/articles/2014-03-06/growing-china-ties-let-sri-lanka-rebuff-u-s-war-inquiry-push; "How Beijing Won Sri Lanka's

Civil War," *Independent*, May 23, 2010, www.independent.co.uk/news/world/asia/how-beijing-won-sri-lankas-civil-war-1980492.html.

4. For an excellent analysis of Sukarno's policies, Washington's attitude toward him, the relationship between anti-Communist Indonesian officers and successive American administrations, and the anti-PKI bloodletting of 1965–1966, see John Roosa, *Pretext for Mass Murder: The September 30th Movement & Suharto's Coup d'État in Indonesia* (Madison, WI: University of Wisconsin Press, 2006), 176–193, for Washington's dealings with the Indonesian army. See also Damien Kingsbury, *Politics of Indonesia* (New York: Oxford University Press, 1998), 57–83.

5. Roosa, *Pretext for Mass Murder*, 193–197.

6. James Dunn, "Genocide in East Timor," in Samuel Totten and William S. Parsons, eds., *Centuries of Genocide: Essays and Eyewitness Accounts*, Fourth Edition (New York: Routledge, 2012), 289.

7. Dunn, "Genocide in East Timor," 288.

8. Romesh Silva and Patrick Ball, *A Profile of Human Rights Violations in Timor-Leste, 1974–1999*, a report by the Benetech Human Rights Analysis Group to the Commission on Reception, Truth and Reconciliation in Timor-Leste (February 9, 2006); Geoffrey Robinson, *"If You Leave Us Here We Will Die": How Genocide Was Stopped in East Timor* (Princeton, NJ: Princeton University Press, 2011).

9. Andrea Hopkins, "Australia Let Indonesia Invade East Timor in 1975," *Guardian*, September 12, 2000; East Timor: Whitlam Was the Culprit," *New Weekly* (Australia), September 23, 2000, http://newsweekly.com.au/article.php?id=340; "Gough Whitlam's 'Indifference' Led to East Timor Occupation—WiKi Leaks," news.com.au, April 11, 2013 (first published two years previously), www.news.com.au/technology/gough-whitlams-indifference-led-to-east-timor-occupation-wikileaks/story-e6frfroo-1226617675503. It is of course impossible to know whether Australian and American efforts to stop the invasion of East Timor would have succeeded. What is clear is that the governments of both countries knew of Suharto's plan but made no effort to oppose it. In the run-up to the invasion, the Indonesian military had waged a fierce propaganda campaign against Fretilin, the leftist pro-independence group, attempted to turn other opposition groups against it, and even instigated one of them, the Timorese Democratic Union (UDT), to stage a coup (which failed). These moves could not have gone unnoticed by Australian intelligence, which kept a close watch on the Indonesian military. See Dunn, "Genocide in East Timor," 283–285.

10. Robinson, *If You Leave Us Here*, 63.

11. John Pilger, "Our Model Dictator," *Guardian*, January 27, 2008; Shane Maloney and Chris Groz, "Gareth Evans and Ali Alatas," *The Monthly*, December 2011–January 2012, www.themonthly.com.au/gareth-evans-ali-alatas-shane-maloney-4304; Robinson, *"If You Leave Us Here,"* 63.

12. Geoffrey Robertson, *Crimes Against Humanity: The Struggle for Human Rights*, Fourth Edition (New York: New Press, 2012), 586–587.

13. Dunn, "Genocide in East Timor," 289.

14. See the declassified documents and commentary in National Security Archive, "East Timor Revisited," December 2001, www.gwu.edu/~nsarchiv/NSAEBB/NSAEBB62/#doc4.

15. See, for example, the Indonesia segment of the April 26, 1978, memorandum written by Vice President Walter Mondale outlining the goals of his upcoming trip to Australia, Indonesia, New Zealand, the Philippines, and Thailand obtained under

the Freedom of Information Act by the National Security Archive, http://nsarchive. gwu.edu/NSAEBB/NSAEBB242/19780426.pdf; and the US Embassy's summary to the Secretary of State of the discussions held between Mondale and Suharto on May 10, 1978, http://nsarchive.gwu.edu/NSAEBB/NSAEBB242/19780510.pdf.

16. Data from William D. Hartung, "US Arms Transfers to Indonesia 1975–1977," *World Policy Institute Report* (March 1997), Table 1.

17. "How British Loans Funded Dictators Arms Spree," *Independent*, May 4, 2013.

18. Robinson, *"If You Leave Us Here,"* 64.

19. Robinson, *"If You Leave Us Here,"* 64.

20. Hehir, *Humanitarian Intervention After Kosovo*, 146.

21. Human Rights Watch, "Justice Denied for East Timor," n.d., www.hrw.org/legacy/ backgrounder/asia/timor/etimor1202bg.htm; Evelyn Rusli, "Indonesian Court Voids 4 Convictions in 1999 East Timor Strife," *New York Times*, August 7, 2004, www. nytimes.com/2004/08/07/world/indonesia-court-voids-4-convictions-in-1999-east-timor-strife.html.

22. Human Rights Watch, "Turkey's Failed Policy to Aid the Forcibly Displaced in the Southeast," *HRW Report*, Vol. 8, No. 9 (D), 1996.

23. For the displacement and the number of homeless people and refugees, as well as the 378,335 figure, see Human Rights Watch, "Still Critical: Prospects in 2005 for Internally Displaced Kurds in Turkey," *HRW Report*, Vol. 17, No 2 (D), 2005, "Introduction," www.hrw.org/reports/2005/turkey0305/turkey0305.pdf.

24. Stephen Zunes, "The United States and the Kurds," *Common Dreams*, October 26, 2007, www.commondreams.org/views/2007/10/26/united-states-and-kurds-brief-history (originally published in *Foreign Policy in Focus*, October 26, 2007).

25. Human Rights Watch, *World Report 1999*, www.hrw.org/legacy/worldreport99/ mideast/algeria.html, mentions the Algerian government's and State Department's figures on the death toll. The report points to the role of the security forces in the violence and, while noting the attacks on civilians by Islamists, also points to killings by the security forces, or allied groups, both sometimes posing as members of the AIG and other violent Islamist groups. For additional details, also see the section on Algeria in Human Rights Watch, *World Report 2002*, www.hrw.org/legacy/wr2k2/ download.html.

26. See Nafeez Mosaddeq Ahmed, "Algeria and the Paradox of Democracy: The 1992 Coup, Its Consequences and the Contemporary Crisis," Algeria-Watch, November 2000, www.algeria-watch.org/en/articles/1997_2000/paradox_democracy.htm.

27. "Bahrain Hardliners to Put Shia MPs on Trial," *Telegraph*, March 30, 2011, www.telegraph.co.uk/news/worldnews/middleeast/bahrain/8416953/Bahrain-hardliners-to-put-Shia-MPs-on-trial.html; Pepe Escobar, "Exposed: The Saudi-US Libya Deal," *Asia Times*, April 2, 2011, www.atimes.com/atimes/Middle_East/MD02Ak01.html; Omar Ocampo, "Regime (Not) Changed: Bahrain, The Arab Spring and Energy Security," *Khamasin*, Department of Political Science, American University of Cairo, May 28, 2014, www.aucegypt.edu/huss/pols/ Khamasin/pages/article.aspx?eid=7; Craig Murray (former British career diplomat and UK ambassador to Uzbekistan), "The Invasion of Bahrain," craigmurray. org, March 14, 2011, www.craigmurray.org.uk/archives/2011/03/the-invasion-of-bahrain/.

28. Hugh Eakin, "The Strange Power of Qatar," *New York Review of Books*, October 27, 2011.

29. Amnesty International, "Annual Report 2012: Egypt," https://web.archive.org/web/20140831064926/https://www.amnesty.org/en/region/egypt/report-2012.

30. "Egypt: More than 41,000 Detainees Since Sisi-Led Military Coup," *Middle East Monitor*, May 27, 2014, www.middleeastmonitor.com/news/africa/11713-egypt-more-than-41000-detainees-since-sisi-led-military-coup; Joe Stork, "Egypt's Political Prisoners," Human Rights Watch, March 6, 2015, www.hrw.org/news/2015/03/06/egypt-s-political-prisoners.

31. Details on the mass arrests and torture and from Tom Stevenson, "Sisi's Way," *London Review of Books*, Vol. 37, No. 4 (February 19, 2015), 3–7.

32. Human Rights Watch, "All According to Plan: The Ra'ba Massacre and Mass Killing of Protestors in Egypt," August 12, 2014, www.hrw.org/reports/2014/08/12/all-according-plan. See also Human Rights Watch, "UN Human Rights Council: Egypt's Human Rights Situation, Repression in China; and Repression in Bahrain," September 17, 2014, www.hrw.org/news/2014/09/17/un-human-rights-council-egypts-human-rights-situation-repression-china-and-arrests-b; Doug Bandow, "Egypt's Al-Sisi Establishes Tyranny Mubarak Only Dreamed of: Washington Should Stop Playing the Fool By Praising Commitment to Democracy," *Forbes*, September 1, 2014, www.forbes.com/sites/dougbandow/2014/09/01/egypts-al-sisi-establishes-tyranny-mubarak-only-dreamed-of-washington-should-stop-playing-the-fool-by-praising-cairos-commitment-to-democracy/; "Sisi Secures Position in Egypt and Abroad Despite Human Rights Record," *Financial Times*, October 6, 2014.

33. See Jean-Pierre Filiu, *From Deep State to Islamic State: The Arab Counter-Revolution and Its Jihadist Legacy* (New York: Oxford University Press, 2015), 180–185.

34. "Britain Resumes Arms Sales to Egypt Despite Commitment to Protect Human Rights," *Middle East Monitor*, November 6, 2013, www.middleeastmonitor.com/blogs/politics/8192-britains-resumes-arms-sales-to-egypt-despite-commitment-to-protect-human-rights; "UK Restores 24 Arms Export Licenses to Egypt," *Daily News* (Cairo), November 3, 2014, www.dailynewsegypt.com/2013/11/03/uk-restores-24-arms-export-licenses-to-egypt/.

35. "US Unlocks Military Aid, Backing President Sisi," *BBC News*, June 22, 2014, www.bbc.com/news/world-middle-east-27961933. On Kerry's statement on the resumption of military aid and on human rights, see "John Kerry Voices Strong Support for Egyptian President Sisi," *Wall Street Journal*, June 22, 2014, www.wsj.com/articles/john-kerry-arrives-in-egypt-on-unannounced-visit-1403426551.

36. "Obama Removes Weapons Freeze Against Egypt," *New York Times*, March 31, 2015, www.nytimes.com/2015/04/01/world/middleeast/obama-lifts-arms-freeze-against-egypt.html?_r=0.

37. "France Concludes €5.2 Billion Arms Deal with Egypt," *Irish Times*, February 17, 2015, www.irishtimes.com/news/world/europe/france-concludes-5-2bn-arms-deal-with-egypt-1.2106261.

38. "Tehran, Iran [sic] Toasts of the President and the Shah at a State Dinner," December 31, 1977, University of California (Santa Barbara), The American Presidency Project, www.presidency.ucsb.edu/ws/?pid=7080.

39. For details on the GCC's air strikes in Yemen, see, for example, Kareem Fahim, "Airstrikes Take a Toll on Civilians in Yemen War," *New York Times*, September 12, 2015; Human Rights Watch, *Yemen: Cluster Munitions Kill, Injure Dozens*, (August 26, 2015), www.hrw.org/news/2015/08/26/yemen-cluster-munition-rockets-kill-injure-dozens; Amnesty International, "Air Strike and Weapon Analysis Shows

Saudi Arabia-Led Force Kills Scores of Civilians," July 2, 2015, www.amnesty.org/en/latest/news/2015/07/yemen-airstrike-analysis-shows-saudi-arabia-killed-scores-of-civilians/.

40. On intelligence and logistical support, see Dan Lamothe, "How US Weapons Will Play a Huge Role in Saudi Arabia's War in Yemen," *Washington Post*, March 26, 2015, www.washingtonpost.com/news/checkpoint/wp/2015/03/26/how-u-s-weapons-will-play-a-large-role-in-saudi-arabias-war-in-yemen/. On the negotiations related to the frigates and other weapons, see Andrea Shalal, "US, Saudi Arabia Near Deal for Two Lockheed Warships: Sources," Reuters, September 2, 2015, www.reuters.com/article/2015/09/02/us-usa-saudi-arms-idUSKCN0R21UF20150902.

41. "Saudi King Meets Obama Amid Concerns Over Iran Nuclear Deal," BBC News, September 5, 2015, www.bbc.com/news/world-us-canada-34153624; Simeon Kerr, "Saudi King Meets Top US Executives in Investment Drive," *Financial* Times, September 7, 2015, www.ft.com/cms/s/0/ff87679e-554f-11e5-8642-453585f2cfcd.html#axzz3mPHBlVsQ.

42. "Obama Signs US Sanctions Law on Venezuelan Officials," Reuters, December 18, 2014, www.reuters.com/article/2014/12/18/us-usa-venezuela-sanctions-idUSKBN0JW2JF20141218.

43. On the background and context of these demonstrations, see International Crisis Group, "Venezuela: Dangerous Inertia," Policy Briefing, No. 31 (September 23, 2014), and Amnesty International, "Venezuela: Lack of Justice for Protest Abuses Gives Green Light to More Violence," March 24, 2015, https://web.archive.org/web/20150518170659/https://www.amnesty.org/en/articles/news/2015/03/venezuela-lack-of-justice-for-protest-abuses-gives-green-light-to-more-violence/.

44. "Venezuela Death Toll Rises Amidst New Protests," Al Jazeera, March 30, 2014, www.aljazeera.com/news/americas/2014/03/venezuela-death-toll-rises-amid-new-protests-201432921437393257.html; "Fresh Street Battles as Venezuela Protest Death Toll Hits 39," RT.com, April 1, 2014, http://rt.com/news/venezuela-clashes-deaths-39-505/; Thabata Molina, "Who Died in Venezuela's 2014 Protests?" *Pan Am Post*, February 11, 2015, http://panampost.com/thabata-molina/2015/02/11/who-died-in-venezuelas-2014-protests/. Molina reports that six protestors "died accidentally."

45. "Fears Spread That Venezuela Is Approaching Bloody Face-Off," *New York Times*, March 11, 2014; "Violent Clashes in Venezuela on Protest Movement Anniversary," *New York Times*, February 12, 2015.

46. "U.S. Declares Venezuela a National Security Threat, Sanctions Top Leaders," Reuters, March 9, 2015, www.reuters.com/article/2015/03/09/us-usa-venezuela-idUSKBN0M51NS20150309. That statement and the sanctions were criticized by South Africa and several Latin American governments.

47. Alexander Cooley, *Great Games, Local Rules: The New Great Power Contest in Central Asia* (New York: Oxford University Press, 2012), 104–105.

48. "'Bullets Were Falling Like Rain': The Andijan Massacre, May 13, 2005," *Human Rights Watch Reports*, Vol. 17, No. 5 (June 2005), esp. 6–33, for an account of the revolt and its suppression. For the casualty estimate, see "Five Years After Andijon Events, Key Questions Remain Unanswered," *Radio Free Europe/Radio Liberty Report*, May 11, 2010; www.rferl.org/content/Five_Years_After_Andijon_Events_Key_Questions_Remain_Unanswered_/2039096.html; "700 Dead in Uzbek Violence," *Guardian*, May 16, 2005, www.theguardian.com/world/2005/may/16/markoliver.

49. Joshua Kucera, "Uzbekistan: Military Aid to Tashkent Would Help Protect NDN—State Department," Eurasianet.org, September 28, 2011, www.eurasianet.org/node/64237.

50. Heather Maher, "Clinton in Central Asia: Seeks Balance Between Realpolitik and Rights," Radio Free Europe/Radio Liberty Report, October 25, 2011, www.rferl.org/content/clinton_in_central_asia_—_seeking_balance_between_realpolitik_and_rights/24370606.html; "Uzbekistan: No Justice 7 Years After the Andijan Massacre," Human Rights Watch, May 12, 2012, www.hrw.org/news/2012/05/11/uzbekistan-no-justice-7-years-after-andijan-massacre.

51. Kucera, "No Longer Under Sanctions, Uzbekistan Gets 300 Armored Vehicles from U.S.," Eurasianet.org, January 22, 2015, www.eurasianet.org/node/71746.

52. Human Rights Watch, "Uzbekistan: No Justice."

53. Alan J. Kuperman, "A Model Humanitarian Intervention? Reassessing NATO's Libya Campaign," International Security, Vol. 38, No. 1 (Summer 2013), 107.

54. "By His Own Reckoning, One Man Made Libya a French Cause," New York Times, April 1, 2011; Kim Wilsher, "Libya: Bernard-Henri Lévy Dismisses Criticism for Leading France to Conflict," Guardian, March 26, 2011, www.theguardian.com/world/2011/mar/27/libya-bernard-henri-levy-france.

55. Ross Douthat, "100,000 Libyan Casualties?," Douthat blog, New York Times, March 24, 2011, http://douthat.blogs.nytimes.com/2011/03/24/100000-libyan-casualties/; Steve Chapman, "Did Obama Avert a Bloodbath in Libya?" Chicago Tribune, April 3, 2011, http://articles.chicagotribune.com/2011-04-03/news/ct-oped-0403-chapman-20110403_1_president-obama-benghazi-barack-obama.

56. Kuperman, "A Model Humanitarian Intervention?," 112.

57. "Gaddafi Tells Benghazi His Army Is Coming Tonight," Al-Arabiya News, February 15, 2011, www.alarabiya.net/articles/2011/03/17/141999.html.

58. For an excellent account of the debates within the Obama administration on Libya prior to the intervention, see Michael Hastings (who mentions the 30,000 figure), "Obama's War Room," Rolling Stone, October 13, 2011.

59. "At Least 30,000 Killed, 50,000 Wounded in Libyan Conflict," Tripoli Post, September 8, 2011, www.tripolipost.com/articledetail.asp?c=1&i=6862.

60. "Gaddafi's Army Will Kill Half a Million, Warn Libyan Rebels," Guardian, March 12, 2011, www.theguardian.com/world/2011/mar/12/gaddafi-army-kill-half-million.

61. "Libya Crisis: EU Agrees Sanctions as UK Warns of 'Day of Reckoning' for Gaddafi," Guardian, www.theguardian.com/world/2011/feb/28/libya-crisis-eu-sanctions-day-reckoning-gaddafi; "Libya: US and EU Say Muammar Gaddafi Must Go," BBC News, March 11, 2011, www.bbc.co.uk/news/world-europe-12711162.

62. "France Becomes First Country to Recognize Libyan Rebels," New York Times, March 10, 2011.

63. "Gaddafi Must Leave, West Tells Libya," Times (London), February 25, 2011, www.thetimes.co.uk/tto/news/world/middleeast/article2925867.ece; "US Imposes Sanctions on Libya in Wake of Crackdown," New York Times, February 25, 2011; Barack Obama, David Cameron, and Nicolas Sarkozy, "Libya's Pathways to Peace," New York Times, April 14, 2011.

64. On Egyptian arms supplies, see "Egypt Said to Arm Libya Rebels," Wall Street Journal, March 17, 2011, www.wsj.com/articles/SB10001424052748704360404576206992835270906; "McCain: I Hope US, Others Arm Libyan Rebels," CBS News, March 22, 2011, citing McCain on Egyptian arms shipments to the rebels, www.cbsnews.com/news/mccain-i-hope-us-others-arm-libyan-rebels/. On the role of

Egyptian commandos, see "Egypt 'Aids Libyan Rebels Against Qadhafi,'" United Press International, March 9, 2011, www.upi.com/Top_News/Special/2011/03/09/Egypt-aids-Libyan-rebels-against-Gadhafi/42161299696518/. The text of UNSCR 1970 is available at www.icc-cpi.int/NR/rdonlyres/081A9013-B03D-4859-9D61-5D0B0F2F5EFA/0/1970Eng.pdf.

65. "Exclusive: Obama Authorizes Secret Help for Libya Rebels," Reuters, March 30, 2011, www.reuters.com/article/2011/03/30/us-libya-usa-order-idUSTRE72T6H220110330. Reuters based its story on information provided by "government sources" who stated that the president had signed the finding "within the last two to three weeks."

66. "SAS Unit Captured in Libya," Guardian, March 6, 2011, www.theguardian.com/world/2011/mar/06/liam-fox-sas-unit-libya; "SAS-Backed Libyan Diplomatic Mission Ends in Humiliation," Guardian, March 6, 2011, www.theguardian.com/world/2011/mar/06/sas-diplomatic-mission-in-libya; "Libya Unrest: SAS Members 'Captured Near Benghazi,'" BBC News, March 6, 2011, www.bbc.com/news/world-middle-east-12658054.

67. "CIA Agents Aid Rebels and Aid Air Strikes," New York Times, March 30, 2011; "US Agents Were in Libya Before Obama Secret Order," Reuters, March 31, 2011, http://af.reuters.com/article/idAFN3110148120110331?sp=true. See also "Libya: US Military Advisors in Cyrenaica," Crethiplethi, February 25, 2011, www.crethiplethi.com/libya-us-military-advisers-in-cyrenaica/usa/2011/.

68. The Wall Street Journal reported in June, "Military advisers from Britain, France, Italy, and Qatar, among other nations, are training some rebel units for a mission that has become as much about regime change as about the United Nations mandate to protect civilians from Col. Gadhafi's forces." Sam Dagher, "To Ease Allies' Fears Rebels Attempt to Rein in Militias," Wall Street Journal, June 13, 2011, www.wsj.com/articles/SB10001424052702304563104576362820981161198.

69. Christopher Chivvis, Toppling Qaddafi: Libya and the Limits of Liberal Intervention (New York: Cambridge University Press, 2014) 157. See also "Italy, France Sending Troops to Advise Libyan Rebels," CNN, April 20, 2011, www.cnn.com/2011/WORLD/africa/04/20/libya.war/.

70. For details, see Chivvis, Toppling Qaddafi, 99, 108, 126–128, 154–155, 157–158, 162; "France Sent Arms to Libyan Rebels," Washington Post, June 30, 2011, www.washingtonpost.com/world/france-sent-arms-to-libyan-rebels/2011/06/29/AGcBxkqH_story.html.

71. Chivvis, Toppling Qaddafi, 154–155.

72. See United Nations, Security Council, "Resolution 1973 (2011)," S/Res/1973 (2011), www.un.org/en/ga/search/view_doc.asp?symbol=S/RES/1973%282011%29.

73. For the various peace proposals and the reaction of the interveners and the opposition, see, for example, "Italy Recognises Libya's National Council," BBC News, April 4, 2011, www.bbc.co.uk/news/world-europe-12961032; "Libya Government Rejects Rebel Ceasefire," Al Jazeera, April 1, 2011, www.aljazeera.com/news/africa/2011/04/201141134110527219.html; "Libyan Rebels Reject Muammar Qaddafi's Ceasefire Offer," Guardian, www.theguardian.com/world/2011/apr/30/libyan-rebels-reject-gaddafi-offer; "Libyan Regime Makes Peace Offer That Sidelines Gaddafi," Guardian, May 26, 2011, www.theguardian.com/world/2011/may/26/libya-ceasefire-offer-sidelines-gaddafi.

74. "Truce Plan for Libya Is Rejected by Rebels," New York Times, April 11, 2011; "Chavez Libya Talks Offer Rejected," Al Jazeera, March 3, 2011, www.aljazeera.com/news/africa/2011/03/201133231925866727.html.

75. The details of the AU's diplomatic efforts are based on the excellent account provided by Alex de Waal, "'My Fears, Alas, Were Not Unfounded': African Responses to the Libyan Conflict," in Aidan Hehir and Robert Murray, eds., *Libya: The Responsibility to Protect and the Future of Humanitarian Intervention* (Basingstoke, UK: Palgrave Macmillan, 2013), 65–72.

76. Simon Tisdall, "The Consensus on Intervention on Libya Has Shattered," *Guardian*, March 23, 2011, www.theguardian.com/commentisfree/2011/mar/23/libya-cease-fire-consensus-russia-china-india; Greg Grandin, "Brazil Stares Down the US on Libya," Al Jazeera, March 31, 2011, www.aljazeera.com/indepth/opinion/2011/03/20113301443583272.html; "China Urges Quick End to Airstrikes in Libya," *New York Times*, March 22, 2011; "Latin American Leaders React to Libya Conflict," *Americas Quarterly*, March 23, 2011, www.americasquarterly.org/node/2341.

77. Hugh Roberts, "Who Said Gaddafi Had to Go?," *London Review of Books*, Vol. 33, No. 22 (November 2011), www.lrb.co.uk/v33/n22/hugh-roberts/who-said-gaddafi-had-to-go. The online edition does not provide page numbers.

78. David Mizner, "Worse Than Benghazi," *Jacobin*, May 17, 2015. www.jacobinmag.com/2015/07/hillary-libya-nato-qaddafi-obama/. Two of the proposals were made through American channels—in one instance an intelligence source used by the Defense Department and in another a former US military officer, who relayed the information to General Carter Ham, head of the US Africa Command (AFRICOM), who was inclined to explore the possibility of negotiations.

79. Kelly Riddell and Jeffrey Scott Shapiro, "Hilary Clinton's WMD Moment: US Intelligence Saw False Narrative in Libya," *Washington Times*, January 29, 2015, www.washingtontimes.com/news/2015/jan/29/hillary-clinton-libya-war-genocide-narrative-rejec/?page=all.

80. Louis Charbonneau, "US Envoy: Gaddafi Troops Raping, Issued Viagra," Reuters, April 29, 2011, www.reuters.com/article/2011/04/29/us-libya-troops-rape-idUS-TRE73S74B20110429; Dan Murphy, "No Evidence of Libya Viagra Rape Claims. But War Crimes? Plenty," *Christian Science Monitor*, June 24, 2011, www.csmonitor.com/World/Backchannels/2011/0624/No-evidence-of-Libya-Viagra-rape-claims.-But-war-crimes-Plenty; Patrick Cockburn, "Amnesty Questions Claim That Gaddafi Ordered Rape as a Weapon of War," *Independent*, June 24, 2011, www.independent.co.uk/news/world/africa/amnesty-questions-claim-that-gaddafi-ordered-rape-as-weapon-of-war-2302037.html.

81. Amnesty International, *The Battle for Libya: Killings, Disappearances and Torture* (2011), 34–52, on the regime's attacks on civilians. Alan J. Kuperman, "False Pretense for War in Libya?," *Boston Globe*, April 14, 2011, www.boston.com/bostonglobe/editorial_opinion/oped/articles/2011/04/14/false_pretense_for_war_in_libya/ and Maximilian C. Forte, "The Top Ten Myths in the War Against Libya," *Counterpunch*, August 31, 2011, www.counterpunch.org/2011/08/31/the-top-ten-myths-in-the-war-against-libya/, challenges the claims that civilians were massacred prior to NATO's intervention.

82. See, for example, "Libya Cracks Down on Protests After Violent Clashes in Benghazi," *Guardian*, February 16, 2011, www.theguardian.com/world/2011/feb/16/libya-clashes-benghazi; "Libya Protests: Second City Benghazi Hit by Violence," *BBC News*, February 16, 2011, www.bbc.co.uk/news/world-africa-12477275; "Witnesses Describe Violence, Chaos in Libyan Cities," CNN.com, February 21, 2011, www.cnn.com/2011/WORLD/africa/02/21/libya.protests.scene/index.html; "Qaddafi Grip

Falters As His Forces Take On Protestors," *New York Times*, February 21, 2011; "Libyan Protestors Say They Will Soldier On Despite Violent Crackdown," CNN, February 19, 2011, www.cnn.com/2011/WORLD/africa/02/19/libya.protests/; "Uprising Flares in Libyan City," Al Jazeera, February 20, 2011, www.aljazeera.com/news/africa/2011/02/201122014 259976293.html.

83. Kuperman, "A Model Humanitarian Intervention?,"110–114.

84. "Libya Rebels Press Attack in Qadhafi's Hometown," *Wall Street Journal*, September 19, 2011, www.wsj.com/articles/SB10001424053111904194604576578703160333090.

85. Human Rights Watch, "World Report 2012: Libya," https://web.archive.org/web/20130310162054/http://www.hrw.org/world-report-2012/world-report-2012-libya. M. Cherif Bassiouni, chair of the UN Human Rights Council's "Libya Commission of Inquiry", *Libya: From Repression to Revolution: A Record of Armed Conflict and International Law Violations* (Leiden: Martinus Nijhoff, 2013), Ch. 15, for details on the battle for Sirte and its aftermath; Maximillian Forte, *Slouching Toward Sirte: NATO's War on Libya and Africa* (Montreal: Baraka Books, 2012), Ch. 2; Seumas Milne, "If the Libyan War Was About Saving Lives, It Was a Catastrophic Failure," *Guardian*, October 26, 2011, www.theguardian.com/commentisfree/2011/oct/26/libya-war-saving-lives-catastrophic-failure; Amnesty International, *Battle for Libya*, 70–78, 82–87.

86. Amnesty International, *Battle for Libya*; David Smith, "Murder and Torture 'Carried Out by Both Sides' of Uprising Against Libyan Regime," *Guardian* www.theguardian.com/world/2011/sep/12/murder-torture-both-sides-libyan-regime.

87. US Department of State, Bureau of Democracy, Human Rights, and Labor, *Country Reports for Human Rights Practices, Libya* (May 24, 2012), 14–18, www.state.gov/documents/organization/186649.pdf.

88. Iris Marion Young, "Violence Against Power: Critical Thoughts on Military Intervention," in Deen K. Chatterjee and Don E. Scheid, eds., *Ethics and Foreign Intervention* (Cambridge: Cambridge University Press, 2003), 270.

89. On how bringing criminal charges against leaders can increase atrocities by obstructing political settlements that include their relinquishing power in exchange for immunity, see Jack L. Snyder and Leslie Vinjamuri, "Trials and Errors: Principles and Pragmatism in Strategies of International Justice," *International Security*, Vol. 28, No. 3 (Winter 2003/2004), 5–44.

90. De Waal, "'My Fears, Alas, Were Not Unfounded,'" 71–72.

91. See, for example, US Department of State, Bureau of Democracy, Human Rights, and Labor, "2010 Human Rights Report: Libya," April 8, 2011, www.state.gov/j/drl/rls/hrrpt/2010/nea/154467.htm. Other reports in this annual series also document severe human rights violations, which continued despite Gaddafi's rehabilitation in the West.

92. Details in Human Rights Watch, *Delivered into Enemy Hands: US-Led Abuse and Rendition of Opponents to Gaddafi's Libya* (September 6, 2012). The treaties violated by torture and renditions include the International Covenant on Civil and Political Rights, the Convention Against Torture, and the Geneva Conventions. Human Rights Watch, "Secret Intelligence Documents Discovered in Libya: Files Show Intimate Relationship Between MI6, CIA, and Libya," September 9, 2011, www.hrw.org/news/2011/09/08/secret-intelligence-documents-discovered-libya.

93. Human Rights Watch, "Secret Documents."

94. Christopher Dickey, "How Gaddafi Friended Bush, Blair, and Berlusconi," *Newsweek*, March 6, 2011, www.newsweek.com/how-gaddafi-friended-bush-blair-and-berlusconi-66117.

95. "Blair Visits Qaddafi, Ending Libya's Long Estrangement," *New York Times*, March 26, 2004.

96. "Tony Blair's Six Secret Trips to Col Gaddafi," *Telegraph*, September 24, 2011, www.telegraph.co.uk/news/politics/tony-blair/8787074/Tony-Blairs-six-secret-visits-to-Col-Gaddafi.html.

97. "Italy's Berlusconi Meets Gaddafi After Islam Storm," Reuters, August 30, 2010; "When Moammer Gadhafi Met Silvio Berlusconi," *Sidney Morning Herald*, June 11, 2009, www.smh.com.au/world/when-moammar-gadhafi-met-silvio-berlusconi-20090610-c3zo.html.

98. "Italy's Bad Romance: How Berlusconi Went Gaga for Gaddafi," *Time*, February 23, 2011, http://content.time.com/time/world/article/0,8599,2053363,00.html; Barbie Natza Nadeau, "Gaddafi's Italian Connection," *Daily Beast*, August 27, 2011, www.thedailybeast.com/articles/2011/08/27/gaddafi-s-connections-to-italy-and-berlusconi.html.

99. For the data (including a spreadsheet that provides details that go beyond the aggregate monetary value of sales per EU country per year), see "EU Arms Exports to Libya: Who Armed Gaddafi," *Guardian*, March 11, 2011, www.theguardian.com/news/datablog/2011/mar/01/eu-arms-exports-libya#data. For background, see Alison Parteger, *Libya: The Rise and Fall of Qaddafi* (New Haven, CT: Yale University Press, 2012), 189; Lindsey Hilsum, *Sandstorm: Libya in the Time of Revolution* (New York: Penguin Press, 2012), 133, 135–140, 188–189; Ethan Chorin, *Exit the Colonel: The Hidden History of the Libyan Revolution* (New York: PublicAffairs, 2012), 135–145, 159.

100. "Libyan Leader Delivers a Scolding in UN Debut," *New York Times*, March 23, 2009.

101. Jeevan Vasagar, "Academic Linked to Gaddafi's Fugitive Son Leaves LSE," *Guardian*, October 31, 2011, www.theguardian.com/education/2011/oct/31/saif-gaddafi-lse-academic. Held introduced Gaddafi's son, Saif ul-Islam, before the latter delivered the Ralph Miliband Lecture at the London School of Economics, as "someone who looks to democracy, civil society, and liberal values as the core of his inspiration." On Giddens's portrayal of Gaddafi, see his article, "My Chat with the Colonel," *Guardian*, March 8, 2007, www.theguardian.com/commentisfree/2007/mar/09/comment.libya?CMP=twt_g.

102. Ed West, "Anthony Giddens on Gaddafi: Looks Like the Prof Is Going to Have to Eat Some Pretty Embarrassing Words," *Telegraph*, March 3, 2011, http://blogs.telegraph.co.uk/news/edwest/100078447/anthony-giddens-on-gaddafi-looks-like-the-prof-is-going-to-have-to-eat-some-pretty-embarrassing-words/; Vasagar, "Academic Linked to Gaddafi's Fugitive Son Leaves LSE"; Michael Burleigh, "Saif Gaddafi: A Monster of Our Own Making," *Telegraph*, November 26, 2011, www.telegraph.co.uk/news/worldnews/africaandindianocean/libya/8915725/Saif-Gaddafi-a-monster-of-our-own-making.html; David Corn and Siddharta Mahanta, "From Libya With Love: How a US Consulting Firm Used American Academics to Rehab Muammar Qaddafi's Image," *Mother Jones*, March 3, 2011, http://m.motherjones.com/politics/2011/03/libya-qaddafi-monitor-group; Ed Pilkington, "The Monitor Group: Gaddafi's PR Firm Used Academics," *Guardian*, March 4, 2011, www.theguardian.com/world/2011/mar/04/the-monitor-groupgaddafi-pr; Pilkington, "US Firm Monitor Group Admits Mistakes Over $3m Gaddafi Deal," *Guardian*, March 3, 2011, www.theguardian.com/world/2011/mar/04/monitor-group-us-libya-gaddafi.

103. See Joseph S. Nye, Jr., "Tripoli Diarist," *New Republic*, December 10, 2007. Nye was taken with Gaddafi's interest in the theory of "soft power," which Nye had developed.

104. Human Rights Watch, "Libya: June 1996 Killings at Abu Salim Prison," June 26, 2006, www.hrw.org/en/news/2006/06/27/libya-june-1996-killings-abu-salim-prison.

105. For details on Gaddafi's murder and that of his son and loyalists, see Human Rights Watch, *Death of a Dictator: Bloody Vengeance in Sirte* (October 2012). Among other things, Gaddafi was apparently sodomized with a knife or stick. CBS News, October 24, 2011, "GlobalPost: Qaddafi Apparently Sodomized After Capture," www.cbsnews.com/news/globalpost-qaddafi-apparently-sodomized-after-capture/.

106. Human Rights Watch, October 24, 2011, "Libya: Apparent Execution of 53 Gaddafi Supporters," www.hrw.org/node/102543.

107. Corbett Dakey, "Clinton on Qaddafi: 'We Came, We Saw, He Died," CBS News, October 20, 2011, www.cbsnews.com/news/clinton-on-qaddafi-we-came-we-saw-he-died/. Forte, *Slouching Toward Sirte*, 130–131, on Western leaders' comments on Gaddafi's death.

108. For details on Sudan's military role in Libya, see Asim Elhag, "The Sudanese Role in Libya 2011," World Peace Foundation, Tufts University, December 17, 2012, https://sites.tufts.edu/reinventingpeace/2012/12/17/the-sudanese-role-in-libya-2011/; de Waal, "'My Fears, Alas, Were Not Unfounded,'" 73–75. For an account that stresses the role of British, French, and Qatari military advisers who were on the ground and played a key role in helping NATO aircraft hit their targets but conspicuously omits mention of the Sudanese contribution, which the NTC freely acknowledged, see Frederic Wehrey, "The Hidden Story of Airpower in Libya (and What It Means for Syria)," *Foreign Policy*, February 11, 2013, http://foreignpolicy.com/2013/02/11/the-hidden-story-of-airpower-in-libya-and-what-it-means-for-syria/.

109. United Nations, Meetings Coverage and Press Releases, "General Assembly Adopts Resolution Stressing Critical Need for Regional Approach to Conflict Resolution in Africa," July 23, 2009, www.un.org/press/en/2009/ga10848.doc.htm.

110. Alex de Waal, "Playing Many Sides, Sudan's Bashir Tries to End His Isolation," *World Politics Review*, March 2, 2015, www.worldpoliticsreview.com/articles/print/15190.

111. "Sudan Joining Saudi Campaign in Yemen Shows Shift in Region Ties," *Bloomberg Business*, March 27, 2015, www.bloomberg.com/news/articles/2015-03-27/sudan-joining-saudi-campaign-in-yemen-shows-shift-in-region-ties; Somini Sengupta, "Sudan Joins Coalition Against Yemen Rebels," *New York Times*, March 26, 2015; Tom Hussain, "Once Iran's Ally, Sudan Sends Advisers for Yemeni Offensive Iran Opposes," McClatchy DC, May 5, 2015, www.mcclatchydc.com/news/nation-world/world/middle-east/article24784117.html.

112. United Nations High Commissioner for Human Rights, "Updated Statistical Analysis of Documentation of Killings in the Syrian Arab Republic," August 2014, www.ohchr.org/Documents/Countries/SY/HRDAGUpdatedReportAug2014.pdf.

113. Micah Zenko, "Syria Civil War Total Fatalities," http://blogs.cfr.org/zenko/2014/04/01/syria-civil-war-total-fatalities/.

114. United Nations High Commission for Refugees (UNHCR), "Stories from Syrian Refugees," n.d., http://data.unhcr.org/syrianrefugees/syria.php; UNHCR, "2014 UNHCR Country Operations Profile—Syrian Arab Republic," n.d., www.unhcr.org/pages/49e486a76.html.

115. "Libyan Revolution Casualties Lower Than Expected, Says New Government," *Guardian*, January 8, 2013, www.theguardian.com/world/2013/jan/08/libyan-revolution-casualties-lower-expected-government; Center for American Progress, Center for Civilians in Conflict, "Issue Brief: Civilian Protection and Harm Response in Post-Conflict Libya," January 2013. As the second report notes, this estimate does not include the tally of pro-regime forces killed and may not account for the total number of civilian deaths. Kuperman, "A Model Humanitarian Intervention," 13, cites a Libyan source to the effect that the number of government forces and supporters killed was probably equal to or slightly less than the total number of civilians and anti-Gaddafi fighters killed.

116. See Rajan Menon, "Beware the Staying Power of the Islamic State," *National Interest* (online), March 23, 2015, http://nationalinterest.org/feature/beware-the-islamic-states-staying-power-13666.

117. "Pentagon Will Send Troops to Train Some Syrian Rebels," *New York Times*, January 16, 2015; "US Reassured Syria's Assad in Back-Channel Message," *Bloomberg*, September 25, 2014, www.bloomberg.com/news/2014-09-25/u-s-reassured-syrias-assad-in-back-channel-message.html; "US-Led Air Strikes Pose Problem for Assad's Moderate Foes," Reuters, September 30, 2014, www.reuters.com/article/2014/09/30/us-mideast-crisis-syria-rebels-insight-idUSKCN0HP0BE20140930.

118. "US Signals Shift On How to End Syrian War," *New York Times*, January 19, 2015.

119. See Sadik J. Al-Azm, "Syria in Revolt: Understanding the Unthinkable War," *Boston Review*, August 18, 2014, http://bostonreview.net/world/sadik-al-azm-syria-in-revolt.

120. "Syria's Deadlocked Civil War: No Solution," *The Economist*, September 27, 2014. On the numbers that appear in the quote: As I have pointed out, the death toll in Syria, the numbers of civilians killed, and the proportion killed by the Assad government remains in dispute; undeniably, tens of thousands of noncombatants have been killed in the war.

121. On the origins and course of Congo's war, see Jason K. Stearns, *Dancing in the Glory of Monsters: The Collapse of the Congo and the Great War of Africa* (New York: PublicAffairs, 2011). The wide range in the estimated number of deaths stems from methodological differences between the International Rescue Committee (the source of the higher estimate) and the *Human Security Report* produced by Simon Fraser University in Vancouver: *Human Security Report 2009/2010* (New York: Oxford University Press, 2011), Part 2, Chapter 7, "The Shrinking Costs of War." For the controversy created by the lower estimate, see "New Study Argues That War Deaths Are Often Overestimated," *Christian Science Monitor*, March 22, 2010; "Study of War's Human Cost Sparks a Conflict of Its Own," *Globe and Mail*, February 9, 2010, www.theglobeandmail.com/news/world/study-of-wars-human-cost-sparks-a-conflict-of-its-own/article4262585/.

122. Details from Human Rights Watch, "DR Congo Chronology," August 21, 2009, www.hrw.org/news/2009/08/20/dr-congo-chronology-key-events and United Nations, "MONUSCO: United Nations Organization Stabilization Mission in the Democratic Republic of the Congo," www.un.org/en/peacekeeping/missions/monusco/facts.shtml. This link is dynamic (updated regularly), so the numbers will change over time. The figures I list here are those available as of May 2015.

123. "In Congo, Even Peacekeepers Add to Horror," *New York Times*, December 18, 2004, www.nytimes.com/2004/12/18/international/africa/18congo.html?pagewanted=2.

124. Nicholas J. Wheeler and Tim Dunne, "Good International Citizenship: A Third Way for British Foreign Policy," *International Affairs*, Vol. 74, No. 4 (1998), 861.
125. Wheeler and Dunne, "Good International Citizenship," 865.

CHAPTER SEVEN

1. Carl von Clausewitz, *On War*, edited and translated by Michael Howard and Peter Paret (Princeton, NJ: Princeton University Press, 1976). See also Eliot A. Cohen and John Gooch, *Military Misfortune: The Anatomy of Failure in War* (New York: Free Press, 1990).
2. For the text, see "Bush Makes Historic Speech Aboard Warship," CNN, May 1, 2003, www.cnn.com/2003/US/05/01/bush.transcript/index.html?iref=mpstoryview.
3. Cohen and Gooch, *Military Misfortunes*, 25. On the persistence of faulty predictions and unexpected occurrences, see Nicholas Naseem Taleb, *The Black Swan: The Impact of the Highly Improbable*, Second Edition (New York: Random House, 2010). See also Robert Jervis, *Perception and Misperception in International Relations* (Princeton, NJ: Princeton University Press, 1976).
4. Miranda Vickers, *Between Serb and Albanian: A History of Kosovo* (New York: Columbia University Press, 1998), 281–290.
5. See Organization for Security and Cooperation in Europe, Office of Democratic Institution and Human Rights, *Kosovo/Kosova As Seen, As Told: An Analysis of the Human Rights Findings of the OSCE Kosovo Verification Mission, October 1998–June 1999* (1999), Ch. 4–14, 22.
6. Ivo Daalder and Michael O'Hanlon, *Winning Ugly: NATO's War to Save Kosovo* (Washington, DC: Brookings Institution, 2000), 12.
7. Human Rights Watch, "The Crisis in Kosovo," n.d., www.hrw.org/reports/2000/nato/Natbm200-01.htm. The DoD report noted that "the Serbs used their system to launch a large number of surface-to-air missiles and antiaircraft artillery at allied pilots. In fact, the average aircrew participating in Operation Allied Force experienced a missile-launch rate three times that encountered by the average Coalition aircrew during Desert Storm. Nonetheless, NATO was able to mitigate the threat. In over 38,000 sorties, only two aircraft were lost to hostile fire … To achieve this result, however, NATO had to devote considerable resources to suppressing the enemy's air defenses. Rather than expend sorties attempting to find and attack the large numbers of man-portable missile and antiaircraft artillery threats, NATO commanders chose to operate most aircraft at altitudes beyond the effective reach of these systems." US Department of Defense, *Report to Congress: Kosovo/Operation Allied Force After-Action Report* (January 31, 2000), xxiii–xxiv.
8. Dana Priest, "Army's Apache Helicopter Rendered Impotent in Kosovo," *Washington Post*, December 29, 1999.
9. Edward N. Luttwak, "Toward Post-Heroic Warfare," *Foreign Affairs*, Vol. 74, No. 3 (May/June 1995), 109–122. For a discussion of how NATO's preoccupation with minimizing risk to its soldiers came at the expense of Kosovar civilians, see Luttwak, "Give War a Chance," *Foreign Affairs*, Vol. 78, No. 4 (July/August 1999), 40–41.
10. Human Rights Watch, "Federal Republic of Yugoslavia: Human Rights Developments 1999," *World Report 1999*, www.hrw.org/legacy/wr2k/Eca-26.htm. For a critical review of various estimates, see Jeffrey St. Clair and Alexander

Cockburn, "Kosovo: Where NATO Bombing Only Made the Killing Worse," *Counterpunch*, Weekend Edition, August 30–September 1, 2013, www.counter-punch.org/2013/08/30/kosovo-where-nato-bombing-only-made-the-killing-worse/.

11. Timothy Garton Ash, "The War We Almost Lost," *Guardian*, September 3, 2000, on the warning of the two presidents.

12. Human Rights Watch, *Under Orders: War Crimes in Kosovo* (New York: Human Rights Watch, 2001), 451; Brian Brady, "Nato Comes Clean on Cluster Bombs," *Independent*, September 16, 2007, www.independent.co.uk/news/world/politics/nato-comes-clean-on-cluster-bombs-402552.html.

13. "NATO Warplanes Jolt Yugoslav Power Grid," *Washington Post*, May 25, 1999, www.washingtonpost.com/wp-srv/inatl/longterm/balkans/stories/belgrade052599.htm.

14. Human Rights Watch, *Under Orders: War Crimes in Kosovo* (New York: Human Rights Watch, 2001), 437–451; Human Rights Watch, *Civilian Deaths in the NATO Air Campaign* (February 2000), www.hrw.org/reports/2000/nato/; Elizabeth Becker, "Rights Group Claims NATO Killed 500 Civilians in Kosovo War," *New York Times*, February 7, 2000, www.nytimes.com/2000/02/07/world/rights-group-says-nato-killed-500-civilians-in-kosovo-war.html.

15. Grant T. Hammond, "Myths of the Air War Over Serbia: Some 'Lessons' Not to Learn," *Air & Space Power Journal*, Vol. XIV, No. 4 (Winter 2000), 84. Garton Ash, "The War We Almost Lost," states that while NATO claimed to have demolished "some 120 Serbian tanks, 220 armored personnel carriers, and 450 artillery and mortar pieces.... the Serbian armoured columns that withdrew from Kosovo looked in remarkably good shape" and that "according to a suppressed US Air Force report obtained by *Newsweek*, Nato verifiably destroyed just 14 tanks, 18 armored personnel carriers, and 20 artillery pieces."

16. Garton Ash, "The War We Almost Lost."

17. Human Rights Watch Report, *Federal Republic of Yugoslavia: Abuses Against Serbs and Roma in the New Kosovo*, August 1999, www.hrw.org/reports/1999/kosov2/#_1_9; Claude Cahn and Tatyana Peric, "Roma and the Kosovo Conflict," European Roma Rights Centre, July 5, 1999. The latter report also discusses abuses suffered by Roma at the hands of Serb police and military.

18. Çeku became KLA Chief of Staff in 1999, served as Kosovo's prime minister from March 2006 to January 2008, and was appointed Security Minister in 2011. He was arrested, but soon released, in Slovenia in 2003, Hungary in 2004, and Bulgaria in 2008 under an Interpol warrant. See "Kosovo Ex-Premier Arrested on War Crimes," *New York Times*, June 24, 2009.

19. BBC News, June 28, 1998, "The KLA—Terrorists or Freedom Fighters?," http://news.bbc.co.uk/2/hi/europe/121818.stm.

20. Council of Europe, Parliamentary Assembly, Committee on Legal and Human Rights, "Inhuman Treatment of People and Illicit Trafficking in Human Organs in Kosovo," December 12, 2010; Amnesty International, "If They Are Not Guilty, Who Committed the War Crimes?" November 29, 2012, www.amnesty.org/en/news/kosovo-if-they-are-not-guilty-who-committed-war-crimes-2012-11-29; Nicholas Schmidle, "Bring Up the Bodies," *New Yorker*, May 6, 2013; "Kosovo PM Is Head of Human Organ and Arms Ring Council of Europe Reports," *Guardian*, December 14, 2010, www.theguardian.com/world/2010/dec/14/kosovo-prime-minister-llike-mafia-boss.

21. Human Rights Watch Report, *Federal Republic of Yugoslavia: Abuses Against Serbs and Roma in the New Kosovo*, Vol. 11, No. 10 (D) (August 1999), http://www.hrw.org/reports/1999/kosov2/#_1_9.

22. For details, see Saïd Haddadt, "The Role of the Libyan Army in the Revolt Against Gaddafi's Regime," Al Jazeera Centre for Studies, March 16, 2011.

23. Christopher Chivvis, *Toppling Qaddafi: Libya and the Limits of Liberal Intervention* (New York: Cambridge University Press, 2014), 134–139.

24. See Mark Kersten, "Negotiating in Libya: What Happens to Justice?," *Justice in Conflict*, July 26, 2011, http://justiceinconflict.org/2011/07/26/negotiating-peace-in-libya-what-happens-to-justice/.

25. For estimate of the death toll, see Milne, "If the Libyan War Was About Saving Lives"; Rachel Donadio, "Italy Says Death Toll in Libya Is Likely Over 1,000," *New York Times*, February 23, 2011.

26. Jeffrey M. Jones, "Americans Approve of Military Action Against Libya 47% to 37%," Gallup.com, March 22, 2011, www.gallup.com/poll/146738/americans-approve-military-action-against-libya.aspx.

27. "Washington Post-ABC News Poll," March 2011, www.washingtonpost.com/wp-srv/politics/polls/postpoll_03142011.html; "CNN Poll: Most Support No Fly Zone in Libya But Not Ground Troops," CNN.com, March 21, 2011, http://politicalticker.blogs.cnn.com/2011/03/21/cnn-poll-most-support-no-fly-zone-in-libya-but-not-ground-troops/.

28. Jeffrey M. Jones, "Americans Shift to a More Negative View of Libya Military Action," Gallup.com, www.gallup.com/poll/148196/americans-shift-negative-view-libya-military-action.aspx.

29. Jijo Jacob, "Majority of Americans Against Sending Ground Troops to Libya," *International Business Times*, March 24, 2011, citing a Reuters-Ipsos poll, www.ibtimes.com/majority-americans-against-sending-ground-troops-libya-276937; "CNN Poll"; "61% Oppose Sending US Ground Troops to Libya," reporting the results of a YouGov/*Economist* Poll, YouGov.com, June 10, 2011, http://today.yougov.com/news/2011/06/10/61-oppose-sending-us-ground-troops-libya/.

30. Chivvis, *Toppling Qaddafi*, 124.

31. Samira Shackle, "Libya Polls Show that British Public Is Divided," *New Statesman*, March 22, 2011, www.newstatesman.com/blogs/the-staggers/2011/03/british-public-support-action.

32. Zsolt Nyiri, "Transatlantic Trends: Public Opinion and NATO," German Marshall Fund, May 16, 2012, www.gmfus.org/commentary/transatlantic-trends-public-opinion-and-nato. The polling data in this study do, however, show higher levels of initial support in the United States, France, and Britain for the intervention as compared to the polls cited above. For the EU as a whole, though, the study reports 48 percent favoring the intervention and 47 percent opposed.

33. See Gary J. Bass, "Jus Post Bellum," *Philosophy and Public Affairs*, Vol. 32, No. 4 (Winter 2004), 382–412; Ruti Teitel, "Rethinking Jus Post Bellum in an Age of Global Transitional Justice," *European Journal of International Law*, Vol. 24, No. 1 (February 2013), 335–342; Michael Walzer, *Arguing About War* (New Haven, CT: Yale University Press, 2004), 19, 76–77, 162–168; Larry May and Andrew Forcehimes, eds., *Morality, Jus Post Bellum, and International Law* (Cambridge: Cambridge University Press, 2012); Larry May, *After War Ends: A Philosophical Perspective* (Cambridge: Cambridge University Press, 2012); Mark Evans, "Moral Responsibilities and the Conflicting Demands of Jus Post-Bellum," *Ethics and International Affairs*, Vo. 23, No. 2 (Summer 2009), 147–164; Annalisa Koeman, "A Realistic and Effective Constraint on the Resort to Force? Pre-Commitment to Jus in Bello and Jus Post Bellum as Part of the Criterion of Right Intention," *Journal of*

Military Ethics, Vol. 6, No. 3 (2007), 198–220; George M. Clifford, "Jus Post Bellum: Foundational Principles and a Proposed Model," *Journal of Military Ethics*, Vol. 11, No. 1 (2012), 42–57; Brian Orend, *Morality of War* (Peterborough, ON: Broadview Press, 2006), Chs. 6 and 7; Benjamin Banta, "'Virtuous War' and the Emergence of Jus Post Bellum," *Review of International Studies*, Vol. 37, No.1 (January 2011), 277–299.

34. See, for example, Jack Snyder, *From Voting to Violence: Democratization and Nationalist Conflict* (New York: Norton, 2000).

35. See Rory Stewart and Gerald Knaus, *Can Intervention Work?* (New York: Norton, 2011). Oddly, the authors stress that special circumstances enabled success in Bosnia, but then invoke its example to make the general case that humanitarian intervention can work. However, the circumstances that made for success in Bosnia will not reliably be present elsewhere, something that the authors concede (see 140–141).

36. Dag Henriksen, *NATO's Gamble: Combining Diplomacy and Airpower in the Kosovo Crisis, 1998–1999* (Annapolis, MD: Naval Institute Press, 2007), 104–105; GlobalSecurity.org, "Croatia—Operation Storm 1995," n.d., www.globalsecurity. org/intell/ops/croatia.htm; Stewart and Knaus, *Can Intervention Work?*, 110–111; Laura Silber and Allan Little, *Yugoslavia: Death of a Nation*, Revised and Enlarged Edition (New York: Penguin, 1997), 360. On the ethnic cleansing carried out by the American-trained Croatian army in Croatia's Krajina regions, see David Salter, "Medak Pocket: Canada's Forgotten Battle," *The Star* (Toronto), September 13, 2013, www.thestar.com/news/insight/2013/09/14/medak_pocket_canadas_forgotten_bat-tle.html; Mark Danner, "Operation Storm," *New York Review of Books*, October 22, 1998, www.nybooks.com/articles/archives/1998/oct/22/operation-storm/.

37. I draw on the incisive discussion of postconflict intervention in Stewart and Knaus, *Can Intervention Work?*, 127–157. See also David M. Edelstein, "Occupational Hazards: Why Military Occupations Succeed or Fail," *International Security*, Vol. 29, No. 1 (Summer 2004), 49–91. Edelstein offers an excellent analysis of the challenges outsiders face in establishing order in postwar societies.

38. For surveys of post-Dayton Bosnia's persistent problems, see Craig Whitlock, "14 Years After War's End Ethnic Divisions Once Again Gripping Bosnia," *Washington Post*, August 23, 2009, www.washingtonpost.com/wp-dyn/content/article/2009/08/22/AR2009082202234.html?sid=ST2009082202479; Patrice C. McMahon and Jon Western, "The Death of Dayton," *Foreign Affairs*, Vol. 88, No. 5 (September/October 2009), 69–83; Steven Woehrel, *Bosnia and Herzegovina: Current Issues and US Policies*, Congressional Research Service, January 24, 2103; International Crisis Group (ICG), *Bosnia's Future* (July 10, 2014).

39. I draw here on Julian Borger, "Bosnian War: 20 Years On: Peace Holds but Conflict Continues to Haunt," *Guardian*, April 4, 2012, www.theguardian.com/world/2012/apr/04/bosnian-war-20-years-on; Jonathan S. Landay, "20 Years After War Began Bosnia Grows More Divided," McClatchy Newspapers, April 25, 2012, www.mcclatchydc.com/2012/04/25/146696/20-years-after-war-began-bosnia.html; "Escalating Ethnic Tensions in Bosnia-Herzegovina," Stratfor, April 13, 2011, www.stratfor.com/analysis/escalating-ethnic-tensions-bosnia-herzegovina; and Alberto Nardelli, Denis Dzidic, and Elvira Jukic, "Bosnia and Herzegovina: The World's Most Complicated System of Government?" *Guardian*, October 8, 2014.

40. Patrice McMahon and Jon Western, "Death of Dayton—How to Stop Bosnia from Falling Apart," *Foreign Affairs*, Vol. 88, No. 5 (September/October 2009), 69–70.

41. On the 2013 ranking: "Comparison: Unemployment Rate," Central Intelligence Agency (CIA) *World Factbook*, www.cia.gov/library/publications/the-world-fact-book/rankorder/2129rank.html?countryname=Bosnia%20and%20Herzegovina&countrycode=bk&regionCode=eur&rank=193#bk; for the 2013 unemployment figure, see "Bosnia and Herzegovina Unemployment Rate, *Trading Economics*," www.tradingeconomics.com/bosnia-and-herzegovina/unemployment-rate; on youth unemployment and emigration; World Bank, "Unemployment, Youth Total (% of Labor Force Ages 15–24)," http://data.worldbank.org/indicator/SL.UEM.1524.ZS; Velma Saric and Elizabeth D. Herman, "Why Bosnia Has the World's Highest Youth Unemployment," *GlobalPost*, October 9, 2014, www.globalpost.com/dispatch/news/regions/europe/141008/bosnia-youth-unemployment-rate; Erol Mujanovic, *Youth Unemployment in Bosnia and Herzegovina: Current Situation, Challenges, and Recommendations* (Sarajevo: Friedrich Ebert Stiftung, 2013).
42. International Crisis Group, *Bosnia's Future* (July 10, 2014), i.
43. International Crisis Group, *Bosnia's Future*, 5.
44. For an overview of the instability and violence, see the panel discussion featuring Frederic Wehrey, Michelle Dunne, Wolfram Lacher, and Faraj Najem, "Libya's Civil War," Carnegie Endowment for International Peace, September 24, 2014; Rajan Menon, "Libya in Chaos," *National Interest*, June 27, 2012, http://nationalinterest.org/commentary/libya-in-chaos-7096. On the upheaval in Fezzan, see Alexander Roeskestad, "Libya's South on the Edge of Chaos," *Al Monitor*, November 2014, www.al-monitor.com/pulse/originals/2014/11/libya-south-chaos-fezzan-tribal-terrorism.html#.
45. See Frederic Wehrey and Wolfram Lacher, "Libya's Legitimacy Crisis: The Danger of Picking Sides in the Post Qaddafi Crisis," *Foreign Affairs*, October 6, 2014, www.foreignaffairs.com/articles/142138/frederic-wehrey-and-wolfram-lacher/libyas-legitimacy-crisis; Human Rights Watch, September 8, 2014, "Libya: Spiraling Militia Attacks May Be War Crimes," www.hrw.org/news/2014/09/08/libya-spiraling-militia-attacks-may-be-war-crimes; Ishaan Tharoor and Adam Taylor, "Here Are the Key Players Fighting the War for Libya, All Over Again," *Washington Post*, August 27, 2014, www.washingtonpost.com/blogs/worldviews/wp/2014/08/27/here-are-the-key-players-fighting-the-war-for-libya-all-over-again/.
46. On the conflict between the militias of Zintan and Misrata, see Patrick Markey and Aziz El Yaakoubi, "Insight—Town Vs. Town, Faction Vs. Faction as Libya Descends into 'Hurricane,'" Reuters, August 1, 2014, http://uk.reuters.com/article/2014/08/01/uk-libya-security-insight-idUKKBN0G023820140801.
47. On Hifter's CIA connections, see "Khalifa Haftar: The Man Who Left Libya to Lead Libya's Rebels," CNN, April 4, 2011, www.cnn.com/2011/WORLD/africa/04/04/libya.rebel.leader/.
48. Abigail Hauslohner and Sharif Abdel Koddous, "Khalifa Hifter, the Ex General Leading a Revolt in Libya Spent Years in Exile in Northern Virginia," *Washington Post*, May 20, 2014, www.washingtonpost.com/world/africa/rival-militias-prepare-for-showdown-in-tripoli-after-takeover-of-parliament/2014/05/19/cb36acc2-df6f-11e3-810f-764fe508b82d_story.html; David Garnstein-Ross, Oren Adaki, and Nathaniel Burr, "Libya: Hifter's Stalled Anti-Islamist Campaign," *War on the Rocks*, July 15, 2014, http://warontherocks.com/2014/07/libya-hifters-stalled-anti-islamist-campaign/#_.
49. Christopher S. Chivvis and Jeffrey Martini, *Libya After Qaddafi: Lessons and Implications for the Future* (Santa Monica, CA: Rand Corporation, 2014), 8, 65.

50. "Two Rival Libyan Governments Claim to Control Oil Policy," Reuters, October 17, 2014, www.reuters.com/article/2014/10/18/us-libya-oil-idUSKCN0I70IV20141018; Frederic Wehrey, "The Battle for Libya's Oil," *Atlantic*, February 9, 2015, www.the-atlantic.com/international/archive/2015/02/the-battle-for-libyas-oil/385285/.

51. Wehrey, "The Battle."

52. Frederic Wehrey, "Is Libya a Proxy War?" *Washington Post*, October 24, 2014, www.washingtonpost.com/blogs/monkey-cage/wp/2014/10/24/is-libya-a-proxy-war/; "Regional Dimensions to the Libyan Conflict," Afro-Middle Eastern Center (Johannesburg), September 24, 2014, http://amec.org.za/articles-presentations/north-africa/472-regional-dimensions-to-the-libyan-conflict; Seumas Milne, "Coups and Terror Are the Fruits of Nato's War in Libya," *Guardian*, May 22, 2014, www.theguardian.com/commentisfree/2014/may/22/coups-terror-nato-war-in-libya-west-intervention-boko-haram-nigeria.

53. "UAE and Egypt Behind Bombing Raids Against Libyan Militants, Say US Officials," *Guardian*, August 26, 2014, www.theguardian.com/world/2014/aug/26/united-arab-emirates-bombing-raids-libyan-militias?CMP=share_btn_link.

54. "Egypt Launches Air Strike in Libya Against ISIS Branch," *New York Times*, February 16, 2015.

55. Tiemoko Diallo and Adama Diarra, "UN Deploys Troops Around Northern Mali After Clashes," Reuters, August 18, 2015, www.reuters.com/article/2015/08/18/us-mali-violence-idUSKCN0QN10D20150818; "Mali's UN Troops Killed in Deadliest Attack," BBC News, October 3, 2014, www.bbc.com/news/world-africa-29475975; "Six UN Peacekeepers Killed When Convoy Attacked in Mali," Reuters, July 2, 2015, http://uk.reuters.com/article/2015/07/02/uk-mali-un-idUKKCN0PC1AE20150702; "Peace Elusive in Mali As More UN Troops Are Killed," Deutsche Welle, www.dw.com/en/peace-in-mali-elusive-as-more-un-troops-are-killed/a-18629032.

56. Katarina Höije, "Thousands Flee Violent Upsurge in Northern Mali," IRIN News, May 29, 2015, www.irinnews.org/report/101561/thousands-flee-violent-upsurge-in-northern-mali; UN Higher Commissioner for Refugees (UNHCR), "Fighting in Northern Mali Forces Thousands to Flee Their Homes," *Briefing Notes*, May 29, 2015, www.unhcr.org/55685b876.html.

57. Oussama Romdhani, "Growing Worries About Libya in the Maghreb," *Al Arabiya*, November 24, 2013, http://english.alarabiya.net/en/views/news/africa/2013/11/24/Growing-worries-about-Libya-in-the-Maghreb.html; Omar Ben Dorra, "Libya Sinking into Chaos," *Al Monitor*, September 1, 2014, www.al-monitor.com/pulse/politics/2014/08/libya.html#. The first attack in Tunisia occurred at the Bardo National Museum in Tunis in March and killed twenty-one people; the second, at a beach resort in Sousse, took place in July, killing thirty-eight. See Howard LaFranchi, "Terrorists in Tunisia Attack Trained at Islamic State Camp in Libya," *Christian Science Monitor*, July 2, 2015, www.csmonitor.com/USA/Foreign-Policy/2015/0702/Terrorists-in-Tunisia-attacks-trained-at-Islamic-State-camp-in-Libya and "Tunisia to Build Anti-Terror Wall on Libya Border," BBC News, July 8, 2015, www.bbc.com/news/world-africa-33440212.

58. Based on Alex de Waal, "'My Fears, Alas, Were Not Unfounded': Africa's Responses to the Libyan Conflict," in Aidan Hehir and Robert Murray, eds., *Libya: The Responsibility to Protect and the Future of Humanitarian Intervention* (Basingstoke, UK: Palgrave Macmillan, 2013), 76.

59. See, for example, "Islamic State Kills Five Journalists Working for Libyan TV Station—Official," Reuters, April 27, 2015, www.reuters.com/article/2015/04/27/

us-libya-security-idUSKBNoNI1V820150427; "Islamic State Militants Claim Attacks on Embassies in Libya," *Guardian*, April 12, 2015, www.theguardian.com/world/2015/apr/13/islamic-state-militants-claim-attacks-on-embassies-in-libya; "Islamic State Murders 30 African Migrants in Libya, While Up to 700 Died Off Coast," *Christian Science Monitor*, April 20, 2015: Frederic Wehrey and Alá Alrabábah, "Rising Out of Chaos: The Islamic State in Libya," Carnegie Endowment for International Peace, March 15, 2015, http://carnegieendowment.org/syriaincrisis/?fa=59268.

60. De Waal, "'My Fears, Alas, Were Not Unfounded,'" 58–76.

61. On Libya as a model intervention, see Ivo H. Daalder and James G. Stavridis, "NATO's Victory in Libya: The Right Way to Run an Intervention," *Foreign Affairs*, Vol. 91, No. 2 (March–April 2012), 2–7; on the Libyan campaign as a "textbook example" of R2P's application, see Nayan Chanda's interview with Gareth Evans, *Yale Global Online*, April 15, 2011, http://yaleglobal.yale.edu/content/gareth-evans-responsibility-protect-transcript.

62. John Stuart Mill, "A Few Words on Non-Intervention," *Fraser's Magazine* (1859), reprinted by the Libertarian Alliance, www.libertarian.co.uk/lapubs/forep/forep008.pdf. This is not to say that Mill ruled out intervention. See also Michael W. Doyle, *The Question of Intervention: John Stewart Mill and the Responsibility to Protect* (New Haven, CT: Yale University Press, 2015), 19–31. As I noted in Chapter 3, Mill does not maintain that intervention should never be undertaken.

63. On the Sunnis and the constitutional drafting process and the January 2005 election, see Joost R. Hiltermann, "Elections and Constitution Writing in Iraq, 2005," European Institute of the Mediterranean (IEMED), *Yearbook 2006*, www.iemed.org/anuari/2006/aarticles/aHiltermann.pdf.

64. Timothy Williams and Duraid Adnan, "Sunnis in Iraq Allied With US Rejoin Rebels," *New York Times*, October 16, 2010.

65. Fred Kaplan, "After Mosul: If Jihadists Control Iraq, Blame Nouri al-Maliki, Not the United States," *Slate*, June 11, 2014, www.slate.com/articles/news_and_politics/war_stories/2014/06/mosul_s_collapse_is_nouri_al_maliki_s_fault_iraq_s_prime_minister_failed.html; International Crisis Group, *Make or Break: Iraq's Sunnis and the State* (August 14, 2013).

66. For details on the expenditures on economic and military aid for Iraq, see Kenneth Katzman, *Iraq: Politics, Governance and Human Rights*, Congressional Research Service, September 15, 2014, 43, Table 4: US Assistance to Iraq: FY2003–FY2015.

67. James Risen, *Pay Any Price: Greed, Power, and Endless War* (Boston: Houghton Mifflin, 2014), Chs. 1–3; R. Jeffrey Smith, "Waste, Fraud and Abuse Commonplace in Iraq," Center for Public Integrity, March 13, 2013, www.publicintegrity.org/2013/03/14/12312/waste-fraud-and-abuse-commonplace-iraq-reconstruction-effort; Special Inspector for Iraq Reconstruction (SIGIR), *Learning From Iraq: A Special Report from the Special Inspector General for Iraq Reconstruction* (2013), esp. Preface and Ch. 1. The $8 billion figure is reported in the preface (*ix*). The office of the SIGIR was created by Congress in 2003 and has issued quarterly reports. This report, covering 2003–2012, was issued under SIGIR William Bowen.

CHAPTER EIGHT

1. There is a mountain of books that demonstrate this reality, though the authors differ dramatically on its causes and consequences of globalization. See, for example,

John Micklethwait and Adrian Wooldridge, *A Future Perfect* (New York: Crown Books, 2000).

2. On the supposed consensus on redefining sovereignty, see the report of the Genocide Prevention Task Force, organized by the United States Holocaust Museum, the American Academy of Diplomacy, and the United States Institute for Peace and cochaired by former Secretary of State Madeleine K. Albright and former US Senator and Secretary of Defense William S. Cohen, *Preventing Genocide*, http://media.usip.org/reports/genocide_taskforce_report.pdf, 101–104. A substantial scholarly literature is dedicated to highlighting the shift in, and power of, norms on sovereignty and human rights. See, for example, Martha Finnemore and Kathryn Sikkink, "International Norm Dynamics and Political Change," *International Studies Quarterly*, Vol. 17 (Autumn 1998), 887–912; Thomas Risse, Stephen Ropp, and Kathryn Sikkink, eds., *The Power of Human Rights: International Norms and Domestic Change* (Cambridge: Cambridge University Press, 1999).

3. Hedley Bull, *The Anarchical Society: A Study of Order in World Politics* (New York: Columbia University Press, 2003). Within the English School a difference (one of many) exists between "pluralists," such as Bull, who believe that the degree of normative agreement is minimal and that efforts to increase it will increase tension and even create conflict in a world of diverse countries, and "solidarists," who see the extent of normative agreement as significantly greater and increasing. See, for example, Hidemi Suganami, "The International Society Perspective on World Politics Reconsidered," *International Relations of the Asia-Pacific*, Vol. 2, No. 2 (February 2002), 1–28, esp. 13–17; Nicholas Wheeler, *Saving Strangers* (Oxford: Oxford University Press, 2002), 33–51, offers a solidarist account of humanitarian intervention, an enterprise about which pluralists are more skeptical.

4. Reinhold Niebuhr, *Moral Man and Immoral Society* (New York: Charles Scribner's Sons, 1932), 49. See also Niebuhr, *The Children of Light and the Children of Darkness* (New York: Charles Scribner's Sons, 1944), Ch. 5, "The World Community."

5. Niebuhr, *Moral Man*, 85.

6. Reinhold Niebuhr, "The Illusion of World Government," *Foreign Affairs*, Vol. 27, No. 3 (April 1949), 379.

7. For an elaboration of this position, albeit in different ways, with respect to international law and norms in general and sovereignty in particular, see Gerry Simpson, *Great Powers and Outlaw States: Unequal Sovereigns in the International Legal Order* (Cambridge: Cambridge University Press, 2004), 4–10; and Wilhelm G. Grewe, *Epochs of International Law*, trans. and revised by Michael Byers (Berlin: Walter de Gruyter, 2000). According to Grewe: "The stronger the leading position of the particular predominant power, the more that State marked the spiritual vision of the age, the more its ideas and concepts prevailed, the more it conferred general and absolute validity on expressions of its national expansionist ideology. In this sense, one can speak of a 'Spanish,' a 'French,' and a 'British' Age in the history of modern international law" (23–24).

8. For skepticism about the extent of global consensus on values—in this instance, those relating to economic justice—and the argument that pluralistic values and the nation-based conception of interest continue to dominate despite the connections born of globalization, see David Miller, "Against Global Egalitarianism," *Journal of Ethics*, Vol. 9, Nos. 1–2 (2005), esp. 67–71.

9. Kofi Annan, "Problems without Passports," *Foreign Policy* (September–October 2002), 30–31. This issue of the magazine features a segment providing different perspectives on the question: "What Is An International Community?"

10. Sadako Ogata, "Guilty Parties," *Foreign Policy* (September–October 2002), 40.

11. United High Commissioner for Refugees (UNHCR), "UNHCR Warns of Funding Shortfall for Syrian Refugees," April 12, 2012.

12. UNHCR, "UNHCR Urgently Needs Funds As It Scales Up Syria Refugee Operations," January 22, 2013, www.unhcr.org/50fe6c159.html.

13. "Lack of Funds: World Food Programme Drops Aid to One-Third of Syrian Refugees," *Guardian*, reprinting an Associated Press news story, September 4, 2015, www.theguardian.com/world/2015/sep/05/lack-of-funds-world-food-programme-drops-aid-to-one-third-of-syrian-refugees.

14. UNHCR, "UNHCR Warns of Winter Crisis for Almost 1 Million Displaced Iraqis and Syrians," November 11, 2014, www.unhcr.org/546f0959.html; "UN Cuts Food Aid to Refugees From Syria," *New York Times*, December 1, 2014; UNHCR, "UN and Partners Seek $8.4 Billion for New Syria Programme in 2015," December 18, 2014, www.unhcr.org/5492a7bb6.html.

15. UNHCR, "2015 UNHCR Country Operations Profile: Syrian Arab Republic," www.unhcr.org/pages/49e486a76.html.

16. "UN Calls On Western Nations to Shelter Syrian Refugees," *New York Times*, April 17, 2015.

17. Aron Lund, "The Betrayal of Syrian Refugees," Carnegie Endowment for International Peace, December 12, 2014, http://carnegieendowment.org/syriaincrisis/?fa=57499.

18. UNHCR, "Resettlement and Other Forms of Admission for Syrian Refugees," March 12, 2015, www.unhcr.org/52b2febafc5.html. The following are the pledges, in descending order, of the countries mentioned, taking into account different forms of admittance: Germany (30,000), Canada (11,300), Australia (5,600), Switzerland (3,500), and Norway (2,500).

19. "Syrian Refugees: Which Countries Welcome Them, Which Ones Don't," CNN, September 10, 2015 update, www.cnn.com/2015/09/09/world/welcome-syrian-refugees-countries/.

20. Rick Lyman, "Eastern Bloc's Resistance to Refugees Highlights Europe's Cultural and Political Divisions," *New York Times*, September 12, 2015.

21. Griff Witte and Karla Adams, "Britain Takes in So Few Refugees They Would Fit in a Subway Train," *Washington Post*, September 1, 2015, www.washingtonpost.com/world/britain-takes-in-so-few-refugees-from-syria-they-would-fit-on-a-subway-train/2015/09/01/af427190-4b34-11e5-80c2-106ea7fb80d4_story.html.

22. "The Guardian View on Syrian Refugees: More Should Be Allowed to Come to the UK," *Guardian*, February 1, 2015, www.theguardian.com/commentisfree/2015/feb/01/guardian-view-syrian-refugees-more-should-allowed-come-here.

23. Amnesty International, *Left Out in the Cold: Syrian Refugees Abandoned by the International Community* (December 2014), www.amnesty.eu/content/assets/Reports/Left_Out_in_the_Cold_Syrian_Refugees_Abandoned_by_the_International_Community_final_formatted_version.pdf. The report does not, in my view, do justice to Sweden's intake of 2,700.

24. Lund, "The Betrayal of Syrian Refugees."

25. This distinction corresponds in some respects to what Rawls described as "liberal" societies on the one hand and "decent hierarchical societies" on the other. John

Rawls, *The Law of Peoples* (Cambridge, MA: Harvard University Press, 1999), esp. 23–29, 59–80.

26. Eric Hobsbawm and Terence Ranger, eds., *The Invention of Tradition* (Cambridge: Cambridge University Press, 1992).

27. See Benedict Anderson, *Imagined Communities: Reflections on the Origin and Spread of Nationalism*, Revised Edition (London: Verso, 2006).

28. On this point, see, in particular, Walker Connor, *Ethnonationalism: The Quest for Understanding* (Princeton, NJ: Princeton University Press, 1994); and Anthony Smith, *Nations and Nationalism in a Global Era* (Cambridge: Polity Press, 1995).

29. See Thomas Nagel, "The Problem of Global Justice," *Philosophy and Public Affairs*, Vol. 33, No. 2 (March 2005), 113–147.

30. See *Preventing Genocide: A Blueprint for US Policymakers* (2008), 106–107.

31. Quite apart from the fact that the P-5 are the major powers, the other ten members of the Council serve two-year terms and do not constitute a permanent presence.

32. "United Nations Peacekeeping Operations: Fact Sheet 31 December 2014," www.un.org/en/peacekeeping/archive/2014/bnote1214.pdf.

33. Council of the City of New York, "Hearing on the 2014 Executive Budget for the Police Department," May 23, 2013, http://council.nyc.gov/downloads/pdf/budget/2014/execbudget/2police.pdf; "Hearing on the Fiscal Year 2014 Executive Budget for the Fire Department," May 14, 2013, http://council.nyc.gov/downloads/pdf/budget/2014/execbudget/fdny.pdf.

34. International Court of Justice, "Contentious Jurisdiction," www.icj-cij.org/jurisdiction/index.php?p1=5&p2=1.

35. The Statute was adopted in 1998 and entered force in 2002 after it was ratified by 60 states. As of 2015, 139 states had signed the treaty, out of which 120 have ratified it. Forty-two states, including China, India, and Indonesia, respectively the world's first, second, and fourth most populous countries, have not ratified it.

36. In agreeing to this arrangement these states may have violated the terms of the Rome Statute. Eric A. Posner and John C. Yoo, "Judicial Independence in International Tribunals," *California Law Review*, Vol. 93, No. 1 (January 2005), 69–70.

37. American Servicemembers' Protection Act of 2002 (Title 2 of Public Law 107–206); approved August 2, 2002, http://legcounsel.house.gov/Comps/aspa02.pdf.

38. For the excellent account by President Clinton's chief negotiator with the ICC on the United States' insistence on special treatment, see David Scheffer, *All the Missing Souls: A Personal History of the War Crimes Tribunals* (Princeton, NJ: Princeton University Press, 2012), Ch. 7, "The Siren of Exceptionalism." Scheffer notes, "Other governments were confused by and annoyed with the US strategy in the talks for the International Criminal Court ... That strategy ended up seeking to protect the United States as a nonparty to the treaty regardless of how its military might wage warfare on foreign territory" (167).

39. David Bosco, *Rough Justice: The International Criminal Court in a World of Power Politics* (New York: Oxford University Press, 2014), 64–66; Ainley, "The International Criminal Court on Trial," *Cambridge Review of International Affairs*, Vol. 24, No. 3 (September 2011), 322–323.

40. Bosco, *Rough Justice*, 119–121.

41. Bosco, *Rough Justice*, 75–76; Ainley, "The International Criminal Court on Trial," 322–323.

42. For details see Bosco, *Rough Justice*, 96–98, 116–118.

43. That military offensive focused initially on insurgents tied to two previous Ugandan presidents, Milton Obote and Lutwa Okello, and later on the LRA. On the anti-LRA counterinsurgency in Acholiland, see Mahmood Mamdani, *Saviors and Survivors: Darfur, Politics, and the War on Terror* (New York: Pantheon, 2009), 279–280; Mamdani, "Responsibility to Protect or Right to Punish?," *Journal of Intervention and State Building*, Vol. 4, No. 1 (March 2010), 58–59. For details on Uganda's manipulation of the Court to squeeze the LRA while exempting itself from scrutiny, see Sarah M. H. Nouwen and Wouter G. Werner, "Doing Justice to the Political: The International Criminal Court in Uganda and Sudan," *European Journal of International*, Vol. 21, No. 4 (2011), esp. 946–954.

44. Adam Branch, "Uganda's Civil War and the Politics of ICC Intervention" *Ethics and International Affairs*, Vol. 12, No. 2 (Summer 2007), 181; Mamdani, *Saviors and Survivors*, 280.

45. Branch, "Uganda's Civil War," 181. On the widespread human rights violations within the camps, see Human Rights Watch, "Uprooted and Forgotten: Impunity and Human Rights Abuses in Northern Uganda," September 2005, 41–46, www.hrw.org/reports/2005/uganda0905/uganda0905.pdf.

46. For details, see Alana Tiemessen, "The International Criminal Court and the Politics of Prosecution," *International Journal of Human Rights*, Vol. 8, Nos. 4–5 (2014), 1–18.

47. Tiemessen, "The International Criminal Court," 15; and Nouwen and Wouter, "Doing Justice to the Political," 943, note that "the Court was created by political decisions, it adjudicates crimes which are frequently related to politics, and it depends on a mysterious and seemingly magical 'political will' for the enforcement of its decisions. The political is not something external to the Court, not just a force which potentially compromises the independence of the Court and needs to be overcome."

48. For critical appraisals of the ICC, see David Kaye, "Who's Afraid of the International Criminal Court? Finding the Prosecutor Who Can Set It Straight," *Foreign Affairs*, Vol. 90, No. 3 (May/June 2011), 118–129; Eric Posner, "The Absurd International Criminal Court," *Wall Street Journal*, June 10, 2012, www.wsj.com/articles/SB10001424052702303753904577452122153205162; Ainley, "The International Criminal Court," 309–333; Jack Goldsmith and Stephen D. Krasner, "The Limits of Idealism," *Daedalus*, Vol. 132, No. 1 (Winter 2003), 47–63; Tiemessen, "The International Criminal Court"; Nouwen and Wouter, "Doing Justice to the Political."

49. By comparison the ad hoc International Criminal Tribunal for the Former Yugoslavia (ICTY) and the International Criminal Tribunal for Rwanda (ICTR) were far more efficient and found over 100 people guilty, many of them senior leaders, including Serbian president Slobodan Milošević and Bosnian Serb leader Radovan Karadžić, and Théoneste Bagosora, the Rwandan colonel who helped form the Interahamwe death squads. Charles Taylor, Sierra Leone's former president, was indicted for war crimes (2003) and sentenced (2013) by a "Special Court" formed following an agreement between the UN and the government of Sierra Leone. For details, see "Special Court for Sierra Leone," www.rscsl.org/.

50. For the texts of the warrants, see www.icc-cpi.int/iccdocs/doc/doc907140.pdf; www.icc-cpi.int/iccdocs/doc/doc639078.pdf.

51. "Decision on the Meeting of the African States Parties to the Rome Statute of the International Criminal Court," Doc. Assembly/13,XIII, July 3, 2009, www.au.int/en/sites/default/files/ASSEMBLY_EN_1_3_JULY_2009_AUC_THIRTEENTH_

ORDINARY_SESSION_DECISIONS_DECLARATIONS_%20MESSAGE_
CONGRATULATIONS_MOTION_0.pdf.

52. The quotations appear in "Often Split, Arab Leaders Unite for Sudan's Chief," *New York Times*, March 30, 2009.

53. "Sudanese Leader Gets Warm Welcome in Qatar as Arab League Ignores ICC Warrant," *Washington Post*, March 30, 2009, www.washingtonpost.com/wp-dyn/content/article/2009/03/29/AR2009032902507.html.

54. See the "Bashir Travel Map," in "Stop Bashir. End Genocide," n.d. (current as of October 2014), http://bashirwatch.org/#turkey.

55. "ICC Prosecutor Shelves Darfur War Crimes Probe," *Guardian*, December 14, 2014, www.theguardian.com/world/2014/dec/14/icc-darfur-war-crimes-fatou-bensouda-sudan; "Omar Bashir Celebrates ICC Decision to Halt Darfur Investigation," *Guardian*, December 14, 2014, www.theguardian.com/world/2014/dec/14/omar-al-bashir-celebrates-icc-decision-to-halt-darfur-investigation.

56. "Alarm Raised Over Violence in Sudan's Darfur," Al Jazeera, March 28, 2014, www.aljazeera.com/news/africa/2014/03/un-raises-alarm-over-growing-darfur-violence-201432723314421433.html; UNHCR, "2015 Country Operations Profile—Sudan," n.d., www.unhcr.org/pages/49e483b76.html; Eric Reeves's blog, January 30, 2015, "Approximately 500,000 People Were Newly Displaced in Darfur in 2015—And This Year Promises to Be Worse," http://sudanreeves.org/2015/01/30/almost-500000-people-were-newly-displaced-in-darfur-in-2014-and-this-year-promises-to-be-worse-2/.

57. In the Kenyan case—which was taken up by the ICC's prosecutor at the request of a Kenyan commission of inquiry rather than by a referral from a state party or the Security Council—the ICC did investigate both of the sides alleged to have been involved in the violence that followed the 2007 presidential elections. See Gabrielle Lynch and Miša Zgonec-Rožej, "The ICC Intervention in Kenya," Chatham House, February 2013.

58. "Uganda's Museveni Calls Upon African Nations to Quit ICC," Reuters, December 12, 2014, www.reuters.com/article/2014/12/12/us-africa-icc-idUSKBN0JQ1DO20141212. On Africa's shifting attitudes toward the ICC, see Kenneth Roth, "Africa Attacks the International Criminal Court," *New York Review of Books*, February 6, 2014.

59. Kate Cronin-Furman, "Managing Expectations: International Criminal Trials and the Prospects for Deterring Mass Atrocity," *International Journal for Transnational Justice*, Vol. 7, No. 3 (November 2013), 434–454.

60. "The LRA in Congo, CAR, and South Sudan," Center for American Progress, "Enough: The Project to End Genocide and Crimes against Humanity," 2015, www.enoughproject.org/conflicts/lra/congo-car-south-sudan; Human Rights Watch, "The Christmas Massacres: LRA Attacks in Northern Congo," February 16, 2009, www.hrw.org/reports/2009/02/16/christmas-massacres-0.

61. "Muslim Group Trapped by Central African Republic Violence Face Dire Situation, Warns UN," UN New Center, December 23, 2014, www.un.org/apps/news/story.asp?NewsID=49673#.VQXjPilUtkg; Krista Larson, "Report: Death Toll in Central African Republic Tops 5,000," *Huffington Post*, September 12, 2014, www.huffingtonpost.com/2014/09/12/central-african-republic-death-toll_n_5810010.html. For a detailed analysis of the conflict in the CAR, see International Crisis Group, "The Central African Republic's Hidden Conflict," Africa Briefing No. 15 (December 12, 2014). On the number of internally displaced people and of refugees, see United

Nations High Commissioner for Refugees, "2015 UNHCR Country Operations Profile—Central African Republic," www.unhcr.org/pages/49e45c156.html.

62. Human Rights Watch, World Report 2015, "Democratic Republic of Congo," www. hrw.org/world-report/2015/country-chapters/democratic-republic-of-congo; Global Centre for the Responsibility to Protect, "Populations in the Democratic Republic of Congo Remain at Imminent Risk of Mass Atrocity Crimes Perpetrated by Armed Groups," (Update of March 15, 2015), www.globalr2p.org/regions/democratic_republic_of_the_congo_drc.

63. UN, Security Council Report, February 2015 Monthly Forecast, "South Sudan (UNMISS)," posted January 30, 2015, www.securitycouncilreport.org/monthly-forecast/2015-02/south_sudan_unmiss.php. On the background of the violence and the 50,00 death toll estimate, see International Crisis Group, "Sudan and South Sudan's Merging Conflicts," Africa Report No. 223 (January 29, 2015), www.crisisgroup.org/~/media/Files/africa/horn-of-africa/south%20sudan/223-sudan-and-south-sudan-s-merging-conflicts.pdf.

64. United Nations Mission in South Sudan (UNMISS), "UNMISS Mandate," n.d., www.un.org/en/peacekeeping/missions/unmiss/mandate.shtml.

65. Julian Ku and Jide Nzelibe make this point in "Do International Criminal Tribunals Deter or Exacerbate Atrocities?," *Washington University Law Review*, Vol. 84, No. 4 (2004), 808.

66. See, for example, Benjamin Valentino, *Final Solutions: Mass Killings and Genocide in the 20th Century* (Ithaca, NY: Cornell University Press, 2005); Valentino, "Final Solutions: The Causes of Genocide and Mass Killing," *Security Studies*, Vol. 9, No. 3 (Spring 2000), 1–59; Alexander B. Downes, "Desperate Times, Desperate Measures: The Causes of Civilian Victimization in War," *International Security*, Vol. 30, No. 4 (Spring 2006), 152–195.

67. Cronin-Furman, "Managing Expectations," 442–443, 453; Ku and Nzelibe, "Do International Criminal Tribunals Deter or Exacerbate Atrocities?", note that perpetrators of atrocities are "high-risk individuals" and that it is not likely that they will abjure violence for fear of being punished by an international court (807).

68. Cronin-Furman, "Managing Expectations," 445, 449, 451–452.

69. Cronin-Furman, "Managing Expectations"; Goldsmith and Krasner, "Limits of Idealism," 55–56; Jack L. Snyder and Leslie Vinjamuri, "Law and Politics in Transnational Justice," *Annual Review of Political Science*, Vol. 18 (May 2015), 303–327; see in particular the concluding section, Ku and Nzelibe, "Do International Criminal Tribunals Deter or Exacerbate Atrocities," who conclude that claims that the ICC and the ad hoc tribunals for the former Yugoslavia (ICTY) and Rwanda (ICTR) deter atrocities are "dubious and debatable" (831), and that these courts have had a "marginal, if not counterproductive, role in deterring humanitarian atrocities in the weak or failing states where such atrocities are likely to occur" (783).

70. The most comprehensive study is by Hyeran Jo and Beth A. Simmons, "Can the International Criminal Court Deter Atrocity?" unpublished paper, draft of December 18, 2014, Social Science Research Network, http://papers.ssrn.com/sol3/papers.cfm?abstract_id=2552820. Jo and Simmons state that: i) there are grounds for "cautious optimism" about the capacity of the ICC to deter atrocities (4); ii) the states concerned about their image at home and abroad are most likely to be deterred, never mind that such states are not likely to commit atrocities to start with (7, 12–14); iii) that the chances that offenders will be punished by the ICC

is "small" (16) though greater than it was before the ICC was created (which is obvious); iv) rebel and insurgent groups are not likely to be deterred (34–36); v) individuals determined to kill or intimidate civilians for personal or political gains "are difficult to deter under any circumstances" (38).

CONCLUSION

1. Steven Pinker, *The Better Angels of Our Nature: Why Violence Has Declined* (New York: Penguin, 2011).
2. Pinker, I should clarify, does not claim that the trend he uncovers will culminate in the end of violence.
3. This is the import of Robert Pape's formula—a combination of realism and just war theory—for humanitarian intervention. He combines the standard just-war checklist with the requirement that the intervening country suffer virtually no casualties, or, in his words, "near zero." These stringent requirements will rule out interventions in many instances. Robert Pape, "When Duty Calls: A Pragmatic Standard of Humanitarian Intervention," *International Security*, Vol. 37, No. 1 (Summer 2012), 41–80.
4. Columbia Law School, Human Rights Clinic, Center for Civilians in Conflict, *The Civilian Impact of Drones* (2012); Stanford Law School (International Human Rights and Conflict Resolution Clinic) and New York University Law School (Global Justice Clinic), *Living Under Drones: Death, Injury, and Trauma to Civilians from US Drone Practices in Pakistan* (September 2012); Kenneth Roth, "What Rules Should Govern US Drone Attacks?" *New York Review of Books*, April 4, 2013; Daniel Brunstetter and Meghan Braun, "The Implications of Drones on the Just War Tradition," *Ethics and International Affairs*, Vol. 25, No. 3 (Fall 2011), 337–358; Mary Ellen O'Connell, "Lawful Use of Combat Drones," testimony before the US House of Representatives, Subcommittee on National Security and Foreign Affairs, April 28, 2010. As for the defense that the drone attacks the United States conducts in countries in which it is not engaged in armed conflict were approved by the governments concerned, O'Connell notes: "States cannot, however, give consent to a right they do not have. States may not use military force on their territory when law enforcement measures are appropriate."
5. Stephen Hopgood challenges this view in *The Endtimes of Human Rights* (Ithaca, NY: Cornell University Press, 2013), arguing that the human rights movement is a product of Western dominance in the post–Cold War era and, as such, is contingent in nature and nonuniversal in scope.
6. Michael Walzer, *Arguing About War* (New Haven, CT: Yale University Press, 2004), 67.
7. Walzer, *Arguing About War*, 73.
8. Nicholas J. Wheeler, *Saving Strangers: Humanitarian Intervention and International Society* (Oxford: Oxford University Press, 2002), 51.
9. Wheeler, *Saving Strangers*, 51.
10. Wheeler, *Saving Strangers*, 39 and footnote 67.
11. NATO, *Secretary General's Annual Report 2014*, January 30, 2015, www.nato.int/cps/en/natohq/opinions_116854.htm.
12. "The US Wants Its Allies to Spend More on Defense: Here's How Much They Are Shelling Out," *Washington Post*, March 26, 2014, www.washingtonpost.com/blogs/

worldviews/wp/2014/03/26/the-u-s-wants-its-allies-to-spend-more-on-defense-heres-how-much-theyre-shelling-out/.

13. This has been shown repeatedly by public opinion surveys. See, for example, Pew Research Center, "The American-Western European Values Gap," November 7, 2011, www.pewglobal.org/2011/11/17/the-american-western-european-values-gap/; Richard Wike (Associate Director, Pew Global Attitudes Project), "Anti-Americanism Down in Europe but a Values Gap Persists," December 4, 2012, www.pewglobal.org/2012/12/04/anti-americanism-down-in-europe-but-a-values-gap-persists/.

14. The gist of cosmopolitan thought is that the focus of our moral concern and obligations ought to be the individual human being, regardless of his or her location or nationality. Cosmopolitans consider borders to be morally arbitrary, and some are even wedded to the concept of "global citizenship." Cosmopolitan theorists are not, however, all cut from the same cloth; moreover, they address various international topics, especially human rights and global economic justice. For an excellent collection depicting the differences among cosmopolitans and presenting the views of their critics, see Joshua Cohen, ed., *For Love of Country?* (Boston: Beacon Press, 1996). For the argument that local loyalties can coexist with, even strengthen, a cosmopolitan outlook, see Kwame Anthony Appiah, *Cosmopolitanism: Ethics in a World of Strangers* (New York: Norton, 2006). For the core principles that unite most cosmopolitans, see William Smith, "Anticipating a Cosmopolitan Future: The Case of Humanitarian Military Intervention," *International Politics*, Vol. 44, No. 1 (2007), 73–74. Other important statements of the cosmopolitan position include Jeremy Waldron, "Who Is My Neighbor?" *Monist*, Vol. 86, No. 3 (2003); Charles Beitz, "Cosmopolitanism and Global Justice," *Journal of Ethics*, Vol. 9, Nos. 1&2 (2005); Simon Caney, *Justice Beyond Borders: A Global Political Theory* (Oxford: Oxford University Press, 2005), esp. Introduction (which draws a distinction between cosmopolitanism and rival perspectives, such as realism and nationalism) and Ch. 2 (which lays out the main ideas of cosmopolitanism and responds to the major criticisms direct against it). Onora O'Neill offers a discussion of the nature and extent of the duties owed to strangers and the conditions that create these obligations in *Toward Justice and Virtue: A Constructive Account of Practical Reasoning* (Cambridge: Cambridge University Press, 1996), 113–121, 197–200, as does Andrew Linklater, "Distant Suffering and Cosmopolitan Obligations," *International Politics*, Vol. 44, No. 1 (January 2007), 19–36. For two different treatments of humanitarian intervention based on a cosmopolitan perspective, see Caney, *Justice Beyond Borders*, Ch. 7, and Toni Erskine, *Embedded Cosmopolitanism: Duties to Strangers in a World of "Dislocated Communities"* (Oxford: Oxford University Press for the British Academy, 2008). See 183–184 for Erskine's definition of "embedded cosmopolitanism," which she offers as an alternative to the conceptions that characterize the works of Brian Barry, Martha Nussbaum, Onora O'Neill, and Thomas Pogge. For a cosmopolitan approach that concentrates largely on economic justice and human rights (in the broad sense) and that emphasizes the importance of creating new institutions to achieve these outcomes, see Thomas Pogge, "Cosmopolitanism and Sovereignty," *Ethics*, Vol. 103, No. 1 (October 1992), 48–75.

15. Daniele Archibugi, "Cosmopolitan Guidelines for Humanitarian Intervention," *Alternatives: Global, Local, Political*, Vol. 29, No. 1 (Spring 2004), 1–21; Archibugi, *The Global Commonwealth of Citizens* (Princeton, NJ: Princeton University

Press, 2008), 192–205. For another cosmopolitan solution, see Thomas Pogge, "An Institutional Approach to Humanitarian Intervention," *Public Affairs Quarterly,* Vol. 6, No. 1 (January 1992), 89–103, and within the context of human rights and economic justice broadly conceived, Pogge, "Cosmopolitanism and Sovereignty," 48–75, esp. 49–52.

16. Smith, "Anticipating a Cosmopolitan Future," 73.

INDEX